Basic Survival Guide

Resources for EN 0103

Second Edition

Mississippi State University

Ann C. Spurlock
Director of Composition

2014

Katie Doughty	Jessica Mann Thompson
Susan Parr	Abigail Voller

2013

Whitney Acton	Cory W. Lockhart
Kathryn Barber	Jessica M. Lockhart
Jessica Burton	Carrie P. Mastley
Kirk A. Cochran, Jr.	Jalesa Parks
Katie Doughty	Rachel Rice
Kiley Forsythe	Tabitha Sheffield
Jen Gordon	Jonathan Smith
John Aaron Grimes	Kayleigh Swisher
Chelsea Henshaw	Jessica Mann Thompson
Carolyn Ellen Hogan	Amanda L. Townsend

Cover image by Frank Tobienne

Cover design by Ellie Moore

Text design by Wilbur Nelson

Books may be purchased for educational purposes.

For information, please call or write:
1-800-586-0330
Fountainhead Press
2140 E. Southlake Blvd., Suite L #816
Southlake, TX 76092

Web site: www.fountainheadpress.com

E-mail: customerservice@fountainheadpress.com

ISBN 978-1-59871-833-1

Printed in the United States of America

Contents

Welcome to MSU:
Getting Started

Introduction

Welcome to Mississippi State University! The transition from high school to college can be challenging and a bit unsettling at times—new environment, new people, difficult coursework—but your time as a college student can also be the best and most memorable experience of your life. You have the opportunity to participate in some amazing social, cultural, and athletic activities while preparing for your chosen career. Decide right now to make the most of your time at MSU by taking advantage of all this university has to offer. With some careful planning, you can excel academically and thrive personally through your undergraduate years. Read and apply the following suggestions to help you succeed.

Tips for Success in College

Academic

Go to class! Arrive on time, with the proper materials, prepared to take notes and ask questions. Class attendance is the most important predictor of academic success.

Follow your syllabus. Each of your instructors should provide a syllabus on the first day of class; this document provides essential information, including course requirements, important dates (tests and assignment deadlines), and reading or other homework assignments. College students are expected to be independent and responsible: this means following a syllabus without reminders.

Keep up. Prepare for each class by completing assigned readings and other homework. Many experts advise students to prepare as though there will be a quiz.

Focus on learning. Be attentive: put away your cell phone, headphones, your latest copy of *The Reflector*, and any other distractions. Remember that learning involves critical thinking and processing information, not memorizing, mindless note-taking, or simply sitting in a room where someone is teaching.

Contribute. If a class involves discussion, participate. At the same time, respect your classmates by listening to what they have to say. An important part of learning is opening your mind to the ideas of others.

Take Responsibility. If you are struggling in a class, talk to your instructor, either during office hours or by appointment. Take steps to get appropriate academic support. For any writing assignment in any academic subject, go to the Writing Center **(see page 5)** for help at any stage of the composition process.

Keep in touch. If you must miss class, e-mail or talk to your instructor, notifying him or her of your situation; provide appropriate documentation (a doctor's excuse, for example) for an excused absence, especially if you need to make up assignments or tests. Remember: it is your responsibility to contact your instructor about missed work.

Make a friend. Get to know at least one person in each of your classes; if you do miss a class, your instructor will not recreate the lecture for you. You will need to rely on someone to provide notes and updates.

Personal

Join. Like most universities, MSU offers a wide range of activities through approximately 320 clubs and other organizations. Explore the Center for Student Involvement page on the MSU website.

Stay healthy. Sleep enough. Eat healthy foods. Exercise. Practice moderation.

Watch your finances. You are probably more independent now in your spending decisions than ever before. Spend wisely, and be cautious about credit card offers. It is easier than you might think to get yourself in debt.

Be safe! Although the MSU campus is a relatively crime-free environment, bad things can happen. So be smart: never walk alone at night, either on campus or in the community; lock your car and put valuables in the trunk or out of sight; lock your dorm room, and do not prop open outside doors; at social gatherings, do not leave your beverage unattended, and do not leave with someone you do not know well and trust.

Campus Resources

Mississippi State University has many resources available to all students, covered through student activity fees. Check them out and consider how they might improve your college experience, both personally and academically. Following are brief descriptions of a few offices; for more options, go to MSU's Academic Advising Center website: **http://www.uaac.msstate.edu**. You will find a wealth of resources available to you as an MSU student.

Student Counseling Services (SCS)
115C Hathorn Hall
(662) 325-2091
http://www.health.msstate.edu/scs

Students are mistaken in thinking that counseling is only for people who are in severe emotional crisis. Although the trained and licensed psychologists, counselors, and social workers at SCS certainly deal with serious issues, they are available to help with so much more: homesickness, stress, test anxiety, relationship issues, and many other aspects of daily life. They work with individuals, couples, and groups; all sessions are voluntary and confidential.

Student Support Services
01 Montgomery Hall
(662) 325-3335
http://www.sss.msstate.edu

Students with documented learning and/or physical disabilities may work through Student Support Services to receive accommodations, such as a quiet test environment, extended time for tests and quizzes, and help with class notes. In addition, the staff provides academic support for students in the TRIO program, a resource for low-income, first-generation college students. These services include advocacy, priority registration, counseling and guidance, career development, supplemental instruction, and tutoring.

Sanderson Center
225 Coliseum Boulevard
(662) 325-7529
http://www.recsports.msstate.edu

The Sanderson Center is a recreational facility designed to encourage and support fitness and an active, healthy lifestyle. Students can swim, play basketball, work out, run/walk, attend exercise classes, and participate in other activities. In addition, the Sanderson Center coordinates a wide variety of intramural sports.

Longest Student Health Center
360 Hardy Road
(662) 325-2431
http://www.health.msstate.edu/healthcenter

Students in need of medical attention can go to the Longest Student Health Center. The staff of doctors, nurses, and technicians provides extensive services, including treatment of illness, routine health exams, physical therapy, and health education. In addition, students have access to lab work and X-ray as well as a pharmacy.

The Learning Center (TLC)
267 Allen Hall
(662) 325-2957
http://www.tlc.msstate.edu

The Learning Center (TLC) is committed to helping MSU students improve their academic performance. The center offers a variety of services to all students: tutoring in a wide range of subject areas, individualized reading and study skills sessions, workshops on subjects ranging from time management to test strategies, access to computer labs, and equipment checkout.

Writing Center (WC)
94 President's Circle
(662) 325-1045
http://www.writingcenter.msstate.edu

Operated by faculty, staff and graduate students in the English Department, the Writing Center is available to any MSU student who is working on a writing assignment in any academic discipline. Students may visit the WC at any stage of the writing process, from generating ideas through editing and proofreading. Tutors will not proofread, change or correct papers; instead, they work with students to guide their progress through the writing assignment. For detailed information on various ways to visit the WC and how to schedule an appointment, **see page 5.**

Department of English

MAIN OFFICE: Lee Hall, second floor
(662) 325-3644
http://www.msstate.edu/dept/english

Most departmental faculty, staff, and graduate teaching assistants have offices in Lee Hall. A few are located in the Writing Center (94 President's Circle). Your composition teacher will give you a syllabus that includes his or her name, office location, office phone number, office hours, and campus e-mail address. You are encouraged to contact your instructor if you have questions about assignments or need help with the course. If you need assistance in contacting your instructor, call the English Department's main office during regular business hours (8:00 a.m.–5:00 p.m., Monday–Friday). Please note that the department staff will not release personal information about instructors, including home addresses, home phone numbers, cell phone numbers, or private e-mail addresses.

Faculty Office Hours

English Department instructors keep regular office hours for the convenience of their students. These times are listed on your syllabus; also, the English Department can provide that information for you. Office hours are designed to help you in many ways. Meeting with your instructor during office hours allows you to receive one-on-one help with any questions or concerns you might have about your progress and personal learning in the course. Students often feel like they should come in during office hours only when they are struggling with an assignment. In truth, visiting during office hours is a great way for you to get regular, personal help or clarification concerning specific questions that you might have about an assignment. Although e-mail is also a viable alternative for contacting instructors, office hours often provide the opportunity for quick and interactive feedback and discussion. Generally speaking, graduating students often wish they had taken better advantage of their instructors' office hours. If your particular schedule does not permit you to come by during regularly scheduled office hours, most instructors are very amenable to setting up a specific appointment that works with the needs of the individual student. Please do not hesitate to expand your education through increased faculty interaction via office hours.

Freshman Composition Courses

All students, regardless of major, must earn six hours of credit in freshman composition (three hours each in Composition I and II). Listed and described below are the general composition courses offered by the English Department at MSU.

EN 0103—Basic English Composition. This is a non-credit course (will not count toward your six hours of composition credit or toward graduation credit) required of any student whose score on the English section of the ACT is below 17 or whose score on the verbal section of the SAT is below 440. This course includes a study of grammar and mechanics as basic to composition, with an emphasis on the development of both paragraphs and full-length essays.

EN 1103—English Composition I. (Prerequisite: a score of 17 or above on the English section of the ACT, 440 or above on the verbal section of the SAT, or successful completion of EN 0103). This course emphasizes logical and rhetorical principles and organizational strategies that contribute to effective writing. It focuses on analysis of argument and concludes with the development of an argument essay.

EN 1113—English Composition II. (Prerequisite: successful completion of EN 1103). This course provides an expanded study of and practice in stylistics and logic, with an emphasis on research, and it includes an analysis of short fiction and poetry. EN 1113 teaches students how to develop strong arguments through the synthesis of multiple sources

MyCourses

MyCourses is MSU's system for delivering course content and supplemental materials online. Use of the system varies by the preferences of individual departments and individual instructors, but you may safely assume that most of your classes will require some use of MyCourses. Instructors may, at their discretion, use MyCourses as a source for:

- class syllabus
- scheduling information
- written class notes
- internet links to required or supplemental materials
- audio-visual materials
- quizzes and tests
- class discussion
- assignment submission and grading
- individual or class e-mail

In addition, you will be required to submit out-of-class writing assignments to either Turnitin.com or Safe Assign. These are both designed to check the originality of student writing against a vast database of other student essays, professional magazines and journals, and pages across the Web. The purpose of these websites is to remind students that plagiarism is not tolerated at MSU and that doing your own work is the best way to learn. Ultimately, they also protect the integrity of your work from unauthorized use by others.

Writing Center

94 President's Circle
(662) 325-1045
http://www.writingcenter.msstate.edu

Hours of operation vary during fall, spring, and summer semesters. Call the Writing Center or visit the website for current hours of operation.

The Writing Center has four locations, so you may schedule an appointment at the location that is most convenient for you. The main location is at 94 President's Circle; additionally, the WC has a location on the ground floor of the Templeton Athletic Academic Center. If you have a quick question and do not require a full session, drop by the Mobile Writing Center (no appointment necessary) between 4:00-6:00 P.M., Monday-Thursday, outside the Dawg House in the Colvard Student Union. Finally, if you are unable to visit one of the physical locations, you may schedule an Online Writing Center appointment, and a staff member will assist you online.

The Writing Center is a free service for all MSU writers—freshmen, sophomores, juniors, seniors, and graduate students—anyone who wants to talk about writing. Writing consultants can help you understand an assignment, coach you through the generative stages of writing, provide feedback on your drafts, and help you in the final stages of your writing. Writing Center staff members will not proofread or edit your work, but they will point out patterns of sentence-level errors and teach you to edit your own work. In addition to helping you with "big-picture" issues—meeting the requirements of the assignment, drafting, revising—writing consultants will help you to solve problems with correctness: sentence structure, punctuation, verb forms, pronoun usage, other points of grammar, and documentation.

MSU students may talk face-to-face or online with staff members about their writing projects in any academic discipline as well as use the Center's computers to write papers, do research, and access grammar and usage resources. Writing consultants will assist students at all skill levels and at any stage in the writing process. Writing consultants can also offer suggestions and feedback for cover letters, personal statements, resumes, and other related writing projects.

About the Staff

The Writing Center is staffed by instructors and lecturers, as well as graduate students earning their M.A.s in English, all of whom teach composition courses in addition to working as writing consultants. Writing consultants are not subject specific tutors—they do not teach history, engineering, or physics—but they have been trained in the theories and practices of effective one-on-one teaching. They will teach you about the choices you have in writing and the consequences of those choices to communicate effectively and meet the requirements of each writing project.

Making an Appointment

Any student may schedule an appointment to visit the Writing Center. To make an appointment, you may either call the Writing Center at (662) 325-1045 or schedule an appointment online yourself. Appointments at our President's Circle and Templeton locations begin on the hour and half-hour and last for 25 minutes. Online appointments begin on the hour and last for 45 minutes. The Mobile Writing Center in the Colvard Student Union does not require appointments, and you may drop by at any time between 4:00-6:00 P.M. Students may visit any of our Writing Center locations up to three times per week for non-consecutive appointments. To schedule an appointment at any of our locations, follow these steps:

1. Go to the Writing Center website: http://www.writingcenter.msstate.edu
2. Select "Click Here to Schedule an Appointment."
3. If it is your first time logging in, select "Click Here to Register" and complete the information in each field.
4. After you register, you may log into the website.
5. After logging in, click "Select Location Here" at the top of the screen in order to select the schedule for the location you wish to visit.
6. On the daily schedule screen, scroll down to the day you wish to make an appointment, or if you wish to make an appointment in the future, click the bottom arrows to take you to a future week or month.
7. Click on a white box during the time you wish to reserve an appointment.
8. After completing the information in each field, click "Save." Your appointment time will be highlighted on the Online Scheduler screen.

If you must cancel a scheduled appointment, follow these steps:

1. Log into the Writing Center scheduling website.
2. Select the "My Control Panel" link in the upper left hand corner. This will list all of your scheduled appointments for the semester.
3. Select the appointment you wish to cancel and click "delete." This will cancel your appointment.

NOTE: You have until the day of your appointment to reschedule. If it is absolutely necessary to cancel an appointment on the day you are scheduled, call the Writing Center and speak to the receptionist: (662) 325-1045.

Please see the following graphics for instructions on making an appointment.

Using the Online Appointment System

After logging in, click "Select Location Here" at the top of the screen in order to select the schedule for the location you wish to visit.

Kate Spr. 13

Fill out the form below in order to save this appointment. Questions marked with a * are required.

Appointment Limits: Appointments must be 30 minutes in length.

Time: REPEAT APPT.	**Thursday, April 18:** 3:30pm ▾ to 4:00pm ▾

| Client: | Search: ___ Select: Henshaw, Chelsea |

This is the class for which you are completing the assignment. If you are not visiting for a class, type N/A.

| Course: | _____ * |

This is the teacher of the class for which you are visiting.

| Instructor: | _____ * |

| Assignment: | _____ * |

This is the type of assignment you are completing.

| Is this your first visit to this MSU WC? | -- please select -- |

| Classification:: | -- please select -- ▾ * |

| What would you like to work on today? | [text area] * |

This is where you let the tutor know what type of writing assistance you need. Please be as specific as possible.

| Admin Options: | Walk-In/Drop-In: ☐ | Missed: ☐ | Placeholder: ☐ ⓘ | Email Client? ☑ ⓘ |

SAVE APPOINTMENT   CLOSE WINDOW

Composition Policies and Procedures

Although composition courses at MSU vary somewhat in topic, readings, and approach, there are several policies that apply to all sections of EN 0103, EN 1103, and EN 1113. These program-wide requirements are explained below. Please consult your course syllabus or speak to your instructor regarding any details you do not understand.

Attendance

Instructors expect all students to attend class regularly and to participate fully in class discussions and activities. Because the department does not have grade penalties in place for excessive absences, the Freshman Composition Committee has agreed on the following policies:

- Instructors will take roll at every class meeting, record all absences, and report them along with midterm and final grades.
- If you miss two class meetings, your instructor will report you to Pathfinders, a campus department that monitors freshman attendance. If you miss two or more classes, expect to hear from a Pathfinders representative. This is not a punitive measure; students who miss class suffer academically, and Pathfinders representatives can often help a student to resolve issues and get back into a routine of going to class.
- If you miss class, regardless of the reason, you may not make up any in-class work that counts as a daily grade (peer response, group work, short quizzes, short writing assignments, etc.). You will receive a zero on any of these activities.
- If you have an excused absence, you may make up major assignments—tests, in-class paragraphs or essays—upon presentation of a valid written excuse. It is your responsibility to contact your instructor and to arrange a make-up time and place with him or her.
- If possible, notify your instructor in advance of any scheduled absence. If you become ill, contact your instructor via e-mail or telephone to make him or her aware of the situation. Most instructors are very reasonable about such matters but only if you behave responsibly by keeping them aware of your situation.

Classroom Behavior

MSU expects students to behave as adults in the classroom, and composition instructors will not tolerate inappropriate behavior that impedes learning. All students have the right to a positive learning environment, and instructors have the right to teach without distraction. The English Department considers the following as disruptive: profanity; abusive, aggressive, or threatening language; excessive noise; cell phone noise; or use of cell phones and other electronic devices without permission. This is not a comprehensive list, but the idea should be clear. If an instructor has asked a student to discontinue disruptive behavior and the student continues to behave inappropriately, the instructor will ask the student to leave the classroom. After class, the instructor will file an incident report with the Dean of Students office, and a representative will contact the student.

Late Work and Failure to Turn in Work

- Unless you have an excused absence, if you miss a deadline for submitting an assignment, you will be penalized 10 percent for every day the assignment is late.
- You will not be permitted to make up assignments that count as daily grades (exercises for homework, peer responses, reading quizzes, and other in-class activities) for any reason.
- If you have a scheduled absence—official university business or travel, for example—talk with your instructor to determine an acceptable plan for submitting work without penalty. It is best to turn in work early, but that is not always possible. Work out a reasonable plan with your instructor.

Plagiarism

Plagiarism is an important issue in any course that requires writing. It is a serious academic crime, and one major objective in all composition courses is to teach students what it means to plagiarize and how to avoid it. Although policies on plagiarism may vary among courses and definitions of plagiarism may be extended in some fields, the following statement offers guidelines and policies on plagiarism that are generally accepted in the liberal arts. Students in freshman composition courses will be asked to read and discuss this policy and sign a statement confirming that they understand it.

Plagiarism Defined

Plagiarism is claiming someone else's work as one's own. Ideas circulate freely in an intellectual community, and intellectual inquiry often depends on the use of ideas borrowed from others. Responsible writers, however, indicate their debt to others by clearly acknowledging any borrowed material. Plagiarism occurs when writers fail to cite their borrowings.

Auto-plagiarism refers to the act of plagiarizing oneself; this occurs by submitting all or part of a document that was originally written for another course (high school or college).

Plagiarized work is often easy to recognize because it does not clearly indicate borrowing. It is full of facts, observations, and ideas the writer could not have developed on his or her own and is written in a style different from that of the writer. By clearly indicating your debts to other writers, you can both avoid plagiarism and call attention to your own original ideas.

Students decide to plagiarize for a variety of reasons: because they find college-level writing to be difficult or intimidating, or perhaps they become frustrated when even hard work results in a low grade. Occasionally, students feel pressure from family, friends, or coaches to make high grades. Concerned about failure, students are sometimes tempted to copy someone else's work or ask a friend to complete an assignment. Many students, especially freshmen, struggle with time management and find themselves overwhelmed with a heavy work load; in these moments of desperation, plagiarism might seem like a reasonable option. It is not. These situations are common, but no matter what, plagiarism is never an acceptable solution.

If you are struggling in this course, seek help from your instructor and/or the Writing Center. As you think about the assignment, start writing, even if the writing begins as a summary of general ideas on the topic; usually, you discover that you have something to say. If you fall behind, talk to your instructor. He or she might penalize you for submitting work late, but that is far preferable to turning in plagiarized work. The penalty for plagiarism is severe, ranging from a zero on the assignment to failure in the course. In addition, your instructor will submit a Student Honor Code Violation form to the Student Honor Code Office. This instance of academic misconduct will be kept on file and could, in the event of a further Honor Code violation, result in dismissal from MSU.

"Incomplete" Grades

The university allows instructors to assign a grade of "I" (incomplete) to a student at the end of a semester in lieu of a final grade, but only under very limited circumstances. This grade is reserved for situations in which a student has completed almost an entire course before a serious illness or injury, a death in the immediate family, or a similar occurrence prevents him or her from completing the course requirements or taking the final examination. Upon verifying the legitimacy of the situation, an instructor may choose to award an incomplete to the student. In this situation, the student has 30 days upon returning to school to complete the required assignments. The instructor will submit a "Change of Grade" form that changes the "I" to the appropriate letter grade. If the student fails to complete the coursework within the 30-day limit, the grade automatically becomes an "F."

Student-Teacher Conferences

Student-teacher conferences are a vital part of MSU's composition classes, and students are often required to meet at least once with their instructors. Studies indicate that students benefit greatly from personal feedback and interaction. As a result, your instructor may schedule times for you to come in for one-on-one conferencing. These conferences are a time for you to receive individualized help with your writing. Although your instructor cannot possibly provide you with all-inclusive feedback in each conference—writing is a process rather than a one-stop visit—these conferences will be very useful in helping you recognize your individual strengths and weaknesses. Conferences are considered to be so important that regular classroom instruction is sometimes cancelled during conference times.

Tips for Conferencing

- **Be punctual**. Arriving late can push things off schedule and limit the attention other students receive (or cut your own session short).
- **Be as prepared as possible**. Read over any feedback you have received on the current essay and jot down a list of questions you want to ask. Do not simply rely on your memory. The more prepared you are for your conference, the more you will learn from your instructor during your conference time.
- **Be proactive**. Students who expect to be told what to "fix" grammatically often leave conferences somewhat disappointed. Instructors are not going to edit your papers. Expect open feedback from your instructor on how you can improve, and look for ways to apply the help that you are given. Taking responsibility for your own writing is vital to good conferencing.
- **Be open-minded**. Remember that feedback from your instructor is important! Students occasionally take conference feedback to mean they are doing something wrong, when in fact the converse is true. The things your instructor will share with you are designed to improve your writing, so stay positive in your conference.
- **Take notes**. It is difficult to remember everything your instructor tells you, and students who do not take notes inevitably struggle to remember the helpful instruction they have received in their conferences.

You are responsible for remembering and being on time to your conference; you may also be required to complete the Writing Conference Form in the back of this book and bring it with you. Most instructors, especially the ones who cancel class during conference weeks, will count you absent and give you a daily grade of zero.

Contacting Instructors by E-mail

Other than talking to your instructor in person, the most effective way to communicate is by e-mail. If you need clarification of an assignment, need to notify your instructor that you must miss class due to illness or family emergency, or need to schedule an appointment prior to the next class meeting, e-mail is the best option. As with any form of written communication, you should follow some basic conventions when writing and sending e-mails to your instructor. E-mail correspondence with instructors is not as informal as e-mailing or texting with friends; you should be courteous, thorough, brief, and professional.

Tips for E-mailing

- Use the subject line and be specific. This helps instructors determine the purpose of your e-mail immediately.
- Address your instructor with a salutation: Dear Mr. Smith, or Hi, Mr. Smith.
- Skip lines between paragraphs, including following the salutation. Skipping lines makes the text easier to read.

- Immediately address your question or problem without being wordy. Be clear in what you want. Provide the proper context (briefly), then ask your question, make your request, or state your information.
- If you miss a class, do not e-mail your instructor to ask, "Did I miss anything important?" or "What did we do in class today?" Composition classes do something important every day, and an instructor cannot re-create an entire class meeting for you.
- Include your first and last names as well as your class and section number. Your instructor is likely your only English teacher, but he or she probably has several sections and possibly even several students with the same first name.
- Proofread your e-mail for typos, misspelled words, and grammatical errors.
- Once you have sent an e-mail, be patient. During the week, you can reasonably expect a reply within 24 hours. On weekends, do not expect a reply until Monday.
- Do not send your instructor chain letters, inspirational stories, jokes, and other miscellaneous messages.

Below is a poorly written e-mail; compare it to the Tips for E-mailing listed above.

```
To: instructor@msstate.edu
Cc: anyonewhoneedsacopy@msstate.edu
Subject: my assignment

hey; and I need to know some things about my assignment from you're class that I
missed yesterday. the reason why is because I got locked out of my dorm room and
couldn't reach my roommate who went home for the weekend and isn't back yet. And I
didn't want to pay the fee. I couldn't come to class without a shower or breakfast,
so I wonder did we do anything important?
Thanks.
Josh
```

Below is a well written e-mail; compare it to the Tips for E-mailing listed above.

```
To: instructor@msstate.edu
Cc: anyonewhoneedsacopy@msstate.edu
Subject: Assignment Request for EN 0103/12

Hello, Mr. Smith -
I missed class yesterday, April 3, and need further instructions so I can finish our
journal assignment that is due Monday. We've discussed several essays in class, but
I need to know exactly which ones we are allowed to write about. Also, is it okay
to use first person?

Thanks for your help.
Josh Elliott
```

EN 0103—Basic Composition

EN 0103 Course Information

EN 0103, Basic Composition, is a non-credit course for MSU students who need reinforcement and support in composition, grammar, and mechanics. Although some students choose to enroll in EN 0103 before taking EN 1103 (Comp I) and EN 1113 (Comp II), it is a required course for any student with an ACT English score below 17 or SAT verbal score below 410. The content of EN 0103 includes instruction in the components of well written paragraphs and essays, focusing on developing main ideas in an organized way using specific details, examples, and explanations. In addition, grammar is emphasized, particularly as it relates to clear and correct written communication.

Required Texts:

Paragraphs and Essays with Integrated Readings, 12th edition—looseleaf format
Basic Survival Guide, 2nd edition—purchase new, not used

Assignments, Points Distribution, and Grading: You will have an opportunity to earn 1,000 points in this class. Your final grade will depend on the total points you earn:

- A = 900–1000
- B = 800–899
- C = 700–799
- D = 600–699
- F = 0–599

You will earn points in the following categories:

Essays: 550 points
Exemplification
- Draft 1   20 pts. (in class)
- Peer Response   10 pts. (in class)
- Draft 2   20 pts. (out of class, typed)
- Final Draft   100 pts.(out of class, typed)

Cause and Effect
- Draft 1   20 pts. (in class)
- Peer Response   10 pts. (in class)
- Draft 2   20 pts. (out of class, typed)
- Final Draft   100 pts. (out of class, typed)

Comparison and Contrast
- Draft 1   20 pts. (in class)
- Peer Response   10 pts. (in class)
- Draft 2   20 pts. (out of class, typed)
- Final Draft   100 pts. (out of class, typed)
- **Final Essay**   100 pts. (in class at designated exam time)

Paragraphs: 90 points
Description	30 pts.
Definition	30 pts.
Process	30 pts.

Grammar: 175 points
Aplia	100 pts.
Grammar Test	75 pts.

Reading and Writing Activities, Quizzes, Classwork, Homework, and Participation: 185 pts.

General Class Policies and Procedures:

Attend all classes. Instructors will take attendance at every class meeting and report all absences. It is your responsibility to contact the instructor if you miss a class, and you are responsible for obtaining any information or assignments. In order to make up essay drafts and tests, you must provide a written excuse that is in accordance with university policy. You may not make up in-class work, homework, or short quizzes even with an excused absence.

Turn in your work on time. You are expected to turn in homework assignments at the *beginning* of class, so be on time; instructors have the right to deny submission if you arrive late or attempt to turn in an assignment at the end of class. If you submit a major assignment late, you will lose 10 percent per day after the due date. Plan ahead! Computer and/or printer problems do not count as valid excuses for late work.

Do your own work. Academic misconduct in any form is a serious offense with heavy consequences. See http://www.honorcode.msstate.edu/ for more details about MSU's honor code policies and sanctions.

Format paragraphs and essays correctly. Here are a few rules about creating and submitting written work:

- Use MLA format on all paragraphs and essays.
- For in-class writing, use blue or black ink and standard notebook paper (not torn from a spiral notebook); skip lines and write on the front side of the paper only.
- For typed assignments, use Times New Roman and a 12-point font.
- For multi-draft assignments, turn in all your materials with the final draft (prewriting, drafts, peer reviews).
- For all writing assignments, submit an electronic copy to Turnitin or Safe Assign via MyCourses.

Stay connected. E-mail is an important communication tool in this class, so check your e-mail frequently. You are responsible for assignments, announcements, or other information that is sent via e-mail. Also, check MyCourses frequently for announcements and assignments.

Come to class prepared to learn. Bring all appropriate materials (textbooks, workbook, paper, pen, etc.) to class every day. Turn off your cell phone and other electronic devices during class. Common courtesy in the classroom is expected and required of you, so any disruptive or disrespectful behavior may result in your dismissal from the day's class.

Ask for help. If you have any questions or concerns about your writing or the class, make an appointment with your instructor or send an e-mail with specific questions and concerns. Also, for extended help, visit one of the Writing Centers on campus.

Know the rules of academic integrity. If you plagiarize any assignment, you will receive a zero on the assignment or an F in the course, depending on the severity of the violation. Further, MSU has an approved Honor Code, which applies to all students: ***"As a Mississippi State University student, I will conduct myself with honor and integrity at all times. I will not lie, cheat, steal, nor will I accept the actions of those who do."***

The team that beat U-of-M #1 & 6 on Thanks — what do you know about that?

EN 0103 Record of Grades

Writing assignments and quizzes become the property of the English Department when submitted for grading. Instructors keep these major assignments on file, but other work will be returned to you. To keep track of your academic standing in this course, record details from your graded assignments below:

DESCRIPTION PARAGRAPH:

Due Date: ____ / ____ / 20____

Points Earned: _____ / 30

Problem Areas: _____   Instructor Comments: _____

_____   _____

_____   _____

_____   _____

DEFINITION PARAGRAPH:

Due Date: ____ / ____ / 20____

Points Earned: _____ / 30

Problem Areas: _____   Instructor Comments: _____

_____   _____

_____   _____

_____   _____

PROCESS PARAGRAPH:

Due Date: ____ / ____ / 20____

Points Earned: _____ / 30

Problem Areas: _____   Instructor Comments: _____

_____   _____

_____   _____

_____   _____

EXEMPLIFICATION ESSAY:

Due Date: ____ / ____ / 20____

Draft 1: _____ / 20

Draft 2: _____ / 20   Instructor Comments: _____

Peer Response: _____ / 10   _____

Final Draft: _____ / 100   _____

Problem Areas: _____   _____

_____

_____

_____

15

CAUSE and EFFECT ESSAY:

Due Date: ____ / ____ / 20____

Draft 1: _____ / 20

Draft 2: _____ / 20

Peer Response: _____ / 10

Final Draft: _____ / 100

Problem Areas: _____

_____

_____

_____

Instructor Comments: _____

_____

_____

_____

COMPARISON and CONTRAST ESSAY:

Due Date: ____ / ____ / 20____

Draft 1: _____ / 20

Draft 2: _____ / 20

Peer Response: _____ / 10

Final Draft: _____ / 100

Problem Areas: _____

_____

_____

_____

Instructor Comments: _____

_____

_____

_____

GRAMMAR

Aplia: ____ / 100 _____

Grammar Test: ____ / 75 _____

OTHER ASSIGNMENTS:

Date:	Assignment:	Grade:
___ / ___	_____	___ /
___ / ___	_____	___ /
___ / ___	_____	___ /
___ / ___	_____	___ /
___ / ___	_____	___ /
___ / ___	_____	___ /
___ / ___	_____	___ /
___ / ___	_____	___ /
___ / ___	_____	___ /
___ / ___	_____	___ /
___ / ___	_____	___ /
___ / ___	_____	___ /

MIDTERM GRADE:

My letter grade at midterm is a(n) _____.

I have earned _____ out of a possible _____ points.

I have _____ absences.

Using the space below, respond to the following writing prompt:

Reflect on your current grade in this course. Are you satisfied? If so, write out a plan for maintaining this grade for the remainder of the semester. Are you dissatisfied? If so, first explain the cause(s) of your low grade; then outline the steps you plan to take to improve the grade.

_____

_____

_____

_____

_____

_____

_____

_____

_____

_____

_____

_____

_____

_____

Student Writing Skills Self-Evaluation

Please take a few minutes to think about your past experience with writing, specifically your previous writing instruction and composition assignments. What do you think you do well? Where do you think you need improvement?

Read each statement below and check the corresponding circle to indicate your level of agreement. Strong agreement indicates extensive skill or knowledge; strong disagreement indicates that, despite instruction and previous writing experience, you have little or no knowledge or skill. All responses should represent how you see your current ability. If a statement asks you to evaluate a skill or knowledge that you have yet to encounter in a classroom, check "N/A" for not applicable.

Statement	Strongly Agree	Agree	Neutral	Disagree	Strongly Disagree	N/A
Rhetorical Skills						
I am able to compose a clear and effective thesis.	○	○	○	○	○	○
I can present appropriate and persuasive reasons to support my thesis.	○	○	○	○	○	○
I have the ability to provide appropriate, specific details to support my reasons.	○	○	○	○	○	○
I can assess my audience and adapt my writing content and style appropriately.	○	○	○	○	○	○
Content						
I present information that has depth and quality; it goes beyond the obvious.	○	○	○	○	○	○
I present a unique perspective in my writing.	○	○	○	○	○	○
I am able to write an introductory paragraph that attracts the reader's interest and narrows gradually to the thesis.	○	○	○	○	○	○
I know how to write a topic sentence that clearly represents a paragraph's content.	○	○	○	○	○	○
In essays, the topic sentences support my thesis.	○	○	○	○	○	○

Statement	Strongly Agree	Agree	Neutral	Disagree	Strongly Disagree	N/A
General Composing Skills						
I have no problem reading and understanding the criteria for writing assignments.	○	○	○	○	○	○
I use transitions effectively to connect general and specific points.	○	○	○	○	○	○
I use transitions effectively between paragraphs.	○	○	○	○	○	○
The sentences I write are clear, understandable, and grammatically correct.	○	○	○	○	○	○
I know how to organize a paragraph or essay to communicate ideas effectively.	○	○	○	○	○	○
Editing/ Proofreading Skills						
I am effective at revising my own drafts.	○	○	○	○	○	○
In my final drafts, all words are spelled correctly.	○	○	○	○	○	○
I use punctuation effectively and correctly.	○	○	○	○	○	○
After proofreading, I am confident that my writing is grammatically correct.	○	○	○	○	○	○
I know how to format an essay using MLA style.	○	○	○	○	○	○

Reflection

After reviewing the completed self-evaluation above, summarize your responses on separate paper. First, note components of the writing process with which you feel comfortable: how have your education and reading habits helped you in these areas? Next, identify the areas of most concern: what aspects of your writing need the most work? Explain why you think it is important to improve your skill level in these areas.

Diagnostic Writing

●

_____   _____   _____
Last Name   First Name   Preferred Name

New at MSU?   ○   ○   Major_____
                Yes   No

_____   _____   _____ _____ _____
Net ID   Hometown, State   Local Phone #

Choose one of the two writing prompts below and, in the space provided, write a well-organized and fully developed paragraph. Provide specific details, and do your best to create complete and logical sentences that are free of errors.

1. Tell the story of something interesting or surprising that you have experienced since coming to MSU. This could involve moving into your dorm, getting acquainted with others, finding your way around campus, or some other experience.
2. What are your goals as a college student? You might consider your preparation for a career, but you could also comment on your desire to transition from being inexperienced and dependent on family to becoming a mature and financially independent adult.

●

●

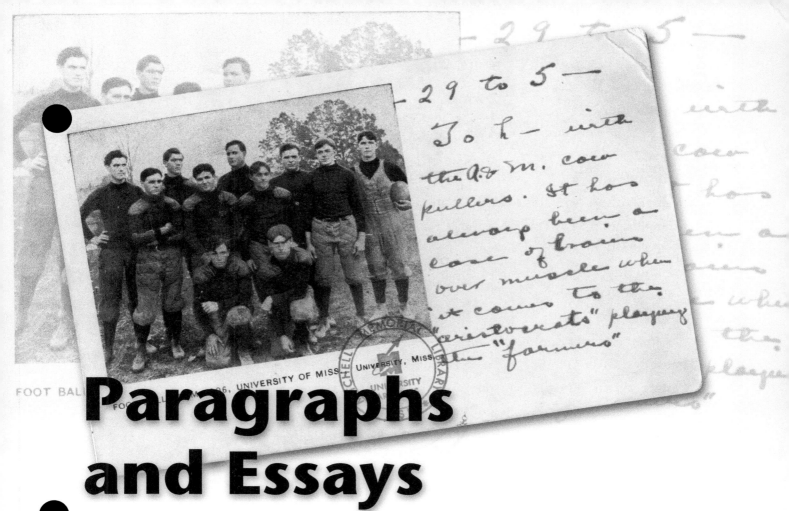

Paragraphs and Essays

Contents

Paragraphs

Description

Student Model Paragraph   Description

The Beach at Apalachicola

In September, I went to a beach in Apalachicola, Florida and saw how beautiful it could be. The beach smelled fresh, the temperature was just a little cool, and the wind blew softly through my hair. The sand was hot and looked like white dust meshed with little specks of gold; it reflected the sun's glow and felt like a grill's hot coals under my feet. I sat on a wide blue and red striped towel in my reclining beach chair under a rainbow umbrella that provided just enough shade. I saw the long, thin sand bar, only inches under the water, in front of me. Many small black and white spotted seagulls ran along the sand bar searching for tiny schools of minnows. At the edges of the sand bar, rainbow coral swayed back and forth in the shallow water; fat yellow fish ducked in and out of the coral as they attempted to hide from bigger, and hungrier, red fish. On the beach, other people laughed and played in the burning sand, and some sat in holes they had dug in order to stay cool. The day went on, and I stayed on the beach long enough to see the sunset, dusky and deep. As the sun set, the beach goers left, and the beach, open and vacant like an amusement park shutting down for the day, was empty. Although the day was over, I was glad I had seen its beauty.

Daniel Scotch

Student Model Paragraph   Description

My Father's Hands

Almost every day of my life before I came to college, I saw my father's hands, but I never really thought about them until now. I see many things in those hands: hard work, sacrifice, power, and love. When I looked at my father's hands last weekend, I saw things that I had never noticed before.

I studied his left hand, and the first thing I noticed was its physical appearance: it is very rugged looking, perpetually tanned by years of hard work in the sun. Although my hand is almost as long as his, his hand is much larger than mine. His fingers are almost as large as my thumb. His palm is thick and callused from many years of hard work. The back of his hand has scars, and a large scar on his thumb reminds me of when he almost lost it to a tractor. His fingernails are thick and rugged but neatly trimmed. On his ring finger, he wears his wedding band. When he takes off the ring, I see a groove that the ring has made over the last twenty years. These physical features are impressive but are nothing compared to what his hands have done. They have received splinters as my father worked in the saw mill as a boy and learned to be a carpenter. They have held a rifle and dug fox holes in Vietnam. For many years, they held a welding rod in a factory so he could support his family. As I continue to study his hands, my focus shifts to the effect they have had on me. I remember looking at his hands as a child and finding both fear and comfort. When my father was angry, one look at those powerful hands would make my heart stop. But when I was scared, he held my small hand in his huge one and made me feel safe. After my last high school football game, I felt a sense of great pride and joy as his hand shook mine. I never gave my father's hands much thought until now. I now

These opening sentences introduce the topic and present a dominant impression.

This is a strong visual description.

What details do you see that explain the accomplishments of these hands? Underline or highlight them.

Throughout the paragraph, note details such as this one. What other specific descriptions can you find that help you visualize the appearance of these hands? Underline or highlight them.

This description moves beyond visual and factual (objective) details to more emotional (subjective) statements. Underline or highlight them.

> These concluding sentences help the reader to focus on the father's importance to his son.

realize that I have looked to those hands for confidence, approval, and justice. Now that I am away from home and in college, the world is a much harder place to live in without his hands to guide me. I miss those hands.

Mike Jones

This essay originally appeared in *Winning Essays*, a publication of the English Department at Mississippi State University.

Student Model Paragraph   Description

A Step into Mammie's World

Since my mother's mother—we called her Mammie—died when I was only five years old, I never really got to know her, that is until my aunt brought me Mammie's trunk last summer. The trunk contains mostly old junk, but I learned a great deal about how life was in her day by rummaging through the contents; spending hours reading old newspapers and books and looking through old letters and clothes helped me get to know her. I looked at old dress patterns and found that many of the clothes my grandmother wore are stylish today: straight skirts, frilly blouses, and spiked heel pump shoes seem to be in style now as they were then. A box of little white gloves was hidden in the corner of the trunk. Mammie must have been a very petite lady because I could barely fit my big hand into her little gloves. A pair of long slinky black gloves was also in the collection. I pictured her looking perfectly radiant in a straight black formal dress with these gloves covering her arms. I saw her laughing and dancing, and then I saw the brassiere. It was all cotton and ugly and it looked like some type of armor instead of a feminine undergarment for a delicate lady with impeccable taste in clothing. I could not imagine wearing such an uncomfortable piece of clothing. Poor Mammie. Looking further, I noticed that the trunk was lined with old newspapers from the 1950's and 60's. They were yellowed with age and very brittle. I found one dated July 14, 1960 which stated that John F. Kennedy had just been nominated as Democratic candidate for president. He had defeated Senator Lyndon B. Johnson from Texas. Looking at an old magazine, I noticed an automobile advertisement from 1952. A new Oldsmobile was priced at $1,095, and a 1951 Studebaker, now a collector's item, with a radio, heater, over-drive, and a beautiful blue finish, cost only $495. Among these old newspapers, I found letters, Christmas cards, and Get Well cards from friends and relatives scattered about in the trunk. I learned about the First Baptist Church in Houston, Mississippi, through minutes of church meetings taken by my grandmother, who was secretary. Old drawings by my mother and her siblings were packed in a box. I could hardly believe that they were once too uncoordinated to stay inside the lines of a coloring book. The trunk itself is kind of tattered and smells old and musty, but it holds Mammie's treasured memories. Through these inexpensive yet priceless items, I grow closer to her every time that I rummage through her collectibles.

Charlotte Springer

This selection originally appeared as a full length essay in *Winning Essays*, a publication of the MSU English Department.

Description—Prompts for Writing a Paragraph

Choose one of the prompts below and write a descriptive paragraph. Remember to develop a dominant impression that you support by providing very specific details, especially ones that you observe using your five senses. Be sure to include both objective (factual) and subjective (your emotional response) details.

Describe a place. Select a place you know well that has a strong emotional meaning (positive or negative) to you: a family vacation spot, a private place you go to think and reflect, a hospital room, a football stadium on game day, your room at home or here at MSU. To develop ideas, ask yourself questions such as the following:

- What is the first thing that comes to mind when you think of this place?
- What makes this place special or important? How does it make you feel?

- In addition to the way this place looks, what other sensory impressions come to mind (smells, sounds, temperature)?
- What details (objects, colors, atmosphere) occur to you?
- What is happening? What are the people around you doing?
- What is your reaction to these details?

Describe a family member, friend, famous person, or pet. Select a person or pet you know well. In addition to physical appearance, think about personality and character. Once you have selected your subject, consider the following:

- Physical aspects: appearance (size, shape, hair and eye color, style of dress), facial expression, and other sensory impressions (soft or rough skin, a particular smell, a unique voice).
- Personality: outgoing/reserved, serious/silly, kind/cruel, generous/stingy, honest/dishonest, etc.
- Your emotional reaction (positive or negative) to this person or pet: why do you feel this way?

Definition

Student Model Paragraph   Definition

Yawnsmit

Sandy sits in the very first row of his English composition class. Usually, he is a very punctual, well-dressed, attentive student. Today, however, with blood shot eyes, he toddles into the classroom about fifteen minutes late wearing a grubby looking, stained t-shirt and a wrinkled pair of blue jeans. Sandy attempts to be inconspicuous as he reads a definition essay in *Guide to Freshman Composition*. Obviously not interested in the class or the assigned reading, he suddenly emits a very boisterous yawn. Immediately, Tim, the guy who sits directly to Sandy's left, does the same. Brianna, the smallest girl in the class, also lets out a thunderous yawn. After that, the entire class erupts into a giant game of follow the leader, with student after student yawning one after another. This is an example of the most common type of yawnsmitting. Yawnsmit is the act of transmitting yawns. The action is not done intentionally but occurs frequently. Most people who yawnsmit have no idea that they are doing it. All it takes for yawnsmitting to occur is a gathering of two or more individuals. One person yawns (Sandy), sending a chain reaction all around, affecting innocent bystanders (Tim, Brianna, the rest of the class). There are two major causes of yawnsmitting: boredom and fatigue. The third and most perplexing cause of yawnsmitting is the "just because cause." This happens with a person is neither tired nor uninterested but yawns just because someone else yawned. These "just because" yawnsmitters are what keeps the transmission going.

Hillary Bingham

This essay originally appeared in *Guide to Freshman Composition*, published in 2007 and utilized by the MSU English Department for EN 1103 instruction.

Student Model Paragraph   Definition

Canoodle?

Most little kids enjoy snuggling with Mom or Dad; as they get older, though, snuggling seems to be too childish and undesirable. "Snuggle" can mean the liquid you use to soften your clothes, or it can be physical closeness which brings comfort, so the use of the word can be confusing. Therefore, I propose the addition of a new word to the English language—"canoodle"—to liven up and bring some clarity to the word snuggle. One may be confused about the actual definition of canoodle, but look no further: the definition is quite simple, fun, and delightful. Canoodle is a new, more personal way of saying snuggle which says, "I want to be comforted." When one is feeling down or irritable, canoodling can be the perfect answer. Now, canoodling is not in any way sexual and can be done with a person of the opposite sex or the same sex. Canoodling can be closely related to the term "spooning," which is widely popular with couples. Instead of using the word "spoon," which sometimes can have a sexual connotation, one can say "canoodle," a fresh new word which only means to feel happy and comforted by having someone else around while one sleeps, watches a movie, or just lounges around. People might also canoodle by snuggling with stuffed animals, as some children do to comfort themselves when tired or emotionally down. Canoodling can occur with anything that brings comfort. Because canoodle is a fresh new word, it is vital to establish its definition so people do not mistake canoodle for something it is not. Walking up to a friend and asking if he or she wishes to canoodle might not be the best idea and could probably cause confusion and a negative reaction. Maybe, instead, a better approach is explaining to friends that canoodle is the new snuggle and asking them to use the term every day. New words, as well as new meanings of old words, pop up frequently, so with a little publicity, canoodle could be used worldwide one day!

Kelsey Myers

This essay originally appeared in *Guide to Freshman Composition*, published in 2007 and utilized by the MSU English Department for EN 1103 instruction.

Student Model Paragraph   Definition

The Power of a Pen

The pen is a humble instrument used for writing or drawing with ink. Some people may look at a pen as only a writing tool. I, however, see it as much more than that. A pen has a powerful ability: to make marks that are permanent. In addition, a pen can also help a person to believe in continuing to move forward and never looking back. I like to think of my life as though I am writing in pen. If I make a mistake, I know I cannot erase it—but I can use it as a learning experience. When writing, if a mistake is made, it is possible to scratch it out with ink, or perhaps even to throw the paper away all together. Even with these corrective options, however, the writing is still there. In my life, I have made errors I wish I could scratch out, but I know I cannot rewrite or erase parts of my life so that bad choices could be altered. Living my life in pen has helped me to understand that I am not anywhere close to perfect. Everyone will make mistakes in life, but those errors can serve as reminders of how to approach a situation differently if the opportunity is presented a second time. Regrets have no place in my life because I do not have the option to change or undo or redo something I have done in the past. I refer to my past, therefore, as my personal guide which I have written in pen: though my past will always be there, I can learn from my misjudgments to make myself a better person for the future. I am able to look at a time when I fell as a lesson to always get back up again. I can learn to stop regretting what has happened and know that there was a reason it did happen. Living my life as though it were written in pen has not only made me appreciate my past and present, but also what is to come in my future.

Alison Jones

Definition—Prompts for Writing a Paragraph

Choose one of the prompts below and write a definition paragraph. Remember to include the word's literal meaning, but make sure to provide your own explanation instead of relying only on a formal definition. Present the definition in your own words and then clarify it with clear descriptions, examples, and comparisons.

Define an emotion or state of being. Select an emotion that you have experienced and define it in terms of its impact on your behavior and outlook as well as how it makes you feel physically. After checking on the official meaning of this emotion, ask yourself a few questions to develop your explanation. Some suggestions:

- What happens to your body when you experience this emotion?
- How does this emotion affect your overall mood?
- Does this emotion affect your appetite, sleep patterns, concentration, or ability to complete tasks?
- How do you behave when you feel this emotion?

Create and define your own word or re-define an existing word. Using your imagination, come up with a new word and create a definition and usage situations for this word. You may also select an existing word and give it new meaning and context.

Be sure to include the following:

- Your own definition of the word; if you choose to re-define an existing word, include the standard definition (in your own words) before explaining your new interpretation.
- An explanation of how this word differs from others with similar meanings.
- A specific situation or context in which the word might be appropriate.
- A few examples that demonstrate your definition.

Process

Student Model Paragraph   Process

A Student's Guide to Getting a Seat on Game Day

On a beautiful autumn Saturday, there is no better place in the world than the student section of Davis Wade Stadium as the Bulldogs of Mississippi State University play football. For students, however, getting a good seat to watch the action can be a challenge. There are several things you must do, and planning is a must. These simple steps will help you think ahead so you can get the perfect seat. First, arrive early at the student entrance, at least 30 minutes. If you wait until just before kickoff, lines will be very long, and once inside the stadium, you will find limited seating. When you get to the entrance, show your ticket and student ID at the gate and receive your wrist band; then enter the stadium. Be sure not to get distracted by the concession stands that are everywhere as you walk towards the student section; purchasing food too early will take away time that you should use to get a good seat. Instead, head straight for one of the multiple ramps that are labeled "Student Section." Before walking up one of these ramps, you will have to show a security guard the wristband you received upon entering the stadium. Once cleared by the guard, walk up the ramp to the seating area. Now you can choose the seat you desire and mark it by placing your cowbell there. Once this is done, you may go back to the concession stand to get your food and drink. Obtaining a good seat at a MSU football game is a challenge, but it is much easier if you follow these simple steps.

Jeffery Mayeaux

Student Model Paragraph   Process

My Grandmother's Mouthwatering Biscuits

Breakfast is said to be the most important meal of the day; it also happens to be my favorite because I love waffles, pancakes, eggs, and another traditional breakfast foods. My grandmother's biscuits, which she taught me to make when I was a little girl, are my absolutely favorite homemade breakfast item; they are fluffy, buttery, delicious, and a breeze to make. Turning a few simple ingredients into yummy biscuits is easy if you follow a few simple steps. First, collect the following ingredients and combine them in a bowl: four cups of self-rising flour, one and a half cups of buttermilk, and two tablespoons of Crisco. Next, thoroughly blend the ingredients. I like to mix with my hands so that I know all the ingredients are completely mixed together. If you do not want to get your hands messy, use a spoon to mix the dough. When you have finished mixing, form the dough into a ball. Next, place the dough on a heavily floured flat surface and, using a rolling pin, roll it out to a thickness of about one-half inch. To prevent sticking, be sure to use plenty of flour, both on the dough and on the flat surface. This also makes the task of cutting the biscuits easier. After rolling out the dough, you are ready to cut it; use either a floured biscuit cutter or the rim of a cup. Cut the biscuits out of the dough and place them on a baking sheet sprayed with Pam. After preheating your oven to 450 degrees, bake the biscuits for thirteen to fifteen minutes, depending on how brown you want them. Once the time is up, you are ready to eat. You can now use these easy steps to make biscuits of your own.

Morgan Gavin

Student Model Paragraph

Process

The Perfect Procedure: Make-up Tips from a Pageant Pro

Ever since I won the Miss Florida Teen USA pageant last year, I have developed the perfect procedure to create a healthy and professional look for photo shoots and public appearances. Anyone can follow this process to achieve a polished and professional look. The first step in creating this look is to apply a face primer; Smash Box is the best brand for the job because it creates a smooth finish. Begin this process by pouring the primer into your hand and rubbing it thoroughly over your face. After applying the face primer, apply an eye primer, preferably Urban Decay, to both eyelids. Once you have primed your entire face, apply makeup, starting with your eyes. You need to apply eye makeup first, so you can avoid dark circles under your eyes, and only apply light colors to your lids and dark colors to the creases of the eye. Next, apply your foundation. Pour a dab of foundation, roughly the size of a nickel, onto a plate. Use the square end of a makeup sponge to dab the foundation from the center of your face to the outer edge until your entire face has been covered. Do not forget to blend the foundation along your hairline, jaw line, and ears. After you have applied foundation, use powder and a blush brush to blot your face. The powder adds a nice glow to your skin under high definition lights or under the sun. Next, swipe bronzer—Sephora is the best brand—above your eyebrows, along your chin bone, and across the highest point of your cheek bone; then, apply blush to the squishiest part of your cheek and along your cheek bones. The last step to achieve a photo finish look is to apply makeup to your lips. Apply the color of your choice, depending on your personal style, and then line your lips with lip-liner. Apply lip gloss if you want to add a nice sheen to your lips. If you follow these steps, you too can achieve a healthy and professional look for photo shoots or public appearances.

Gracie Simmons

Process—Prompts for Writing a Paragraph

Choose one of the prompts below and write a process paragraph. Remember, process is written in chronological, or time, order. There are two types of process: explanation and instruction. Explanation seeks to educate or inform readers about how something works or happens; writers of process explanations do not expect readers to perform the process. On the other hand, instruction provides readers with step-by-step information on how to perform a particular task or activity.

Describe a self-improvement process. Select a process that, if followed, will result in a person becoming healthier, more physically fit, more attractive, more efficient, or more accomplished. This could be a particular diet strategy, an exercise routine, or creating and following a set pattern of behavior. In your explanation, be sure to emphasize the positive outcome of this process; also, be specific, providing details for each step and helpful hints where appropriate.

Instruct readers on how to get what they want from others. Think of something that you might want – permission from your parents or some other authority figure, a higher grade, getting to do what you want with a group of friends – and provide carefully thought out steps to achieve this goal. This prompt requires you to explain to your readers how they must consider the audience so that each step has the intended outcome. You might also write this in first person, explaining how you go about getting what you want, but make sure to explain so that a reader could follow your advice.

Provide instructions on how to perform a task with a specific outcome. Select an activity with a desired outcome and instruct readers in a clear way. This includes a wide variety of activities, such as creating the perfect playlist, cooking a particular food item, going on a long distance run, or navigating a particular website. Use your imagination, but make sure to select a task that you know very well. Break down the activity into manageable steps, and speak directly to the reader. For example, you might command a reader in the following way: "Be sure to measure the ingredients accurately" or "Next, inflate the tire to the manufacturer's recommended pressure."

Essays

Exemplification

Student Model Essay   Exemplification

Unrealistic Advertisement

Nowadays, many people obsess over trying to reach an unrealistic goal of physical perfection. In some cases, women spend thousands and thousands of dollars to achieve that goal, believing that what they see in advertisements is reality. However, advertisements attempt to persuade women into believing that they need to have perfect bodies or flawless features in order to obtain happiness or appeal to the opposite sex. As a reaction to this common misconception, Dove created a campaign, called "Real Beauty," to show women how misleading advertisements can be. Dove took an ordinary woman and transformed her into what most people would find appealing. Step by step, viewers see what advertisers do in order to make a woman look "perfect" and "flawless." By the end of the process, Dove has totally transformed her face with the help of makeup and technology. Generally, magazine and television advertisements create unrealistic expectations and can be misleading.

Many advertisements in magazines deceive women and create unrealistic expectations. Typically, about half the pages in a magazine are advertisements, so women can assume there are bound to be a few false ads in an ordinary fashion magazine, but what about in a health magazine? Misleading ads are found everywhere, even in places one normally would not expect them to be. For instance, *Health Magazine* is all about new ways to stay healthy and fit, but little do people know that it too has false advertisements. In this magazine, there is a "Healthy and Smart" ad that provides what the magazine calls a smart way to diet. This ad shows a young woman who appears happy to have a perfect body and looks fit. Along with the photo, there is a diet plan that consists of consuming between 1200–1300 calories a day for a week or more, even with exercising daily. In reality, this diet plan is not a smart way to lose weight. Consuming so few calories while also exercising could put a body into starvation mode. Women are often tricked into believing that because such information appears in a health magazine, it must be right and healthy for them. It does not help when women see the picture of the young woman with a perfect body representing the diet plan. This fools women by leading them to assume that if they follow this diet plan, then they too will be happy with themselves and will turn out like those young women, which, in reality, is a false claim.

In addition to appearing on the pages of magazines, misleading advertisements are shown on television as well. Commercials with false beauty information appear all the time. Women see celebrities and assume they normally look that way. Advertisers also tend to hire women who are considered "perfect" and appealing to the opposite sex. Actually, these celebrities and ordinary women are made to look perfect by applying makeup, fixing hair, and air-brushing. In fact, a makeup commercial featuring actress Julia Roberts was banned in Britain. British authorities said the Lancôme ad was misleading because Ms. Roberts does not normally look that way. In the commercial, she appears vibrant, young, and flawless; in reality, she is much older than she appeared, and the suggestion that makeup could take years off her face is false; therefore, it was banned. This is a prime example of how the advertising industry has distorted people's perception of beauty. Another example is a commercial for Crest toothpaste: a very attractive and flawless-looking woman uses Crest and has a better and brighter smile. The commercial also suggests that using Crest might have a positive effect on the opposite sex by showing the woman walk by her ex-boyfriend. As she strolls by, he takes one glance at her and says, "Wow," indicating he should have never let her go. This commercial misleads women into believing that using Crest toothpaste will make one's smile bigger and brighter, therefore making one appealing to the opposite sex. This suggestion is false and misleading.

Advertisements today are everywhere, and they leave people wondering what is real and what is fake. Misled by these idealistic images, women strive to achieve perfection because of what they see in magazines and on television. What is hard for most women to grasp, though, is there is no "perfect body" out there; it is all an illusion. Advertisements make women appear "flawless," but, in reality, no one is perfect. That is exactly the reason Dove created the "Real Beauty" campaign. It shows the true side of women and how they normally look before advertisements ruin natural beauty with makeup and technology. It is no wonder that women's perceptions of beauty are distorted. Women have to be more aware of misleading advertisements and more aware of their own real beauty.

Tara Nash

Student Model Essay   Exemplification

Place of My Dreams

"Philly will either make you or break you," is what the locals say. In my case, Philadelphia *made* me who I am today. Philadelphia is the one place that makes me feel like I can truly be myself because it is where I was introduced to most of my closest friends. It also holds a special place in my heart because my favorite sports teams are located in this area. Another aspect that I find special is that the United States declared its independence from Britain in Philadelphia; it is the true birthplace of America. There is no other place like Philadelphia in the world. Because of its friendly people, professional sports, and deep history, someday I hope to call Philadelphia my home.

For starters, the people of Philadelphia are very passionate and strong-willed individuals. They are the kind of people who are proud of where they come from. Growing up, I heard many stories about the meanness and coldness of the locals' personalities. However, that is not the case. Everyone I met in Philly has always been very kind to me. Many people I encountered were nice enough to show me the sights and sounds of the city. Those people really wanted me to fall in love with their city, just as they did when they were young. In addition, my friend, Octavious, grew up in Philly and introduced me to new people; these people eventually became my friends. Each one of my friends has a deep South Philly accent that I love and appreciate. However, more than anything, I appreciate a quality they all share, lovingness. They are so kind to one another and to me as well. My friends took me in as one of their own, and they made me feel a part of their Philly family. In fact, the only rude individuals I found in this city were the commuters from New Jersey. As my friend, James, always says, "No one in Philly likes them folks from Jersey." Philadelphians dislike these commuters because they are usually very hostile. New Jersey "invaders" are especially harsh when discussing their favorite sports teams, so discussions are problematic because people from Philly are equally as passionate about their beloved sports.

Because Philadelphia has a rich background in sports, professional sports teams are central to Philadelphian culture. For example, The Philadelphia 76ers (basketball) have won three NBA titles, the last one in 1983. The Phillies (baseball) have won two World Series championships, and they are the most recent team in Philly to earn a championship trophy. Philly also has professional football and hockey teams, the Eagles and Flyers respectively. Neither team has earned a title, but the fans are still very hopeful. The most important thing to realize about Philadelphia's sports is to never count on a team to win a championship. Philly's teams have broken many hearts because they so often come very close to winning but rarely succeed. Nevertheless, Philadelphians are die-hard supporters of their teams. Many of these fans were pleasantly surprised when the Phillies won the 2008 World Series; the city was ecstatic after twenty-eight years of disappointment. This accomplishment definitely brought pride back to the City of Brotherly Love and added another achievement to Philly's rich history.

Another important aspect of Philadelphia is its place in American history. For instance, the birthplace of America is located in the Old City District at Independence Hall. Independence Hall is an old brick building that looks very similar to a church. Its striking green-blue roof is what stands out most about this two-hundred-year-old building. Knowing that this place is where the America's forefathers composed the Declaration of Independence and the U.S. Constitution is a surreal feeling. Also, seeing the Liberty Bell with the large crack down its shiny, bronze side is much more thrilling to see in person rather than in a history book. Walking through the Old City District and taking in the historic sites makes me feel like I am back in the 1700s and a part of history.

Because of the friendly people, exciting sports, and rich history, the city of Philadelphia will always have a place in my heart. There is not one thing that I would change about that city; Philly is my dream location. Not a day goes by that I do not think about my friends, family, sports teams, and landmarks that fill the city. Once I complete my undergraduate degree, I plan to start a whole new life in this place that I want to call home. Home is where someone can feel like oneself and be around people and things that he or she loves. Philly is definitely my home.

Luke Cunningham

Student Model Essay

Exemplification

Selfish America

We are a nation comprised of unbelievably selfish individuals. Americans consider no one or anything that is beyond their immediate family or interests. The vast number of people who inhabit this great nation are given many opportunities to help people who are less fortunate than they are, but hardly anyone takes advantage of such opportunities. Furthermore, Americans spend a large amount of money on useless things that they never use for more than a month or two before throwing them in the trash. America is seen as a great and powerful nation, where people come to seek freedom and opportunities, but under this false appearance lies the black heart of selfishness at the very center of its core.

Many Americans do not ponder life outside of their family home or their interests. The thoughts of an average person consist of television, dating, religious views, music, and parties. These people are also preoccupied with impressing others, attending popular events, and buying expensive gadgets. However, these "good" people rarely consider what they could do to make the world a better place. For instance, they are not concerned with world hunger, global warming, economic crises, or foreign affairs. Such things are not important to these individuals unless their lives are directly affected.

In order to make up for the lack of consideration, there are many different ways for Americans to help their fellow man. Americans have the chance to volunteer their services in many different ways. There are organizations such as Stewpot, which is a service that accepts donated food and then cooks food for people who cannot afford to feed themselves or their families. Another group is Gateway Rescue Mission, where clothes are donated and then sold for extremely low prices so people can afford to clothe themselves. Most Americans think that they have better things to do with their free time. Only a small percentage of Americans actually take advantage of these opportunities. Also, some Americans complain because we send troops across the ocean to help less able countries defend and take care of themselves. The people of this nation only care about the fact that these soldiers are risking their lives. Individuals do not realize the possibility that this mission is for a greater cause. It is very noble for a person to give his or her life so that an entire country will have a chance to survive, but most Americans refuse to see it this way.

After the failure to help their fellow man, Americans have further proven their selfishness by purchasing extravagant items that they do not need. The average American will spend two hundred dollars on something trivial, like new shoes or the latest style of clothing. Most will not consider that instead of buying yet another outfit to add to an already extensive collection, they could have donated that money to help feed a village in a third world country. Also,

---

Annotations:

The writer is using a shocking statement as a hook to get readers' attention.

Wordy phrase. How could you state the same idea in fewer words?

This is an example of how you can go beyond the three-point thesis. This thesis tells readers the essay will be about American selfishness, but we have to read on find out which particular examples of selfishness the writer will focus on.

Readers should expect to see specific examples of these three activities at some point in this essay. What examples occur to you?

Good transition

Does this topic sentence support the thesis? Does it reflect the content of this paragraph? How could you make it stronger?

What transition belongs here?

These are specific examples that support a general statement.

Good transitional sentence - it reflects on the main idea of the previous paragraph.

when these individuals are done with these items, in many cases barely used, most will simply throw these belongings in the garbage instead of donating them to help someone less fortunate. Americans waste their money on so many different things such as food, electronic devices, and clothes. For instance, many people eat out roughly once a week and do not eat half of what they order. Americans could help so many others, including their fellow countrymen, by doing simple things, such as donating clothes, recycling, and giving food to a local charity.

> This statement summarizes the information previously presented in the essay. Is it effective? Why or why not?

> The writer ends with a statement of significance to inspire readers to think about the serious nature of the topic. You can also end an essay with a suggestion or recommendation. What kind of call to action might work at the end of this essay to inspire readers to do something about this problem?

People of other countries have looked up to this nation for many years. They see America as a beacon of hope that stands for freedom and opportunity. However, this country has not lived up to its reputation. We, the people of this country, are entirely too selfish. We think only of ourselves and our needs and wants or those of our families and friends. We do not consider the effects that our actions (and sometimes inaction) have, outside and within this nation. Most Americans indulge in expensive items and entertainment and consider their time too valuable to help others. The world is a sad place when people can get away with such atrocities and not be held accountable.

> What is the definition of this word? It has a strong meaning; does it seem appropriate in this context?

Sarah Speelman

Exemplification—Prompts for Writing an Essay

Choose one of the prompts below and write an exemplification essay. Exemplification writing seeks to prove a point by using examples to "show" the reader, so remember to support your points by providing multiple examples that are followed with specific details.

Explain the value of playing video games. This essay could go in one of several different directions; for example, you might focus on increased skill levels (in such areas as eye-hand coordination, critical thinking, problem solving) or the benefit of playing video games over watching television or even reading a book. Plan your essay carefully, and make sure to include the names of specific games that might have value, focusing on particular aspects of each game.

Explain people's morbid fascination with grizzly or gruesome events. Using specific examples, support the idea that people enjoy viewing events that involve injury or even death. You might consider television shows and movies, pointing out the popularity of those that present graphic depictions of violence. Do people watch car races primarily to witness the wrecks or boxing matches to see the blood? If so, be sure to bring up a specific driver or boxer in a particular competition. Also, think about how people behave when driving by the scene of a traffic accident or passing by the scene of a crime.

Explain how people are influenced by the media. You could frame your essay around the marketing of a particular product (cars), or you might want to focus on a specific product's advertising campaign (Toyota Prius). Other options: think about the objectivity of news reporting of a particular network (Fox News or MSNBC, for example) OR the representation of a particular group of people (women, African Americans, Muslims, the elderly) in television programming.

Explain the qualities of a successful professional. Using detailed examples, show how certain characteristics (physical attributes, personality, habits, behaviors) contribute to success in a specific profession. Focus on one type of professional (athletes, artists, business professionals, academics, politicians) and identify specific members of that profession.

Exemplification Essay Peer Response

Provide thorough and thoughtful responses to the following questions. **Yes and No answers are insufficient**, so comment, explain, or offer suggestions for all responses. You may also write on the draft and mark grammar and punctuation mistakes.

Read the Title:

1. How does the title grab your interest? In what way does it predict the content of the essay?

Read the Introduction:

2. Does the introduction have a hook (opening sentence) that is a surprising statement, interesting fact, relevant quotation, or thought provoking question? After reading the introduction, predict what you expect to find in the body.

3. Underline the thesis. What specific and significant claim does the thesis make?

Read the Body Paragraphs:

4. Underline the topic sentence in each body paragraph. Does each topic sentence support the thesis sentence? What do you predict each body paragraph will add to this essay?

5. Number the examples used in each body paragraph. Identify any examples that do not support the author's main point or that could be explained in greater detail. Are there enough examples in each body paragraph? Note these on the paper.

6. Circle the transitions in each body paragraph. Note any location you think may need additional (or different) transitional words or phrases.

7. Do you see any information that should be moved to another paragraph or perhaps removed entirely? Explain your reasoning.

Read the Conclusion:

8. How does the conclusion relate to the thesis?

9. List the points the author has included in the conclusion. Identify any points that do not relate to the thesis. What points are missing from the conclusion?

10. What final thoughts does the author leave with the reader?

11. What was your favorite part of the essay? Explain.

Exemplification Essay Peer Response

Provide thorough and thoughtful responses to the following questions. **Yes and No answers are insufficient**, so comment, explain, or offer suggestions for all responses. You may also write on the draft and mark grammar and punctuation mistakes.

Read the Title:

1. How does the title grab your interest? In what way does it predict the content of the essay?

Read the Introduction:

2. Does the introduction have a hook (opening sentence) that is a surprising statement, interesting fact, relevant quotation, or thought provoking question? After reading the introduction, predict what you expect to find in the body.

3. Underline the thesis. What specific and significant claim does the thesis make?

Read the Body Paragraphs:

4. Underline the topic sentence in each body paragraph. Does each topic sentence support the thesis sentence? What do you predict each body paragraph will add to this essay?

5. Number the examples used in each body paragraph. Identify any examples that do not support the author's main point or that could be explained in greater detail. Are there enough examples in each body paragraph? Note these on the paper.

6. Circle the transitions in each body paragraph. Note any location you think may need additional (or different) transitional words or phrases.

7. Do you see any information that should be moved to another paragraph or perhaps removed entirely? Explain your reasoning.

Read the Conclusion:

8. How does the conclusion relate to the thesis?

9. List the points the author has included in the conclusion. Identify any points that do not relate to the thesis. What points are missing from the conclusion?

10. What final thoughts does the author leave with the reader?

11. What was your favorite part of the essay? Explain.

Cause and Effect

Student Model Essay

Losing It All But Gaining More

Two years ago, I was forty pounds overweight. Because of this, I lacked confidence in myself and felt extremely depressed about my appearance. Most of the time, I never felt like I fit in with my friends. Not only did I lack confidence, but daily activities, such as walking up a flight of stairs or walking to my next class, were a struggle for me. In addition, my doctor told me that I was also putting myself at risk of developing diabetes and heart problems in the near future. Being overweight definitely put a damper on my life; therefore, I realized I had to do something to make positive changes. I decided I wanted to begin exercising because I knew exercising would release endorphins to make me feel happy rather than depressed and lower my risk of developing serious diseases. Exercising made me feel better about myself and gave me the confidence I needed.

As I began exercising daily, I noticed a difference in my energy level. My day-to-day activities became easier. For example, I did not find myself short of breath after walking to class or up a flight of stairs. The exercise that had the most impact on my energy level was running. Running gave me so much more energy than I had before, and I felt much healthier as a result. Exercise was beginning to change my life, and I was pleased with my progress. I loved not being tired at the end of the day. In addition, I was able to do so much more. I thought exercising would make me feel exhausted; instead, it did the opposite and provided me with an abundance of energy.

After a few months passed, I began to feel my confidence improving. Because of my strenuous exercise routine, I was losing weight and gaining confidence. When I spent time with my friends, I noticed that I felt more comfortable around them. In the past, they would all go shopping, and I would feel terrible as I watched them try on cute clothes that I could not fit into. However, after losing weight, I was able to experience the same fun they were having on shopping trips. Before starting an exercise routine, I never went to the beach with my friends because I was afraid to wear a bathing suit in front of everyone; I was too embarrassed about being overweight. Now, when they ask me to join them at the beach, I do not hesitate to accept their invitation. In fact, I feel much more confident about the way I look. In this way, exercising made a drastic difference in my self-esteem and in my confidence around others.

Although I am happy about my increased energy level and improved appearance, the most important effect exercising had on me was improving my health. After exercising helped me get fit, I returned to the doctor, and he gave me some very good news: because of my improved health, I now have a longer life expectancy and am at very low risk of developing diabetes or heart disease. Furthermore, my blood pressure and cholesterol levels have returned to normal. I am in the best health of my life! Small tasks that had once been a battle for me, such as walking my dog and picking up the mail, are now simple tasks, as they should be.

Looking back at my life two years ago and comparing it to my life now makes me grateful for the changes exercise has made in my life. There is no greater feeling than being able to do the things I want to do without having low energy or low self-esteem holding me back. Now, I am an avid runner who encourages other people to get in shape by exercising daily. Exercise has given me the energy I need and everything I have ever wanted. Ultimately, it has helped me live the life I was always meant to live.

Christine Field

Student Model Essay

Adolescent Violence

As society evolves over time, young generations continue to be exposed to many adult issues. In the United States, it seems that murder is barely given a second thought, and violence is a part of day-to-day life. Sadly, the world has turned into a community of hate, malice, and violence. As the saying goes, our children are the future. However, what lessons are kids learning these days? If society expects youth to be the leaders of tomorrow and succeed in a productive nation, positive influence is essential. Because children's minds are being fueled with what modern society deems as "cool," their collective understanding of what is acceptable is being corrupted; therefore, violence is steadily increasing. Increased violence among children in the United States is mainly due to glorification of war, media, and video games.

The glorification of war has become increasingly apparent in modern society. In America's early history during the late 1700s, colonists fought in the Revolutionary War so that the colonies could become an independent nation. Clearly, the act of war has been a part of life since America's founding. For example, when males turn eighteen, they are required to register with Selective Service, so they can be drafted into the military if needed. Often, war is seen as the only way to correct problems. In return, this often leads to war being glorified beyond its original intent, and a significant contributor to this problem is the media. On television, there are commercials showing brave, powerful, and courageous military men with guns in their hands, standing on top of mountains. The message conveyed to many young viewers through these commercials is that these are "real men." The media's portrayal of military recruitment has become an image of power that many young boys dream of and wish to achieve.

In addition to advertising's positive representation of military life, other forms of the media cause an increase in violence. For example, news programs aid in the glorification of war; in addition, almost every show on television shows some form of violence or abuse. It seems that people cannot go anywhere or do anything without seeing some act of violence. Every night, the evening news shows murder, armed robbery, and other violent crimes committed by young people. Furthermore, a movie is not deemed award winning unless some form of violence is added to its action-packed theme; even a romantic flick is judged incomplete without someone dying a tragic death. The reality is that youth are exposed to negative influences in everyday life. For example, many kids who are raised in violent households often end up roaming the streets and committing crimes. In many children's minds, there is no other alternative to getting by in life without using violence, and the media reinforces and supports this idea. Even what is considered children's entertainment contributes to violence in the form of video games.

Video games are a specific form of entertainment that aid in embedding seeds of violence in children's minds. Society has become more technologically advanced, and as a result, young people are brought up in an environment where the latest gadgets are within arm's reach at the local store. Video game companies have combined their marketing with the entertainment industry by inventing visually stimulating, real-life interaction that entrances many young viewers. Even though there are a handful of educational games, they are heavily outweighed by the number of violent video games available. As statistics show, most young children spend more time sitting in front of the television than playing outside; as a result, children are spending more time playing violent games than is necessary. Because children are playing these negative video games, violent images become embedded in their minds. If video games are a main source of learning problem solving skills, children are likely to use these violent means to solve their real-life predicaments. Therefore, children who follow tactics that they see in video games usually do not solve their problems in positive, non-violent ways. These visually stimulating games are clearly one of the many forms of entertainment that portray acts of violence.

Violence has become a serious issue that society must strive to reduce. The three main causes of violence in the lives of American children include the glorification of war, the media, and video games. Children should not be exposed to acts of violence at such a young age when they are so impressionable and looking for role models. Clearly, it is apparent that violence is a serious problem in American society. We must keep our futures in mind and begin to ensure safe lives for children.

Tracy Anderson

This essay originally appeared in *Guide to Freshman Composition*, published in 2007 and utilized by the MSU English Department for EN 1103 instruction.

Student Model Essay   Cause and Effect

The Strangulation of Education by the Economy

Evaluate this first sentence. It introduces the topic, but what is it lacking? Think of ways you might edit this sentence to make it more effective.

Think about the wording in the introduction: how could you edit it to eliminate repetition?

As the American economy takes a turn for the worse, public education is suffering and will continue to suffer under this financial hardship. Among these academic institutions are this country's colleges and universities. Due to lack of funds, all colleges and universities across the United States have had to make difficult decisions to make up for the lack of financial resources. These decisions include hiring a smaller number of qualified faculty and skilled staff, doing away with some campus perks, and lowering the enrollment standards.

How does this sentence narrow the focus as the introduction moves gradually to the thesis?

As less and less money is being funded to colleges and universities due to the current economic crisis, these institutions will lower their budgets and hire less qualified faculty. This will lead to significant changes in the educational standards that students have begun to expect from their academic institutions. The quality and variety of courses offered will be greatly reduced because there will not be enough teachers to handle the large number of classes, and there will also be fewer upper level courses offered to the students due to the under-qualified individuals teaching in the classrooms. As a result, because teachers are less qualified for their positions, the institutions can pay them less. Therefore, a lower budget at colleges and universities not only hurts the faculty; it also creates problems for students.

This is a strong topic sentence that relates directly back to the thesis.

This sentence is worded as a definite consequence of reduced funding. Why could this be a problem? Think about ways to reword this statement to make it more valid.

This strong concluding sentence summarizes the point of the paragraph and points towards significance.

Not only will the classrooms suffer because of the financial crisis, but the overall maintenance of the campuses will decline. There will be fewer staff members, like janitors and grounds keepers, to take care of such large establishments and the grounds around them. There will not be enough money to support the number of workers needed to maintain such large campuses. The various buildings that make up a campus will eventually fall into disrepair due to the lack of manpower and the absence of sufficient funds needed to maintain those buildings. The grass will no longer be green, and the trees and the flowers will not be nicely trimmed and arranged because the colleges and universities will not be able to employ the staff needed to accomplish these things. Also, there will be no one to pick up after the students when they make messes on campus. Why would campus maintenance workers want to clean up after messy people when they will not be paid enough to support themselves and their families? This financial decline will not only affect job opportunities for staff, it will also eventually lead to lower enrollment because no one wants to attend a school that is not appealing to the eye.

This topic sentence is a strong transition that introduces the main idea of the new paragraph.

This question can lead to logic issues because it questions work ethic and attitude and suggests pay reductions.

Be careful of absolute language (no one, everyone, etc.): "many people may not want" or "few people want."

On campus, other than the financial difficulties, life is fairly easy for the students because there are always people to cook for them, to clean up after them, and to entertain them, but when the colleges and universities begin to receive smaller amounts of money from the government and sponsors, students will have to start doing certain things for themselves and dealing with the loss of many perks that they have come to enjoy. There will be no kind cafeteria workers preparing delicious food for everyone and picking up after the students when they are in a hurry and leave their food on the tables. The workers will be angrier due to smaller wages, and the food will begin to resemble little more than frozen T.V. dinners. Furthermore, there will be no more campus funded movies, concerts, sporting events, and artistic performances. If they happen at all, students will be charged a fee. The students at Mississippi State University, for example, enjoy many perks that are free to them.

Evaluate the structure of this topic sentence. Does it function well as a transition? Does it introduce the topic of this paragraph? What is your opinion of its length?

Consider the supporting information in this paragraph. Is the writer drawing illogical conclusions about attitude that might be unrelated to financial issues?

There is a campus funded gym, the Sanderson Center, which is free to all full time students, a free bus route that transports students to all areas of the campus, and a campus newspaper that is free of charge. Things such as these are expensive to maintain. Gyms need exercise machines and have to employ people to care for them, buses need fuel and repairs, and newspaper departments need money for paper, ink, and printing. Ultimately, lack of funds will drastically affect perks for the students at colleges and universities.

> Good concluding sentence.

To be able to pay the faculty and staff that make colleges and universities function and to make up for the loss of students due to the weakening of the school, the enrollment standards will also have to be lowered a great deal. The academic institutions will have to be less selective about whom they accept so that more students and more tuition money will be coming in. Lowering the standards will lead to a higher failure and dropout rate because a greater number of students will not be able to handle the course load at a college or university. Furthermore, tuition prices will have to be raised to keep up with financial demands, and this will put more of a financial strain on the students and their families who are already struggling to make ends meet. Overall, lowering enrollment standards will affect many people and the school negatively.

> This paragraph is essentially a causal chain. Although the ideas are logical, it nearly becomes a slippery slope.

The falling economy is forcing the leaders of establishments to make many difficult decisions that will make those establishments lower the standards of themselves and their institutions. Colleges and universities are such establishments, and they are being hit hard by the financial crisis that is plaguing this country. They will have to come to terms with their inability to fund a large number of highly qualified faculty and staff, make campus life as comfortable as possible for the students, and accept the best and the brightest students. These decisions will affect everyone attending and working at academic institutions. Colleges and universities make these difficult decisions so that people who want to better themselves and the world around them will have a place to learn and to grow as people, even if they are not going to be as content doing so any longer.

> Overall, this conclusion summarizes the essay and restates the thesis; however, the wording is a bit awkward in places. Evaluate (or even rewrite) this paragraph to improve the presentation of ideas.

Sarah Speelman

Cause and Effect—Prompts for Writing an Essay

Choose one of the prompts below and write a cause and effect essay. Cause and effect writing explores why something occurs and what results follow. Remember that chronologically, causes precede an event and effects follow. In your essay, be sure to mention both causes and effects, but you may focus more heavily on one or the other.

Discuss either peer pressure or bullying. For either of these topics, you might find it easy to evaluate the effects (low self esteem, inability to embrace an individual identity), but do not ignore the causes. For example, ask yourself why certain children become bullies or why others are targets for bullying. Why are some people highly susceptible to peer pressure, yet others think and act independently?

Discuss academic misconduct (cheating). Why do students resort to plagiarism or cheating on tests? What factors cause them to resort to behavior that they know is wrong? The effects of cheating are more obvious, but remember to mention them as well. Be sure to consider the consequences of cheating at the college level, which typically are more severe than K-12 penalties.

Discuss a time when you had difficulty in a relationship. Identify the specific relationship: academic (teacher, principal, coach), familial (a parent, sibling, grandparent), or social (friend, teammates). What kind of difficulty did you have? Was it a one-time argument or a disagreement that had been building for a while? Think about the causes of this difficulty: what factors influenced this situation? If you prefer to focus on the effects, consider how both you and the relationship changed: has your life changed, and do you have a better understanding of yourself and the other(s) involved?

Discuss the impact of social media on personal relationships. Consider the positive or negative ways that social media sites (Facebook, Twitter, Instagram) can impact personal relationships. Think about specific components of the site, such as pictures and postings.

Cause and Effect Essay Peer Response

Provide thorough and thoughtful responses to the following questions. **Yes or no answers are insufficient**, so comment, explain, or offer suggestions for all responses. You may also write on the draft and mark grammar and punctuation mistakes.

Read the Title:

1. How does the title grab your interest? In what way does it predict the content of the essay?

Read the Introduction:

2. Does the introduction have a hook (opening sentence) that is a surprising statement, interesting fact, relevant quotation, or thought provoking question? After reading the introduction, predict what you expect to find in the body.

3. Underline the thesis. In your own words, identify the cause/effect relationship. What specific and significant claim does the thesis make? Will the writer focus more on causes or effects?

Read the Body Paragraphs:

4. Underline the topic sentence in each body paragraph. Does each topic sentence support the thesis sentence? What do you predict each body paragraph will add to this essay?

5. List the causes and effects the author includes in the essay. Draw an arrow from each cause to each effect. In what ways is the relationship clear? In what ways is it unclear?

6. Does the author focus more on causes or effects, or an equal combination? Why does this choice make sense, considering the topic?

7. Look at the structure and organization of the essay. Does the author switch back and forth between cause/effect, or have more than one cause and then an overall effect? Explain why you think the organization is or is not appropriate.

8. Circle the transitions in each body paragraph. Note any location you think may need additional (or different) transitional words or phrases.

9. Do you see any information that should be moved to another paragraph or perhaps removed entirely? Explain your reasoning.

Read the Conclusion:
10. How does the conclusion relate to the thesis?

11. List the points the author has included in the conclusion. Identify any points that do not relate to the thesis. What points are missing from the conclusion?

12. What final thoughts does the author leave with the reader?

13. What was your favorite part of the essay? Explain.

Cause and Effect Essay Peer Response

Provide thorough and thoughtful responses to the following questions. **Yes or no answers are insufficient**, so comment, explain, or offer suggestions for all responses. You may also write on the draft and mark grammar and punctuation mistakes.

Read the Title:

1. How does the title grab your interest? In what way does it predict the content of the essay?

Read the Introduction:

2. Does the introduction have a hook (opening sentence) that is a surprising statement, interesting fact, relevant quotation, or thought provoking question? After reading the introduction, predict what you expect to find in the body.

3. Underline the thesis. In your own words, identify the cause/effect relationship. What specific and significant claim does the thesis make? Will the writer focus more on causes or effects?

Read the Body Paragraphs:

4. Underline the topic sentence in each body paragraph. Does each topic sentence support the thesis sentence? What do you predict each body paragraph will add to this essay?

5. List the causes and effects the author includes in the essay. Draw an arrow from each cause to each effect. In what ways is the relationship clear? In what ways is it unclear?

6. Does the author focus more on causes or effects, or an equal combination? Why does this choice make sense, considering the topic?

7. Look at the structure and organization of the essay. Does the author switch back and forth between cause/effect, or have more than one cause and then an overall effect? Explain why you think the organization is or is not appropriate.

8. Circle the transitions in each body paragraph. Note any location you think may need additional (or different) transitional words or phrases.

9. Do you see any information that should be moved to another paragraph or perhaps removed entirely? Explain your reasoning.

Read the Conclusion:

10. How does the conclusion relate to the thesis?

11. List the points the author has included in the conclusion. Identify any points that do not relate to the thesis. What points are missing from the conclusion?

12. What final thoughts does the author leave with the reader?

13. What was your favorite part of the essay? Explain.

Comparison and Contrast, Point-by-Point

Student Model Essay   Comparison and Contrast, Point-by-Point

Testing My Limits

Now that I am in college, what I do now versus what my parents had me do is completely different. Almost everything has changed since I left home. At my house, someone told me what to do and when to do it, but now, I'm lucky if I get out of my bed on the weekends. My parents had rules and made suggestions about everything: what I could do on the weekends, what I could wear, what time I came home, what time and what foods I ate, and when I cleaned. Although I feel that my parents' rules and suggestions about my curfew, my chores, and my eating habits were fair, my rules for myself are more reasonable now because I'm getting older, I'm more mature, and I'm living on my own.

While I lived at home with my parents, I had a curfew of 11:30. I had a problem with this curfew because all of my friends were older and had later curfews or none at all, so most of the time I had to leave when social gatherings were still going on. I can remember only a few times when my parents let me break curfew, and that was because I worked late, and sometimes I really needed to get away from the stress of school and work. In college, however, I come and go as I please. Now when I'm hanging out with friends and it's getting late, my parents aren't calling my cell phone constantly. I give myself a reasonable curfew, so I can go to parties, hang out, and potentially meet people and become more social, since I didn't get those opportunities in high school.

Just as my social life has changed, so has my environment. At home, my room always had to be spotless. My parents were very particular about how my room looked. Everything had its own place; nothing could be on the floor, and even the pillows had to be fixed just right. When I go home for the weekends now, I feel that I should be the golden child because my parents don't get to see or talk to me for long periods of time. However, I still have to clean my room, wash the dishes, and vacuum as though I still live there. Unlike at home, in my dorm room, I don't have anyone yelling at me to make my bed every day, and there is no one questioning why my clothes are on the floor or why I haven't taken out the trash. In more than one way, it isn't bad that my parents were strict about cleaning and chores; now that I am living with a roommate, I am more relaxed about when chores are completed, but they still get done.

Although I enjoy being more flexible about keeping my room neat and clean, the one rule my parents made that I wish had not changed since I left home is my eating habits. My mom always had complete control regarding eating. She didn't let us eat at restaurants much. Mom always made our plates, and we always ate what she cooked, no matter what it was. In college, though, fast food has become convenient. When I don't have time to sit in the Perry Cafeteria to eat, I get Panda Express or Chick-fil-a and eat in my room. If I'm studying for a test or doing homework, I usually snack on popcorn or chips. Eating unhealthy and fast food is extremely abnormal for me, and it is a bad habit that I regret deeply. This negative change in my eating habits is definitely not reasonable on my part. If my habits don't change soon, the freshman fifteen will turn into the freshman thirty.

Several parts of my life have changed since I left home to attend college. I have started to drift away from my parents' rules and set my own limits. Although I am getting older and more mature, I am always going to have my parents' teachings to rely on. I am learning to take their rules and make them my own; at the same time, now it is my turn to venture out, make my own mistakes, and hopefully learn from them in the end.

Zacarah Cox

Student Model Essay

Comparison and Contrast, Point-by-Point

Sports Here and There

People of every age all over the world participate in sports. The type of sport, the reason for playing it, and the aim varies from person to person. Many adults are active because they want to be fit or lose weight; in contrast, children want to have fun or possibly become professionals one day. In the United States, when children or teenagers go to school or college and want to play sports, they usually try out for their high school or college team, whereas in Germany they join a sports club. Although sports in German clubs and in American colleges have some similarities, they are very different when coaches, teammates, and practice methods are considered.

Although the word "coach" is the same in Germany and the U.S., there are some important differences between club coaches and college coaches. In Germany, coaching is usually only a side job or hobby, so coaches usually have other full-time jobs. For example, they are often teachers, officers, or venders. Although coaches get little money for their work, they still coach because they love the sport and enjoy being a part of it. However, it is sometimes difficult to have enough coaches and to recruit new ones in sports clubs. In contrast, American college coaches have full-time jobs as coaches, so they have to focus on only one job and can earn more money by coaching. However, if they do not want to coach anymore, it is more difficult for them to quit because they have no other jobs to support themselves financially. While American coaches are considered professionals in their field, German coaches do their jobs more for personal satisfaction.

In addition to a difference in the role of coaches, the actual teams themselves are very different. In Germany, almost every city has at least one sports club; therefore, pupils normally choose to go to the club which is closest to their residence or to their school. However, not every athlete of a club goes to the same school or college because sports and education are separate from each other. At colleges in the United States, college athletes are part of a team that represents their university, and most athletes get athletic scholarships so that they do not have to pay for tuition or food. In addition, not everybody can choose to join a college team; an athlete must already have a high skill level, and only the best are selected to play for a university. Also, American athletes at the college level always go to school with their teammates; this may not be the case in Germany.

Just as the teams are structured very differently, so is the practice schedule. In German clubs, practice time is during the week, usually in the late afternoon or evening around six o'clock since coaches and athletes are busy during the day with work and school. In addition, athletes practice only three or four times a week with their coaches and teammates, so they practice and work out on their own other days. In contrast, an American college's daily practice is in the morning before classes or in the afternoon around three o'clock. The teammates practice together almost every day while the coach makes announcements and gives advice. The aim of a college sports team is to be good as one unit and to represent the university; for clubs, it is more focused on the individual.

The systems of sports in German clubs and in American colleges are quite different regarding coaches, athletes, and practices. Although American athletic systems integrate education with athletics, German sports systems allow student athletes to separate their participation in sports from other aspects of their lives. However, both Germany and America are quite successful in athletic competitions, and their successes demonstrate how both systems can be effective.

Cornelia Griesche

Student Model Essay

Comparison and Contrast, Point-by-Point

A Perfect Match?

These are effective bridge sentences, moving from general to specific.

A question can be an effective way to get the reader's attention.

These sentences narrow the topic further, introducing the writer's parents and leading readers to the thesis.

Have you ever wondered if there is a person who is a perfect match for you? All people are individuals with different traits, so the possibility is small that two people with common characteristics will find each other. Even if a man and a woman get married after falling in love, as they get to know each other, their differences will become obvious. When my parents first got married, they seemed to be a match made in heaven and had many common interests, such as swimming, walking, and enjoying their work. However, over time they have come to recognize their differences in certain

This effective topic sentence begins with a transition, states both of the subjects, and lists one point.

This topic sentence provides a transition from the previous body paragraph and introduces the next point.

Now that you have read two carefully constructed body paragraphs, evaluate this one on your own. Focus on the topic sentence, the discussion of each subject, and the transition between subjects. What does this paragraph do well? How can it be improved?

The first sentence of the conclusion provides a solid restatement of the thesis in new words.

The thesis is clearly stated and provides a framework for the essay.

This transition smoothly moves the reader from Subject A to Subject B.

These sentences focus on both Subject A and Subject B simultaneously, illustrating how the two subjects interact and further developing the paragraph's main idea.

This transition takes the reader from Subject A to Subject B.

This is an effective transition to take the reader from individual subjects to both subjects simultaneously. Doing this creates parallelism between the first and second body paragraphs.

These sentences provide a brief summary of the essay's main points, transitioning from Subject A to Subject B.

areas of life. Although they share some similarities, they are miles apart when it comes to certain leisure activities.

First of all, my mother and father have very different tastes in watching television. My father likes watching sports. When he was younger, he was good at playing baseball, so he enjoys watching Major League Baseball, especially the New York Yankees. Whenever a baseball game is on TV, he watches all nine innings. On the other hand, my mother likes dramas and does not like watching sports. She sometimes identifies with the female lead, and if the female lead falls in love with the handsome guy, she also pretends to fall in love. When my father and mother watch TV together, some arguments happen. For example, when my mother is watching a show she enjoys, my father will sometimes grab the remote control and change the channel to sports. Her viewing is disrupted, and she misses some important scenes because of my father. Therefore, they argue about who has top priority. No one ever wins these arguments, and they continue to have completely different tastes when watching TV.

Just as they differ in their TV watching habits, my father and mother have very different approaches to shopping. My father does not like to go shopping. If he goes to a department store or big outlet mall, he always checks where the break area is. After he looks around in four or five stores, he goes to the break area and waits there until my mother and I finish browsing. In contrast, my mother really enjoys shopping. Even though she does not buy too many clothes or other things, she enjoys window-shopping. Whenever new items come out, she is good at finding them. Then, she checks the price and quality before comparing them to the previous ones. She is a very good shopper. On the other hand, when we all go to a big outlet mall, my father sits in the break area for hours while my mother and I shop. If I were he, I would be very bored, but he told me that he just likes taking a rest. Just like their differences with TV watching, when my parents go shopping together, no one knows that they are a couple because it is hard for them to be together in a shopping mall.

In addition to their different TV watching habits and shopping styles, my father and my mother also have attitudes about traveling. My father does not like traveling. He really hates leaving his hometown for very long because the preparation for and inconvenience of traveling annoys him. Because of this, he has never been to many famous places in South Korea. When he does agree to travel, he just looks around, takes a few pictures, and is ready to go home. In contrast, my mother is really crazy about traveling. She has visited almost every town and city in South Korea, and now she is ready to explore other countries. She believes that traveling gives people a broad perspective and understanding of life. When I was younger, we were planning a family trip for summer vacation. At that time, my mother suggested going to another country to experience a new culture. However, my father refused to leave South Korea, so we just went to the beach near my hometown. Clearly, they have very different opinions about traveling.

Overall, my father and mother are different even though they have lived together for twenty-three years. My father likes watching sports but does not like to shop or travel. On the other hand, my mother likes watching dramas on TV, browsing in stores and visiting new places. They have such different opinions about these things that sometimes I am very surprised that they are still happily

> The author moves from a specific relationship to ideas about relationships in general, which is opposite to the introduction. How does this effectively conclude the essay?

married and that their lives are going well. However, whenever I see them argue, I think that they would be a match made in heaven if they were considerate of each other's interests. It might take a long time for one couple to be perfect; however, these difficulties are a natural process of people's relationships because all human beings are very different.

Hyeonji Lee

Comparison and Contrast, Subject-by-Subject

Student Model Essay   Comparison and Contrast, Subject-by-Subject

Mother and Daughter: Sorting It Out

Relationships between parents and their children can be complicated. There are always bumps and curves on the road of life. Unlike some families, my mother and I did not have a strong mother-daughter bond; we never talked or did anything together, even when I was a young child. Because our relationship was so distant from the start, we grew even further apart as I got older. Although the relationship I have with my mother started out shaky, it has changed drastically in the past few years, due in part to a horrible tragedy which brought us together.

When I was a young child, my mother never took any interest in the things I liked or wanted to do. Because of our different interests, our relationship was distant. As I grew older and more independent, my mother and I grew further and further apart. We never talked, laughed, or held a casual conversation about each other's day. We simply lived in the same house and spoke only when necessary. For example, if I mentioned that I was going to a friend's house over the weekend or after school, my mom would respond by telling me that I needed to do chores or help her with something. We spoke only when necessary, and this was our very limited form of communication. We had nothing in common. Eventually, I began to like sports, and my mother enjoyed shopping and cooking, activities that did not interest me. My newfound passion did not help with our relationship; my mother wanted me to be "girly," but I wanted to go outside and play with my friends. I believe that our different personalities and opposite interests caused angry disagreements and drove us apart.

When I came to my teenage years and began high school, we were merely tolerant of each other. We did what he had to do to keep the peace and live in the same home. Then suddenly, when I turned fourteen, my mother sat me down and told me that she wanted a closer relationship with me. I was not fond of the idea at first because I had built up so much resentment from my early childhood. However, after talking to her for an hour, I slowly grew a little bit closer to her. We began doing a little of what we both liked to do. She started coming to my soccer games, and I, in turn, began to go shopping and cook dinner with her. I enjoyed this time with her, and our relationship improved a bit. However, when I turned fifteen, a tragedy in our family brought us closer than I ever thought possible. A few months after my fifteenth birthday, my two-year-old sister drowned in our pool while I was babysitting her. Because of this horrible accident, my mom and I wanted to support each other in any way possible as we worked to survive the terrible grief. Today, we have an appreciation for each other, and our relationship is incredibly strong.

Considering my mother and I never used to speak, it is important now that we speak every day, usually for at least an hour. I am able to talk to my mom and tell her everything about my life and not have to worry about her judging me. My mom and I try to do everything possible together. I am now happy to come home, and I try to be home as much as possible. I am so happy to know that I have such a strong relationship with my mom because not many people are able to have that. Unlike in our past, my mom tries to be involved and supportive with my activities. She comes to my soccer games, and she watches me play sports. We try to be there for each other as much as possible. Now, it is important for me to make decisions and act in a way that makes her proud because I care what she thinks. I try to cook, and I shop with her. Today, my mom and I have a strong relationship. I respect her so much, and I feel that no matter what happens in our lives we will always have a feeling of comfort because we know we will always have each other.

Although our relationship was rough when I was growing up, we have grown to have the strongest bond possible for a mother and daughter. Also, I believe that if my mother and I did not have a troubled relationship at the beginning, we would not be as close as we are today. The challenges and tragedy that we have endured together have been the worst and the best things that could happen to a mother and a daughter. My mom and I will be able to take on any problem that comes to us in life because we know we will always have each other's back. The difference between our relationship at the beginning and the one we have now shows that the mother and daughter bond is strong and can overcome any obstacle.

Sophya Dragos

Student Model Essay   Comparison and Contrast, Subject-by-Subject

Ruby Hall Versus Traditional Housing

Last summer, I had the privilege of coming to Mississippi State University to work in the Mechanical Engineering Department for three weeks. While I was here, I stayed in a place called Hull Hall. This building is a traditional style dormitory, with community showers, very thin doors that allow almost zero privacy, and rooms furnished with very cheap and unattractive furniture. Basically, Hull is one of the oldest dorms on campus and has not seen a renovation in quite some time, if ever. This environment sounds like a nightmare, right? In contrast, this semester I am living in the newest dormitory on campus—Ruby Hall, the "Cadillac" of college dormitories. Ruby is definitely the nicest dorm that I have seen on this campus and other campuses in Mississippi. Slowly but surely, this campus and several other campuses around the nation are leaving behind dorm plans like Hull Hall and transforming traditional-style housing into newer apartment styles, causing students to miss out on a very important aspect of college. Even though Ruby Hall is decorated with matching furniture of much higher quality than the cheap furniture of lesser dorms like Hull Hall and allows

its residents to have their own private bathrooms, it is missing one of the key elements that a person needs in college: interaction with other students. This housing transition that provides nicer and safer facilities might actually affect college students in negative ways.

One seemingly small characteristic that has been included in the newer dormitory room is a door that closes automatically. This type of door may not seem like a big problem to the newer generation of students who have never experienced a door that shuts manually, but because the doors in Ruby Hall shut automatically, students miss out on the opportunity to make life-long friends. After all, it is hard to create a friendship with someone if his or her door is always closed. But I have worked hard to solve this problem by propping the door open with a doorstop every time I am in my room to give people the chance to come by to say hello.

Even though the doors to Hull Hall's rooms are not as thick and new as Ruby's, they do have to be shut manually. Anyone who lives or has lived in Hull Hall knows that most of the doors stay open most of the time. This openness allows for a sense of unity and togetherness that is missing in the newer dorms like Ruby Hall. Granted, most of the time the residents of an older dorm talk only about the poor living conditions in that particular dorm, but they are partaking in conversation nonetheless. If a person wants to shut the door to the room, he or she must do so physically, and as everyone knows, college students do not want to exert any extra energy where they do not see a need. This laziness allows residents of traditional-style housing to become better acquainted with their hall neighbors. But this opportunity also arises in other locations in the dorm.

In Ruby Hall, students have their own personal shower and bathroom. This may sound like a benefit of living in a newer dormitory, but it is just another way that these new dorms have promoted the hermit lifestyle. Residents of Ruby Hall are quite lucky to have their own personal space. They never have to talk to anyone they do not want to or share anything that they do not want to. But therein lies the problem.

One of the most commonly heard complaints about living in an older dorm is that one may have to share a community shower with several other inhabitants, and rightly so. Sharing something as personal as a shower can get just that: very personal. But what people often overlook is the fact that having to share something so intimate can really create a sense of unity among those that have to go through with it. Therefore, those of us who shared a community shower in Hull Hall will always feel that common bond toward each other.

In my opinion, the quality of a residence dorm does not rely upon its luxuries; the quality relies on the friendships built by the people who inhabit it. Even though Ruby Hall may offer a better living environment than that of an older dorm such as Hull Hall, the residents of the newer dorm are missing out on one of the joys of being in college. As college housing becomes more upscale, interaction and unity among the residents becomes weaker.

Andrew Telle

This essay originally appeared in *A Guide to Freshman Composition*, published in 2006 and utilized by the MSU English Department for EN 1103 instruction.

Student Model Essay   Comparison and Contrast, Subject-by-Subject

You've Got Mail

> The title grabs the attention of the reader and clearly connects to the lead in the introduction.

> This writer draws in readers by immediately situating them in time and place before moving gradually to the essay's topic: communication.

The year was 1991, the Internet was in its infancy, cellular phones were expensive and as big as bricks, and email was a distant dream. American troops were deploying to Kuwait to support Operation Desert Storm; to say communication with loved ones was limited would be an understatement. Since then, technology has changed the way the deployed American soldier communicates with family and friends. Today's soldier has a myriad of technologies that allow him to communicate instantly with loved ones, unlike the soldiers of Desert Storm who wrote letters on cardboard food cartons.

> In comparison and contrast essays, a thesis should always present both subjects. What are the two subjects of this essay?

> Although this is a comparison/contrast essay, the writer has utilized an additional rhetorical strategy: narration. Is this effective? Why or why not?

> This is an effective second point, but it is not fully developed like the first point is. How could you develop it further?

A young Marine boarded the Navy ship *USS Tuscaloosa* headed for Operation Desert Storm in 1991. As the ship pulled away, the Marines and sailors knew that they would not hear from their loved ones again for weeks. Letters were sent to the next port where the ship was scheduled to stop. The next mail call would be in Hawaii, two weeks away. Lying in bunks stacked four high, Marines and sailors wrote letters on paper, cardboard, or whatever they could find. When the letters were finished, they addressed them and wrote "free mail" where the stamp goes and sent them off via "snail" mail. After arriving in a port, the first order of business was always to find a pay phone. People were willing to wait hours in line to talk to loved ones for a few short minutes.

> The writer begins with an effective first point, letters, which is further developed with specific examples for clarification of "snail mail."

> This is a transitional paragraph that creates a bridge between subjects. It summarizes the first subject before moving to the second one. Does this paragraph accomplish that goal? How could you make it stronger?

Upon arrival in the desert, mail was delivered to the front lines weekly by helicopter. Service members prayed for care packages or letters and pictures. The person who received a care package was the man of the week. Usually, a care package consisted of grandma's freshly baked (now two weeks old) cookies, melted candy, magazines, and cigarettes. After months of eating dehydrated MREs (Meals Ready to Eat), eating grandma's stale cookies was like having Thanksgiving dinner. These hardships and feelings of being disconnected are now distant memories thanks to technological improvements.

This topic sentence presents a transition, then introduces the second subject.

Thirteen years later, a soldier boards a bus to deploy to Operation Iraqi Freedom. This soldier is armed with all the latest technologies. He is carrying a high tech cell phone, a laptop computer with wireless Internet capability, and a webcam. He is able to call his wife or parents while he is waiting at the airport, when he arrives at his destination, and any other time he wants. Today, communication is instant for the American soldier, even in combat zones. Iraq has cell phone towers, and Internet connections can be set up in tents. Soldiers use programs like Windows Messenger or Yahoo Messenger to chat and use webcams with little delay. This technology has greatly improved communication for the deployed service person. Morale is greatly boosted because soldiers know they can see the faces of their spouses and children daily instead of waiting weeks for pictures in the mail. In addition, email makes writing letters more efficient because the letters are delivered instantly, and pictures can be attached to the emails. All of this new technology, resulting in instant communication, is great for the soldier and the family, but is it good for the government and the military at war?

Identify the points discussed by this writer. Do they correspond with the points mentioned in his description of 1991? Are all points well developed?

Avoid questions to begin or end body paragraphs; instead, turn a question into a statement to create a clear transition to the next body paragraph.

With every advance in technology, negative events also occur. Operational security is very important to the military. Communicating times and locations of movements over unsecured cell phones and Internet connections can be detrimental to the military mission. Cell phone interceptors and hackers can retrieve messages and plan attacks if they know when and where units are going to be, which could cost the military many lives. Military members are trained not to give out this information over unsecured means of communication or to unauthorized personnel. Training and discipline are the keys to maintaining good operational security. As long as each soldier knows what not to talk about, instant communication provided by technology is a great benefit.

While this is an interesting point to make about this topic, it does not connect to the essay's main idea. How could the writer make this relevant to his thesis?

Readers learn here that the writer has a personal connection to his subject. In what way(s) would the essay be strengthened if he had presented this information much earlier?

Technological advances have made the military service person's life much more convenient and enjoyable while away from home. A smile from a wife or child, even over a webcam, can make a soldier's day. So drop that pen and paper and send me an email, or call me on the cell phone because technology has made our communication instant. Thank you, technology, for all you have done for the United States military.

The writer restates the main idea of the essay clearly. However, it lacks certain components of a strong conclusion. What are they?

Scott E. Hilligoss

Comparison and Contrast—Prompts for Writing an Essay

Choose one of the prompts below and write a comparison and contrast essay. Remember that "contrast" evaluates differences, and "comparison" examines similarities. Compare and contrast writing seeks to draw attention to unexpected, rather than obvious, similarities or differences. Comparison/contrast essays are organized in one of two ways: point-by-point or subject-by-subject.

Think about the food consumption of college students. When students attend college, they probably live away from home. As a result, their eating habits might change because they do not have ready access to a kitchen and someone to prepare meals for them. Do they still eat about the same amount and types of food on a regular schedule? To prepare for this topic, make a list of the foods students eat in a typical day, including when and where meals are consumed.

Reflect on "then" and "now." Select an experience that you have had more than once and write about how the event itself or your reaction to the event has changed over the years. This could be an annual celebration (birthday or specific holiday), a recurring event (first day of school, summer vacation, pre-season practice), or a major event that you have experienced at least twice (birth or death of a loved one, winning an award, competing against the same opponent at different times).

Compare or contrast two public figures. Select two people who are well known for similar reasons; make sure to choose comparable subjects. These people could be talk show hosts, athletes (playing the same sport and even the same position), musical performers, actors, politicians, or a number of other identities. The possibilities for this writing assignment are extensive, so choose carefully and make sure you have a strong basis for comparison.

Comparison and Contrast Essay Peer Response

Provide thorough and thoughtful responses to the following questions. **Yes or no answers are insufficient**, so comment, explain, or offer suggestions for all responses. You may also write on the draft and mark grammar and punctuation mistakes.

Read the Title:

1. How does the title grab your interest? In what way does it predict the content of the essay?

Read the Introduction:

2. Does the introduction have a hook (opening sentence) that is a surprising statement, interesting fact, relevant quotation, or thought provoking question? After reading the introduction, predict what you expect to find in the body.

3. Underline the thesis. In your own words, identify the two subjects. What specific and significant claim does the thesis make? Will the writer focus more on comparison or contrast?

Read the Body Paragraphs:

4. Underline the topic sentence in each body paragraph. Does each topic sentence support the thesis sentence? What do you predict each body paragraph will add to this essay?

5. Based on your observations, what is the writer's organizational strategy (subject-by-subject or point-by-point)? How is the organization successful or unsuccessful?

6. Identify the writer's points (at least three) about the two subjects. What points does the writer make about each? If you can think of alternate or additional points the writer could have considered, list them below.

7. Look at the structure and organization of the essay. Does the writer switch back and forth between comparison/contrast or focus on only one strategy? Explain why you think the organization is or is not appropriate.

8. Circle the transitions in each body paragraph. Note any location you think may need additional (or different) transitional words or phrases. If the writer has chosen subject-by-subject structure, has he or she included a transitional paragraph? How is the paragraph successful or unsuccessful?

9. Do you see any information that should be moved to another paragraph or perhaps removed entirely? Explain your reasoning.

Read the Conclusion:
10. How does the conclusion relate to the thesis?

11. List the points the author has included in the conclusion. Identify any points that do not relate to the thesis. What points are missing from the conclusion?

12. What final thoughts does the author leave with the reader?

13. What was your favorite part of the essay? Explain.

Comparison and Contrast Essay Peer Response

Provide thorough and thoughtful responses to the following questions. **Yes or no answers are insufficient**, so comment, explain, or offer suggestions for all responses. You may also write on the draft and mark grammar and punctuation mistakes.

Read the Title:

1. How does the title grab your interest? In what way does it predict the content of the essay?

Read the Introduction:

2. Does the introduction have a hook (opening sentence) that is a surprising statement, interesting fact, relevant quotation, or thought provoking question? After reading the introduction, predict what you expect to find in the body.

3. Underline the thesis. In your own words, identify the two subjects. What specific and significant claim does the thesis make? Will the writer focus more on comparison or contrast?

Read the Body Paragraphs:

4. Underline the topic sentence in each body paragraph. Does each topic sentence support the thesis sentence? What do you predict each body paragraph will add to this essay?

5. Based on your observations, what is the writer's organizational strategy (subject-by-subject or point-by-point)? How is the organization successful or unsuccessful?

6. Identify the writer's points (at least three) about the two subjects. What points does the writer make about each? If you can think of alternate or additional points the writer could have considered, list them below.

7. Look at the structure and organization of the essay. Does the writer switch back and forth between comparison/contrast or focus on only one strategy? Explain why you think the organization is or is not appropriate.

8. Circle the transitions in each body paragraph. Note any location you think may need additional (or different) transitional words or phrases. If the writer has chosen subject-by-subject structure, has he or she included a transitional paragraph? How is the paragraph successful or unsuccessful?

9. Do you see any information that should be moved to another paragraph or perhaps removed entirely? Explain your reasoning.

Read the Conclusion:
10. How does the conclusion relate to the thesis?

11. List the points the author has included in the conclusion. Identify any points that do not relate to the thesis. What points are missing from the conclusion?

12. What final thoughts does the author leave with the reader?

13. What was your favorite part of the essay? Explain.

Drafting and Revision— The Process of Composition

Writing as a Process

In composition classes—this one as well as EN 1103 and EN 1113—you will be expected to write more than one draft of most essays in order to arrive at a final version that is well developed, appropriately organized, and grammatically correct. Unfortunately, many students write an essay once and consider themselves finished with the assignment, but that is not the case. A first draft is just one step of a process that allows you the opportunity to refine and improve your writing through feedback from both your classmates and instructor. In EN 0103, as well as EN 1103, you will write three drafts of all essays except the one you write during the final exam. Typically, you will go through four stages in order to complete one essay assignment:

- Prewriting—In this phase, you narrow a topic, generate ideas, and plan your organizational strategy. Prewriting typically begins with brainstorming, clustering, or freewriting to develop ideas. Once you complete this step, you will create an outline in order to organize the presentation of these ideas.
- Draft 1—For the first draft, you move from the outline to sentences and paragraphs. In this phase, you need to focus on content more than correctness. As you write the first draft, try to include all main ideas and most specific details. Make sure to present a thesis in the introduction as well as topic sentences in all body paragraphs. Work to create a conclusion that summarizes the essay and restates the thesis. At this point, your ideas might not be as fully developed or clearly worded as you would like, but the most important priority is to include them. You will have the opportunity to expand, edit, and proofread later.
- Draft 2—You will receive feedback from either your classmates or instructor (sometimes both) before writing the second draft. During this stage of the writing process, you should focus on a few main activities: reviewing your organization, adding content (specific details, examples, and descriptions), making sure your sentences communicate the idea you intend, and connecting ideas through the addition of transitional words and phrases.
- Final Draft—At this point, your essay should be fully developed and well organized. Now is the time for final editing—checking for clear expression of ideas, exact word choice—and proofreading. When you proofread, you are checking for grammatical and mechanical errors.

To complete each essay assignment, you must submit all materials (prewriting, peer response, drafts) along with the final draft to your instructor. In addition, you must upload a copy of your final draft to Turnitin.com or Safe Assign.

The following essay demonstrates the work of a student in EN 1103. He wrote a literacy narrative, the first essay assigned in Comp I. This assignment asks students to tell the story of some aspect of their lives involving literacy, typically defined as the ability to read and write. Through a series of three drafts, this student reveals a childhood experience that continues to impact his attitude toward reading. The final draft is presented in MLA format; you may use this as a formatting model when writing your own essays.

Student Model Essay   Literacy Narrative

Draft 1

Reading

    I personally don't consider reading an enjoyable pastime, as a matter of fact, if I was given a choice of reading a novel or jumping into a pool of starving piranhas, the piranhas would win every time. I am a math nerd, and I find reading literature for substance and hidden meanings a waste of time. I much prefer the straight forward and factual realm of numbers over the ambiguous and round about language of literature. While I understand that generally the more one reads the more well-spoken and cultured the individual becomes, I still simply can't bring myself to even fathom experiencing satisfaction from reading a novel.

My strong distaste for reading began when I entered fourth grade. My school was heavily focused on AR points, which were earned by reading a book and later passing a quiz on it's contents. My teacher required that each student earn 46 AR points per nine weeks. To accomplish this goal, I had to read for nearly 4 hours each and every night. My mother also strongly supported the AR point system and put even more pressure on me to get more AR points. Every day I would come home, do homework, eat dinner and begin reading. Consequently, I couldn't spend time with my friends, play with my toys, or even just enjoy the innocence of youth, because it kept me from having the life of a normal fourth grade, I began to form a sort of grudge against reading that would last for much longer than anticipated. A few months into the fourth grade, I found myself nine years old and drowning in a sea of chapter books. As the year wore on, the pressure to get the final AR points was amplified by a constant bombardment of reminders from both school and my mother. After several stressful nights, reading became a necessity, almost a habit, rather than an outlet for pleasure and imagination. By the end of the year, I had reached my goal of 46 AR points but the toll of those nightly readings had already impacted me. I recall being so overjoyed by the fact that I did not have to earn any more AR points that I vowed to myself that I would never read a books again—unless I was required to by a class.

Even now, I still hold onto my dislike for reading. When I read, I fell as though I am being forced to comprehend every minute detail the author includes. If a book is assigned in class, immediately I have contempt for the novel as well as the teacher. I compare reading to an overly complicated jigsaw puzzle in which not all of the pieces fit perfectly together.. However, hopefully as time goes on and the pressure to read from classes lessens, I will be able to enjoy immersing myself into the puzzle of literature. I consider people who enjoy reading to be talented in a way that I am not. I am amazed by those individuals who can, willingly, sit in a crowded room and read all whilst managing to block out the hum of life that is taking place around them. They become so wholly captivated by a work of fiction also surprises me; how a individual can form emotional ties to a fictional character and feel the characters sympathy, pain or joy is a phenomena I am unable to explain. In the future, maybe one day I might find myself completely fascinated by the intricate weaving of characters, setting and plot that make up the ever changing world of novels, to strive towards this goal I will have to become much more open-minded about reading and I will have to allow myself to fall into the trap of an author's greatest masterpiece – his story. Eventually, I hope I will be able to read to my children with as much fervor as my mother read to me, but as of right now I find reading a "have to" and not a "want to".

Student Model Essay   Literacy Narrative

Draft 2

Reading is a Puzzle

I personally do not consider reading an enjoyable pastime. As a matter of fact, if I was given a choice of reading a novel or jumping into a pool of starving piranhas, the piranhas would win every time. As a self-proclaimed math nerd, I find reading literature for substance and hidden meaning a massive waste of time. I much prefer the straight forward and factual realm of numbers over the ambiguous and round about language of literature. While I understand that generally the more one reads the more well spoken and cultured the individual becomes, I still can not bring myself to even fathom experiencing satisfaction from reading a novel. For me, the eventual decline into my hatred of reading has its origins in the fourth grade.

> The first draft includes only three paragraphs; the second draft has five paragraphs: a clear introduction, three body paragraphs with clear topic sentences, and a clearly identifiable conclusion.

> In the introductory paragraph, the student adds a clear thesis statement: "For me, the eventual decline into my hatred of reading has its origins in the fourth grade."

My strong distaste for reading began when I entered fourth grade. My school was heavily focused on AR points, which were earned by reading a book and later passing a quiz on it's contents. My teacher required that each student earn 46 AR points per nine weeks. To accomplish this goal, I had to read for nearly 4 hours each and every night. My mother also strongly supported the AR point system and put even more pressure on me to get more AR points. Every day I would come home, do homework, eat dinner and begin my marathon of reading. Consequently, I couldn't spend time with my friends, play with my toys, or even just enjoy the innocence of youth, because it kept me from having the life of a normal fourth grade, I began to form a sort of grudge against reading that would last for much longer than anticipated.

> No apostrophe is needed in the word "its" in this sentence.

A few months into the fourth grade, I found myself nine years old and drowning in a sea of chapter books. Unfortunately, I began to look at the next *Junie B. Jones* or *Magic Tree House* book as a shackle that kept me from truly enjoying reading. As the year wore on, the pressure to get the final AR points was amplified by a constant bombardment of reminders from both school and my mother. After several stressful nights, reading became a necessity, almost a habit, rather than an outlet for pleasure and imagination. By the end of the year, I had reached my goal of 46 AR points but the toll of those nightly readings had already impacted me. I recall being so overjoyed by the fact that I did not have to earn any more AR points that I vowed to myself that I would never read a books again – unless I was required to by a class.

> After the topic sentence, the student adds specific examples.

Even now, as a college freshman, I still hold onto my dislike for reading. When I read, I fell as though I am being forced to comprehend every minute detail the author includes. If a book is assigned in class, my inner rebel comes to life and immediately I have contempt for the novel as well as the teacher who assigned the reading. As I flip through each page, partially taking in the context, I cannot help but mourn the time I am loosing. My mind wanders through all the activities I would rather be doing like spending time with friends, playing video games or completing my math-based assignments. Even as the reading is discussed in class I cannot help but scoff at the overly evasive way the author reveals symbols or character or tone.

> There is a misspelled word: "fell" instead of "feel"

> Another misspelled word: "loosing" instead of "losing"

I compare reading to an overly complicated jigsaw puzzle in which not all of the pieces fit perfectly together. In this puzzle, each piece could be interpreted differently by different individuals who shape the piece to fit anywhere they deem fit. However, hopefully as time goes on and the pressure to read from classes lessens, I will be able to enjoy immersing myself into the puzzle of literature. I consider people who enjoy reading to be talented in a way that I am not. I am amazed by those individuals who can, willingly, sit in a crowded room and read all whilst managing to block out the hum of life that is taking place around them. They become so wholly captivated by a work of fiction also surprises me; how a individual can form emotional ties to a fictional character and feel the characters sympathy, pain or joy is a phenomena I am unable to explain.

> The student has combined information ("I compare reading to an overly-complicated jigsaw puzzle...") from one of the larger unorganized paragraphs of draft 1 and focused it in the last body paragraph of the second draft.

In the future, maybe one day I might find myself completely fascinated by the intricate weaving of characters, setting and plot that make up the ever changing world of novels, to strive towards this goal I will have to become much more open-minded about reading and I will have to allow myself to fall into the trap of an author's greatest masterpiece – his story. Eventually, I hope I will be able to read to my children with as much fervor as my mother read to me, but as of right now I find reading a "have to" and not a "want to".

> The conclusion has evolved into a separate paragraph; in the first draft, the concluding ideas were part of a larger body paragraph.

Tyler Hassell

Courtney Kimbrough

EN 1103-11

11 February, 2013

Reading: The Hopeless Puzzle

I personally do not consider reading an enjoyable pastime; as a matter of fact, if I were given a choice of reading a novel or jumping into a pool of starving piranhas, the piranhas would win every time. As a self-proclaimed math nerd, I find reading literature for substance and hidden meanings a massive waste of time. I much prefer the straightforward and factual realm of numbers over the ambiguous and roundabout language of literature. While I understand that generally the more one reads the more well-spoken and cultured the individual becomes, I still simply cannot bring myself to even fathom experiencing satisfaction from reading a novel. For me, the eventual decline into my hatred of reading has its origins in the fourth grade.

My strong distaste for reading began when I entered fourth grade. My school was heavily focused on AR points, which were earned by reading a book and later passing a quiz on its contents. My teacher required that each student earn forty-six AR points per nine weeks. To accomplish this goal, I had to read for nearly four hours every night. My mother was also a strong proponent of my reading as she believed it would bring to life my inner scholar; so naturally, she heavily supported the AR point system and put even more pressure on me to get more AR points. To reach my goal, every day I would come home, do homework, eat dinner and begin my marathon of reading. Consequently, I was unable to spend time with my friends, play with my toys, or just enjoy the innocence of youth. Because it kept me from having the life of a normal fourth grader, I began to form a sort of grudge against reading that would last for much longer than anticipated.

A few months into fourth grade, I found myself nine years old and drowning in a sea of chapter books. Unfortunately, I began to look at the next *Junie B. Jones or Magic Tree House* book as a shackle that kept me from truly enjoying reading. As the year wore on, the pressure to get the final AR points was amplified by a constant bombardment of reminders from both school and my mother. After several stressful nights, reading became a necessity, almost a habit, rather than an outlet for pleasure and imagination. Of all the nights I spent holed up in my room, one in particular stands out to me: the night I realized I truly hated reading. I do not remember what I was reading, but I do remember the feeling I got after I read an entire chapter and could not even recall the context of what I read. Then and there, I understood just how systematic my readin. had become. I was not reading to immers. myself in a fantasy, but to satisfy the demand. of my teacher and my mother. For me, reading had truly lost all of its mystery and pleasure. I read to pass the test, and I simpl. moved on to the next book.

By the end of the year, I had reached my goal of forty-six AR points, but the toll of those nightly readings had already impacted me. Sure, my mom and teacher were satisfied, but I just knew that next year in fifth grade I would have to start the entire AR process all over again. This prediction of next year's struggles enforced my bitterness even more; I realized that school was always going to thrust books upon me, and there was nothing that I could do to change my fate. However, I also realized that the AR point system ended before middle school. I recall being so overjoyed that I did not have to earn any more AR points after fifth grade that I vowed never to read a book again unless I was required to by a class.

Today, I compare reading to an overly complicated jigsaw puzzle in which not all of the pieces fit together properly. In this puzzle, each piece could be interpreted differently by various individuals who shape the piece to fit anywhere they deem. In fourth grade, I lost my passion for reading. The pressure put on me by my mother and teacher to earn my AR points overwhelmed me entirely, and books became a hindrance of which I resented completely. However, hopefully as time goes on and the pressure to read from classes lessens, I will be able to enjoy reading. In the future, maybe one day I might find myself completely fascinated by the intricate weaving of characters, setting and plot that make up the ever changing world of novels. To strive towards this goal, I will have to become much more opened-minded about reading, and I will have to allow myself to fall into the trap of an author's greatest masterpiece. his story. Eventually, I hope I will be able to read to my children with as much fervor as my mother read to me, but as of right now I find reading a "have to" and not a "want to."

OLD DORMITORY. MISSISSIPPI A. & M. COLLEGE.

Composition:
The Stages of Writing

Chapter Contents

Reading

Finding the Main Points: Essay

This exercise is designed to help you with close reading of an assigned essay or article. Read the work through once without stopping. Read it a second time, completing this form as you go. As you read, look for connections, transitions, and supporting evidence.

Rewrite the thesis sentence in your own words.

_____

_____

_____

Write the topic sentence for each body paragraph in your own words. Next, list the supporting details for each topic sentence. If the essay has more than four body paragraphs, record this information at the end of this worksheet.

Body Paragraph 1:

Topic Sentence: _____

_____

Supporting Details: _____

_____

_____

Body Paragraph 2:

Topic Sentence: _____

_____

Supporting Details: _____

_____

_____

Body Paragraph 3:

Topic Sentence: _____

_____

Supporting Details: _____

_____

_____

Body Paragraph 4:

Topic Sentence: _____

_____

Supporting Details: _____

_____

Did you find body paragraphs without topic sentences? If so, identify them.

_____

_____

_____

Read the conclusion. Write the restated thesis statement. List the points that summarize the body. Identify any new information that did not appear in the introductory or body paragraphs.

_____

_____

_____

_____

_____

Reading Actively

When instructors assign readings, they expect you to focus intently enough to gain more than a superficial understanding of content. You should process the information well enough to reflect on its greater meaning, both to society in general and to you individually. Complete this activity as you read an assigned essay or article for the first time. As you complete each step, record your level of interest on a scale of 1 (completely uninteresting) to 5 (very interesting).

Read the title. **STOP.** Predict what the topic and approach will be. Interest Level: _____

_____

_____

_____

Read details about the author (if provided). **STOP.** Record whatever information you see (education, professional position). Did this article or essay originally appear in a different publication? If so, record the original source of publication. How does this information affect your expectations on what you are about to read? Interest Level: _____

_____

_____

_____

_____

_____

Read the introduction. **STOP.** Predict what the rest of the essay will discuss. List supporting evidence you expect to find in the rest of the essay. Interest Level: _____

_____

_____

_____

_____

_____

_____

Read the body paragraphs. **STOP**. What is the author's purpose? Write a sentence about the tone of the essay; is it serious or lighthearted? Interest Level: _____

_____

_____

_____

_____

_____

_____

_____

Read the body paragraphs again. Was the topic carried through? Were your predictions correct? Has your interest level changed? If so, why did it change, and what is it now?

Interest Level: _____

_____

_____

_____

_____

_____

_____

Focus on the conclusion. What does it have in common with the introduction?

_____

_____

_____

_____

_____

Prewriting

Generating Ideas

Clustering Practice

Using the diagram below, generate ideas as to support the assertion that the physical makeup of a classroom influences the learning atmosphere. Use at least three of the spaces provided, and be sure to think of specific details.

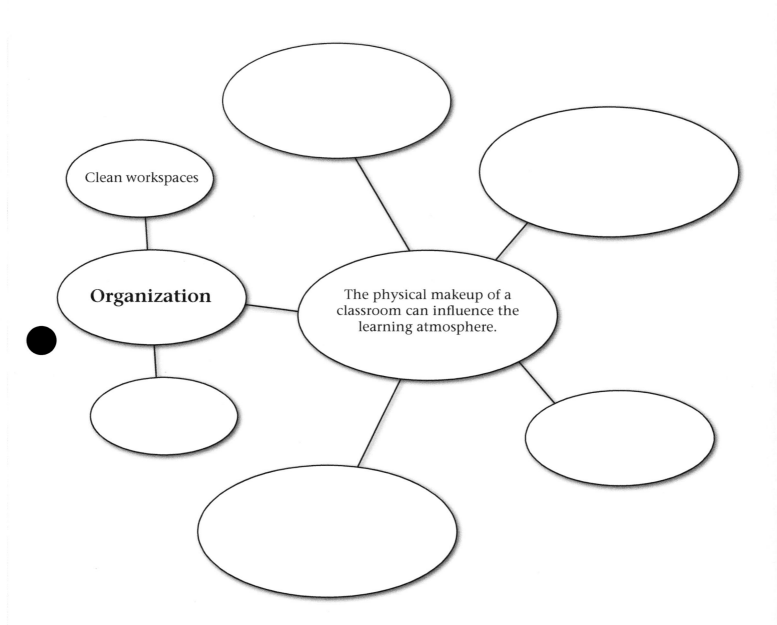

Clustering Worksheet

Use the diagram below to organize your ideas. Place the subject that interests you in the center oval. Use at least three of the spaces provided. In addition, create additional boxes to expand your ideas with specific details.

Name: _____ Date: _____

Clustering Worksheet

Use the diagram below to organize your ideas. Place the subject that interests you in the center oval. Use at least three of the spaces provided. In addition, create additional boxes to expand your ideas with specific details.

Clustering Worksheet

Use the diagram below to organize your ideas. Place the subject that interests you in the center oval. Use at least three of the spaces provided. In addition, create additional boxes to expand your ideas with specific details.

Essay Organizer

Use the designated spaces below to organize your essay ideas. Be sure to utilize each space by listing the points you plan to make in each paragraph of your essay.

Introduction

Body

Point 1   Point 2   Point3

Conclusion

Essay Organizer

Use the designated spaces below to organize your essay ideas. Be sure to utilize each space by listing the points you plan to make in each paragraph of your essay.

Introduction

Body

Point 1　　　　　　　Point 2　　　　　　　Point3

Conclusion

Essay Organizer

Use the designated spaces below to organize your essay ideas. Be sure to utilize each space by listing the points you plan to make in each paragraph of your essay.

Introduction

Body

Point 1   Point 2   Point3

Conclusion

Cause and Effect Brainstorming Practice

The best way to begin generating ideas for an effective Cause and Effect essay is by proposing your topic as a question. For example: *What are the major causes of automobile accidents?*

Using the chart provided below, fill in the spaces to generate responses to the question above. Follow the example. Use at least three of the spaces. Your ideas may also extend beyond the available space.

Condition	Cause	Effect
weather	-rain -high winds -ice/snow	-poor tire traction -reduced visibility
traffic		

Cause and Effect Brainstorming Worksheet

Using the spaces below, narrow and focus your topic. Then write your topic in the form of a question, one that includes "why" or "how." List causes and effects in the boxes; completing this exercise should help you generate ideas and provide focus for your cause and effect essay.

My Topic: _____

_____

Topic Question: _____

_____

Cause	Effect
-rain -high winds -ice/snow	-poor tire traction -reduced visibility

Comparison and Contrast Brainstorming

To write an effective comparison and contrast essay, you must first spend time generating and organizing your ideas. In the space below, identify your chosen subjects. Next, generate as many details as possible that you might want to include in your essay.

_____   _____

Subject A   Subject B

Brainstorming: Developing Ideas

_____   _____

_____   _____

_____   _____

_____   _____

_____   _____

_____   _____

_____   _____

Now that you have some good ideas about your subjects, organize them into categories. List each group of ideas in the spaces provided below. Be sure to create at least three points.

Point 1: _____   Point 3: _____

_____   _____

_____   _____

_____   _____

_____   _____

Point 2: _____   Point 4: _____

_____   _____

_____   _____

_____   _____

_____   _____

Thesis

Reviewing your list of points, which are more interesting and relevant: similarities or differences? Once you have decided, use the space below to write a draft of your thesis statement. This statement should acknowledge either the similarities or differences but also make it clear that you are focusing on the other.

Examples:

Even though my identical twin sister and I are alike in many ways, obviously in our appearance but also in our moral values and love of music, we have always been dissimilar in our willingness to take risks in certain situations, such as wearing certain clothes, obeying our parents, and becoming involved in relationships.

Acknowledgement: The subjects (the author and her sister) have some things in common: physical appearance, moral values, and love of music.

Focus of Essay: The subjects (the author and her sister) are fundamentally different in the way they dress, obedience to their parents, and willingness to become involved in a relationship (points of contrast).

Although kindergarten and college are miles apart in terms of academic rigor and personal freedoms, as I begin my new life at MSU it is clear that I am still that excited and terrified young boy who let go of his mother's hand at the classroom door. The same concerns about leaving home, learning a new routine, and fitting in with my peers confronted me at the door of my room in Ruby Hall.

Acknowledgement: The subjects (the author as he began kindergarten and as he begins college) are very different in the difficulty of subjects and in the amount of freedom students have.

Focus of Essay: The subjects (the author as he began kindergarten and as he begins college) are strikingly similar in how the author feels about leaving home, learning a new routine, and fitting in (points of comparison).

Thesis Statement: _____

_____

_____

_____

_____

_____

Considering Audience

When writing anything—a text, an e-mail, a letter, an essay, or paragraph—it is important to think about your audience. Who will read this document? What is your purpose? Whom are you trying to convince? What is the best way to convince that audience? What do you need to adjust in order to communicate effectively with a specific audience?

Develop the statement below in order to convince each audience of the argument you are making:

1. Argument: *Panama City, Florida is the best place to visit for Spring Break.*

Audience 1: Friends

_____

_____

_____

_____

Audience 2: Parents

_____

_____

_____

_____

Audience 3: Employer

_____

_____

_____

_____

Argument	Audience 1: Friends	Audience 2: Parents	Audience 3: Employer

Outlining

Paragraphs—Creating a Topic Sentence

A topic sentence clearly indicates the main idea of a paragraph. The topic sentence typically gives an idea of what the paragraph will discuss, but it is not a statement of fact or an announcement. Create a clear topic sentence for the paragraph you would write if given the topics provided below.

Example:

Topic: How is community service beneficial to college students?

Possible Topic Sentence: Community service should be required for all college students because it teaches good time management and responsibility.

1. Topic: What is one thing you cannot live without?

   Possible Topic Sentence:

   _____

   _____

   _____

2. Topic: What makes a healthy diet?

   Possible Topic Sentence:

   _____

   _____

   _____

3. Topic: How do you plan a successful surprise party?

   Possible Topic Sentence:

   _____

   _____

   _____

4. Topic: What animal would make a great pet? Why?

   Possible Topic Sentence:

   _____

   _____

   _____

Paragraphs—Writing a Topic Sentence

Topic sentences tell the reader what a paragraph is about. Following you will find short, relatively undeveloped paragraphs that are missing topic sentences. Read the paragraphs and write a topic sentence that clearly states what the paragraph is about.

Example:

Paragraph: Huskies are beautiful dogs. They are soft and fluffy. Huskies are friendly and easy to care for. They like going on walks and being outside, so they are fun to have around. Huskies do not have a special diet, which makes them great pets.

Possible Topic Sentence: The Siberian Husky is my favorite animal.

1. Paragraph: Online classes allow students to do assignment on their own time. Students can work during the day and do classwork at night or during free time. This type of education allows even someone with a full-time job to earn a degree without having to travel to a college campus. People can sit as home in their pajamas and still be "in" the classroom. Online classes are also cheaper, which makes them available to more people.

   Possible Topic Sentence: _____

   _____

   _____

2. Paragraph: Exercise helps people maintain a healthy weight, which reduces weight-related health risks. It reduces the risk for heart attack. Exercise leads to lower cholesterol and lower blood pressure. It reduces stress, making people happier and more productive. Exercise creates a happier and healthier society.

   Possible Topic Sentence: _____

   _____

   _____

3. Paragraph: Fall weather is my favorite. It's not too hot and not too cold; jeans and a light sweater is all that's needed. Football season is in the fall, which is always entertaining. Campus is busy with football fans and tailgating on the weekends. The leaves on the trees change color in the fall, making campus really beautiful. Thanksgiving also takes place during the fall. I love Thanksgiving because I get to eat great food and spend quality time with my family. Of all the seasons, fall is my favorite.

   Possible Topic Sentence: _____

   _____

   _____

4. Paragraph: Disney World is clean and well organized. It is easy to find trash cans, restrooms, and food stands. I enjoy shopping in the Disney shops and buying souvenirs for family and friends. The candy shops are enjoyable because there are lots of delicious Disney-themed sweets. I also love the rides at Disney World. There are plenty of rides for all ages. My favorite rides are the smaller roller coasters and the water rides. Disney World is fun because there is something for everyone.

Possible Topic Sentence: _____

_____

_____

5. Paragraph: The first floor of my dream home would have a large kitchen, a large, open living room, a guest bedroom and bathroom, and a laundry room. The living room would have two doors that open out onto the massive backyard with a patio that has an outdoor kitchen, seating area, and fire pit. The second floor would have the master bedroom and bathroom, a home office and library, and another bedroom and small bathroom. My dream home would be in Northeast Mississippi surrounded by woods.

Possible Topic Sentence: _____

_____

_____

6. Paragraph: I always enjoyed my English classes in middle school and high school. I did not like learning grammar, but I loved reading and writing about what I had read. It should have been easy for me to pick a major, but I had to change my major several times before I finally decided to pursue a degree in English. I loved the composition and literature classes I had to take my freshman year of college. I am very glad I chose English because I learn something new everyday and I love the classes I get to take.

Possible Topic Sentence: _____

_____

_____

Paragraphs—Description Paragraph Outline

Once you have finished brainstorming, fill in this outline to help you develop your description paragraph. Remember that a strong descriptive paragraph creates a dominant impression through the use of vivid sensory details: sight, smell, sound, taste, and touch. When you begin writing your paragraph, organize these details logically (order of importance, spatially).

Begin by identifying the dominant impression you intend to convey in this paragraph. While outlining your paragraph, refer back to this statement to make sure the details you've selected support the dominant impression.

Dominant Impression: _____

_____

_____

_____

_____

Topic Sentence: _____

_____

_____

_____

_____

Sight Detail: _____

_____

_____

_____

_____

Smell Detail:_____

_____

_____

_____

_____

Sound Detail: _____

_____

_____

Taste Detail: _____

_____

_____

_____

_____

Touch Detail: _____

_____

_____

_____

_____

Summary Statement: _____

_____

_____

_____

_____

Paragraphs—Definition Paragraph Outline

Once you have finished brainstorming, fill in this outline to help you organize your definition paragraph. Remember that definition paragraphs usually define a commonly used word in a different way, or they define a word of your own creation. The topic sentence should include the word you are defining and your definition. Then you will support your definition by explaining why you have defined the word this way, giving examples and making comparisons.

Topic Sentence: _____

_____

_____

_____

Explanation: _____

_____

_____

_____

Example: _____

_____

_____

_____

Comparison: _____

_____

_____

_____

Summary Statement: _____

_____

_____

_____

Paragraphs—Process Paragraph Outline

Once you have finished thinking carefully about the steps involved in your selected activity, fill in the outline to help you organize your process paragraph. Remember, the process paragraph tells the reader how something works or how to do something. Fill in the outline using at least six steps. If more steps are needed you may add them. Be sure to provide helpful hints where appropriate and add transitions as you move from one step to the next.

Topic Sentence:

_____

_____

_____

Step 1:

_____

_____

Step 2:

_____

_____

Step 3:

_____

_____

_____

Step 4:

_____

_____

Step 5:

_____

_____

Step 6:

_____

_____

Step 7:

_____

_____

_____

Step 8:

_____

_____

_____

Step 9:

_____

_____

_____

Step 10:

_____

_____

Summary Statement:

_____

_____

Now that you have completed your outline, read your topic sentence and summary statement. Does your topic sentence identify the process you are discussing? Does your summary statement indicate why this process is necessary, or how this process may be useful? If not, what changes do you need to make and why?

_____

_____

_____

_____

Focusing on the steps of your process, are they easy to understand? When you follow them do you get the same result every time? Have you left out any steps? How can you add clarity?

_____

_____

_____

_____

Essays—Creating a Thesis Statement

A thesis statement clearly indicates the main point of an essay. It is more than a statement of fact or an announcement and should state an opinion. Also, a thesis sentence should be specific and clearly worded. Using the topics and supporting details listed below, create effective thesis statements for each topic.

Example:

Topic: Are required college courses beneficial to students?

Supporting Details: improved writing skills and necessary understanding of math

Possible Thesis Statement: Required college courses are beneficial to all students because they improve reading and writing skills and give a necessary understanding of math.

1. Topic: Is reality television harmful to viewers?
   Supporting Details: strong language, encourages greed, creates stereotypes, unrealistic expectations
   Possible Thesis Statement:

   _____

   _____

   _____

2. Topic: Why is it important to vote?
   Supporting Details: voice opinion, select government officials, civil responsibility
   Possible Thesis Statement:

   _____

   _____

   _____

3. Topic: Who is your role model? Why?
   Supporting Details: Martin Luther King, Jr.; dedication to civil rights, nonviolent protests, passionate leader
   Possible Thesis Statement:

   _____

   _____

   _____

4. Topic: Why is college important?
   Supporting Details: education, learn responsibility, learn social skills, prepare for future job
   Possible Thesis Statement:

   _____

   _____

5. Topic: Where is your favorite place? Why?
   Supporting Details: Disney World; roller coasters, characters, souvenirs, parades
   Possible Thesis Statement:

   _____

   _____

   _____

6. Topic: What are some consequences of relying too much on technology?
   Supporting Details: poor face-to-face interactions, poor communication skills, poor spelling, terrible writing skills, lack of critical thinking skills
   Possible Thesis Statement:

   _____

   _____

   _____

7. Topic: What makes a good football team?
   Supporting Details: recruiting, strong media presence, and good coaching and play calling
   Possible Thesis Statement:

   _____

   _____

   _____

Essays—Writing a Thesis Statement

The thesis statement informs the reader of what the essay is about. You have been provided with the following topic sentences for an essay. Read the topic sentences and create an effective thesis statement for that essay.

Example:

Topic Sentence 1: I have matured over the course of the semester.

Topic Sentence 2: I have become more independent this semester.

Topic Sentence 3: I also learned how to be more responsible this semester.

Possible Thesis Statement: During my first semester of college, I learned how to be more mature, more independent, and more responsible.

1. Topic Sentence 1: Reality TV teaches children to be disrespectful.
   Topic Sentence 2: Reality TV encourages children to use curse words.
   Topic Sentence 3: Reality TV pressures children to be sexually active.
   Possible Thesis Statement:

   _____

   _____

   _____

2. Topic Sentence 1: Stress can be harmful because it causes a decrease in appetite.
   Topic Sentence 2: Sleep deprivation is another harmful effect of stress.
   Topic Sentence 3: Stress also causes chronic health problems.
   Possible Thesis Statement:

   _____

   _____

   _____

3. Topic Sentence 1: Playing video games too often can lead to antisocial behavior.
   Topic Sentence 2: Violent video games teach children to be aggressive.
   Topic Sentence 3: Video games prevent children from succeeding in school.
   Possible Thesis Statement:

   _____

   _____

   _____

4. Topic Sentence 1: School uniforms prevent students from wearing inappropriate clothes.
   Topic Sentence 2: School uniforms encourage focus on academics.
   Topic Sentence 3: School uniforms reduce peer pressure for students.
   Possible Thesis Statement:

   _____

   _____

   _____

5. Topic Sentence 1: Taking notes in class helps students succeed in college.
   Topic Sentence 2: Participating in class and asking questions aids in understanding, which leads to success.
   Topic Sentence 3: Studying for tests and turning assignments in on time ensures college success.
   Possible Thesis Statement:

   _____

   _____

   _____

6. Topic Sentence 1: Mississippi State should expand its parking lots in order to accommodate the increased student population.
   Topic Sentence 2: MSU needs to renovate outdated classrooms in order to enhance the learning experience.
   Topic Sentence 3: Mississippi State should include more dining options for students.
   Possible Thesis Statement:

   _____

   _____

   _____

7. Topic Sentence 1: Traveling is important because it allows individuals to interact with people from different backgrounds.
   Topic Sentence 2: Traveling allows people to see different parts of the world.
   Topic Sentence 3: Traveling improves the overall health of individuals.
   Possible Thesis Statement:

   _____

   _____

   _____

Essays—Exemplification Essay Outline

Once you have finished brainstorming, complete this outline to help organize your exemplification essay. Remember that exemplification essays use specific examples to express or clarify a more general idea. The specific examples support the general idea stated in your thesis. When organizing examples, be sure to put them in a logical order (least important to most important or general to specific, for example).

Introduction

Hook: _____

_____

_____

Bridge Details (Narrowing down): _____

_____

_____

Thesis Statement: _____

_____

_____

Body Paragraph 1

Topic Sentence: _____

_____

Example 1: _____

_____

_____

Example 2: _____

_____

_____

Example 3: _____

_____

_____

Body Paragraph 2

Topic Sentence: _____

_____

Example 1: _____

_____

_____

Example 2: _____

_____

_____

Example 3: _____

_____

_____

Body Paragraph 3

Topic Sentence: _____

_____

Example 1: _____

_____

_____

Example 2: _____

_____

_____

Example 3: _____

_____

_____

Conclusion

Restatement of Thesis:_____

_____

_____

Summary of Topics: _____

_____

_____

Significance/Suggestion: _____

_____

_____

Essays—Cause and Effect Essay Outline

Once you have finished prewriting, complete the following outline to help you organize your cause and effect essay. Remember, cause and effect essays help readers understand why something happened or how one thing affects another. Be sure to mention both causes and effects, but emphasize one more than the other; make sure the thesis indicates the focus of your essay. Also, remember to organize your essay in a logical order (for example, least important to most important, immediate or remote).

Introduction

Hook: _____

_____

_____

Bridge Details (Narrowing down): _____

_____

_____

Thesis Statement: _____

_____

_____

Body Paragraph 1

Topic Sentence: _____

_____

Detail 1:_____

_____

_____

Detail 2:_____

_____

_____

Detail 3:_____

_____

_____

Body Paragraph 2

Topic Sentence: _____

_____

Detail 1:_____

_____

_____

Detail 2:_____

_____

_____

Detail 3:_____

_____

_____

Body Paragraph 3

Topic Sentence: _____

_____

Detail 1:_____

_____

_____

Detail 2:_____

_____

_____

Detail 3:_____

_____

_____

Conclusion

Restatement of Thesis:_____

_____

_____

Summary of Topics: _____

_____

_____

Significance/Suggestion: _____

_____

_____

Essays—Comparison and Contrast Essay Outline: Point-by-Point

Once you have finished your prewriting, complete the outline below to help you organize your comparison and contrast essay. Remember that comparison shows the similarities and contrast presents differences. You may organize a comparison and contrast essay in one of two ways: point-by-point or subject-by-subject or. Use this outline format for point-by-point organization.

Introduction

Hook: _____

_____

Bridge Details (Narrowing down): _____

_____

_____

Thesis Statement: _____

_____

_____

Body Paragraph 1—Point 1

Topic Sentence: _____

_____

_____

Subject A: _____

_____

_____

_____

Subject B: _____

_____

_____

_____

Body Paragraph 2—Point 2

Topic Sentence: _____

_____

_____

Subject A: _____

_____

_____

_____

Subject B: _____

_____

_____

_____

Body Paragraph 3—Point 3

Topic Sentence: _____

_____

_____

Subject A: _____

_____

_____

_____

Subject B: _____

_____

_____

_____

Conclusion

Restatement of Thesis: _____

_____

_____

Summary of Points: _____

_____

_____

Significance/Suggestion: _____

_____

_____

Essays—Compare and Contrast Essay Outline: Subject-by-Subject

Once you have finished your prewriting, complete the following outline to help you organize your comparison and contrast essay. Remember that comparison shows the similarities and contrast presents differences. You may organize a comparison and contrast essay in one of two ways: point-by-point or subject-by-subject or. Use this outline format for subject-by-subject organization.

Introduction

Hook: _____

_____

_____

Bridge Details (Narrowing down): _____

_____

_____

Thesis Statement: _____

_____

_____

Body Paragraph 1—Subject A

Topic Sentence—Introduce Subject A _____

_____

_____

Point 1: _____

_____

_____

Point 2: _____

_____

_____

Point 3: _____

_____

_____

Body Paragraph 2—Transition between Subjects

Subject A Conclusion: _____

_____

_____

Transitional Statements: _____

_____

_____

_____

Subject B Introduction: _____

_____

_____

_____

Body Paragraph 3—Subject B

Topic Sentence—Subject B: _____

_____

_____

Point 1: _____

_____

_____

Point 2: _____

_____

_____

Point 3: _____

_____

_____

Conclusion

Restatement of Thesis: _____

_____

_____

Summary of Topics: _____

_____

_____

Significance/Suggestion: _____

_____

Drafting

First Draft

Creating a Strong Introduction

The introduction is one of the most important components of an essay: it must draw the reader's interest, introduce a topic, and make a strong claim. Use the following outline to plan your introduction.

Topic—Choose a topic, and write it on the line below.

_____

Hook—The hook is the reader's first impression of an essay. A strong hook consists of one or more sentences that use lively and original language to draw the reader's interest and introduce the topic. Hooks take many forms, such as questions, brief narratives, and surprising statements. On the lines below, write two different kinds of hooks.

Hook 1: _____

_____

_____

Hook 2: _____

_____

_____

Thesis Statement—The thesis statement is the heart of the essay; in the thesis statement, the writer reveals the claim he or she intends to prove in the essay. A strong thesis statement makes a specific claim about a topic and reveals the writer's plan for supporting that claim by listing his or her main points. On the lines below, write a thesis statement for your topic.

_____

_____

_____

_____

Bridge Sentences—Bridge sentences narrow the subject from general, as it appears in the hook, to specific, as it appears in the thesis statement. Strong bridge sentences reveal the relationship between the hook and the claims made in the thesis statement. On the lines below, create a strong introduction by writing a hook, bridge sentences, and a thesis statement.

Rewrite one of the hooks you wrote in the spaces above.

_____

_____

_____

Write at least three sentences to narrow your subject and connect the hook above to your thesis statement.

_____

_____

_____

_____

_____

_____

_____

_____

_____

_____

_____

Rewrite your thesis statement from the front of this worksheet.

_____

_____

_____

_____

Creating a Strong Introduction

The introduction is one of the most important components of an essay: it must draw the reader's interest, introduce a topic, and make a strong claim. Use the following outline to plan your introduction.

Topic—Choose a topic, and write it on the line below.

_____

Hook—The hook is the reader's first impression of an essay. A strong hook consists of one or more sentences that use lively and original language to draw the reader's interest and introduce the topic. Hooks take many forms, such as questions, brief narratives, and surprising statements. On the lines below, write two different kinds of hooks.

Hook 1: _____

_____

_____

Hook 2: _____

_____

_____

Thesis Statement—The thesis statement is the heart of the essay; in the thesis statement, the writer reveals the claim he or she intends to prove in the essay. A strong thesis statement makes a specific claim about a topic and reveals the writer's plan for supporting that claim by listing his or her main points. On the lines below, write a thesis statement for your topic.

_____

_____

_____

_____

Bridge Sentences—Bridge sentences narrow the subject from general, as it appears in the hook, to specific, as it appears in the thesis statement. Strong bridge sentences reveal the relationship between the hook and the claims made in the thesis statement. On the lines below, create a strong introduction by writing a hook, bridge sentences, and a thesis statement.

Rewrite one of the hooks you wrote in the spaces above.

_____

_____

_____

Write at least three sentences to narrow your subject and connect the hook above to your thesis statement.

_____

_____

_____

_____

_____

_____

_____

_____

_____

_____

_____

Rewrite your thesis statement from the front of this worksheet.

_____

_____

_____

_____

Creating a Strong Introduction

The introduction is one of the most important components of an essay: it must draw the reader's interest, introduce a topic, and make a strong claim. Use the following outline to plan your introduction.

Topic—Choose a topic, and write it on the line below.

_____

Hook—The hook is the reader's first impression of an essay. A strong hook consists of one or more sentences that use lively and original language to draw the reader's interest and introduce the topic. Hooks take many forms, such as questions, brief narratives, and surprising statements. On the lines below, write two different kinds of hooks.

Hook 1: _____

_____

_____

Hook 2: _____

_____

_____

Thesis Statement—The thesis statement is the heart of the essay; in the thesis statement, the writer reveals the claim he or she intends to prove in the essay. A strong thesis statement makes a specific claim about a topic and reveals the writer's plan for supporting that claim by listing his or her main points. On the lines below, write a thesis statement for your topic.

_____

_____

_____

Bridge Sentences—Bridge sentences narrow the subject from general, as it appears in the hook, to specific, as it appears in the thesis statement. Strong bridge sentences reveal the relationship between the hook and the claims made in the thesis statement. On the lines below, create a strong introduction by writing a hook, bridge sentences, and a thesis statement.

Rewrite one of the hooks you wrote in the spaces above.

_____

_____

_____

Write at least three sentences to narrow your subject and connect the hook above to your thesis statement.

_____

_____

_____

_____

_____

_____

_____

_____

_____

_____

_____

_____

Rewrite your thesis statement from the front of this worksheet.

_____

_____

_____

_____

Creating a Strong Conclusion

The conclusion is a very important component of an essay. A good conclusion shows how the writer has proved his or her point and why the essay is important. Readers often judge the effectiveness of the entire essay by the conclusion. Use the following outline to plan a conclusion.

Summary Statement—The summary statement shows readers how you have proved your point. A good summary statement consists of two parts: a summary of the major points and a restatement of the thesis. It is important to remember that a summary statement uses new language but never includes new details.

Restatement of the Thesis—Write your original thesis statement.

_____

_____

_____

Now, restate your thesis, using either new language or new sentence structure or both.

_____

_____

_____

Summary of the Major Points—Write the topic sentences of your body paragraphs.

Topic Sentence 1: _____

_____

_____

Topic Sentence 2: _____

_____

_____

Topic Sentence 3: _____

_____

_____

Now, restate your topics, using either new language or new sentence structure or both.

Topic Sentence 1: _____

_____

_____

Topic Sentence 2: _____

_____

_____

Topic Sentence 3: _____

_____

_____

Concluding Remarks—Concluding remarks are your last opportunity to make a good impression on the reader. Your concluding remarks will show why your essay is significant. Concluding remarks can take many forms, such as a narrative, a recommendation, a quotation, or a prediction. On the lines below, write two different kinds of concluding remarks.

Concluding Remarks 1: _____

_____

_____

Concluding Remarks 2: _____

_____

_____

Bridge Sentences—While an introduction narrows from general to specific information, a conclusion broadens from specific to general. Between your summary statement and concluding remarks, you need to write bridge sentences to show the relationship between the two while broadening the scope of the information. First, circle one of the types of concluding remarks you have written. On the lines below, write at least three sentences to connect your summary statement to the concluding remarks you circled.

_____

_____

_____

Creating a Strong Conclusion

The conclusion is a very important component of an essay. A good conclusion shows how the writer has proved his or her point and why the essay is important. Readers often judge the effectiveness of the entire essay by the conclusion. Use the following outline to plan a conclusion.

Summary Statement—The summary statement shows readers how you have proved your point. A good summary statement consists of two parts: a summary of the major points and a restatement of the thesis. It is important to remember that a summary statement uses new language but never includes new details.

Restatement of the Thesis—Write your original thesis statement.

_____

_____

_____

Now, restate your thesis, using either new language or new sentence structure or both.

_____

_____

_____

Summary of the Major Points—Write the topic sentences of your body paragraphs.

Topic Sentence 1: _____

_____

_____

Topic Sentence 2: _____

_____

_____

Topic Sentence 3: _____

_____

_____

Now, restate your topics, using either new language or new sentence structure or both.

Topic Sentence 1: _____

_____

_____

Topic Sentence 2: _____

_____

_____

Topic Sentence 3: _____

_____

_____

Concluding Remarks—Concluding remarks are your last opportunity to make a good impression on the reader. Your concluding remarks will show why your essay is significant. Concluding remarks can take many forms, such as a narrative, a recommendation, a quotation, or a prediction. On the lines below, write two different kinds of concluding remarks.

Concluding Remarks 1: _____

_____

_____

Concluding Remarks 2: _____

_____

_____

Bridge Sentences—While an introduction narrows from general to specific information, a conclusion broadens from specific to general. Between your summary statement and concluding remarks, you need to write bridge sentences to show the relationship between the two while broadening the scope of the information. First, circle one of the types of concluding remarks you have written. On the lines below, write at least three sentences to connect your summary statement to the concluding remarks you circled.

_____

_____

_____

Creating a Strong Conclusion

The conclusion is a very important component of an essay. A good conclusion shows how the writer has proved his or her point and why the essay is important. Readers often judge the effectiveness of the entire essay by the conclusion. Use the following outline to plan a conclusion.

Summary Statement—The summary statement shows readers how you have proved your point. A good summary statement consists of two parts: a summary of the major points and a restatement of the thesis. It is important to remember that a summary statement uses new language but never includes new details.

Restatement of the Thesis—Write your original thesis statement.

_____

_____

_____

Now, restate your thesis, using either new language or new sentence structure or both.

_____

_____

_____

Summary of the Major Points—Write the topic sentences of your body paragraphs.

Topic Sentence 1: _____

_____

_____

Topic Sentence 2: _____

_____

_____

Topic Sentence 3: _____

_____

_____

Now, restate your topics, using either new language or new sentence structure or both.

Topic Sentence 1: _____

_____

_____

Topic Sentence 2: _____

_____

_____

Topic Sentence 3: _____

_____

_____

Concluding Remarks—Concluding remarks are your last opportunity to make a good impression on the reader. Your concluding remarks will show why your essay is significant. Concluding remarks can take many forms, such as a narrative, a recommendation, a quotation, or a prediction. On the lines below, write two different kinds of concluding remarks.

Concluding Remarks 1: _____

_____

_____

Concluding Remarks 2: _____

_____

_____

Bridge Sentences—While an introduction narrows from general to specific information, a conclusion broadens from specific to general. Between your summary statement and concluding remarks, you need to write bridge sentences to show the relationship between the two while broadening the scope of the information. First, circle one of the types of concluding remarks you have written. On the lines below, write at least three sentences to connect your summary statement to the concluding remarks you circled.

_____

_____

_____

Second Draft

○ ## Providing Vivid Descriptions

Answer the questions following each sentence in order to make the action or object more detailed and precise. Rewrite each sentence, transforming the general statement into a very specific one. You may write each sentence in either the first or third person. Avoid the verb "to be." For help with word choice, refer to the suggestions at the end of the worksheet.

Example: *The city is old.*

What is the name of the city? How old is it? What evidence of aging can be seen in the city? Natchitoches, Louisiana, was founded in 1714, and some of the city's buildings are beginning to crumble from years of weathering and lack of maintenance.

1. 1. The bird flew.
   What kind of bird? What color is the bird? How fast is it flying? What direction is it going? What has caused it to take flight? What is its "emotional" status?

2. The child looked out the window.
   Is the child a boy or a girl? What expression is on the child's face? What type of room (or building) is the child in? Why is the child in this room, and what does he or she see? What is the child's reaction to the scene outside the window?

3. The teacher said that she would not accept late papers.
   What, **exactly**, did the teacher say (think about using a direct quotation)? What is the teacher's name? What kind of tone did she use? How did the students respond?

○ 4. The room was dirty.
   What type of room is this? Why is the room dirty? How dirty is it? How does it smell? What objects or materials are contributing to the room's dirtiness? Who should have cleaned this room? Why didn't this person clean it?

5. The food is delicious.
   What kind of food is it? How and where was it prepared? Who prepared it? What does the food smell like? What is the texture of the food? How is it presented on the plate?

6. He has not slept in days.
   What is his posture? What is his facial expression? What do his eyes look like? How does his voice sound? What is his disposition? Is he making sense when he talks? What do his clothes look like? Does he look freshly showered and cleaned up?

Examples of words that clarify meaning with sensory detail:

SMELL: odor, stench, stink, fragrance, aroma

TASTE: sweet, saccharine, bitter, savory, rancid, tangy

TOUCH: rough, smooth, blistering, freezing, fuzzy, soft, coarse

SIGHT: bright, dim, dull, radiant, gory

SOUND: blasting, ringing, sizzling, bubbling, whispering, hissing, shouting

Examples of active verbs for describing action vividly:

○ trudge, stroll, bustle, zip, whistle, sigh, carry, speed, zoom, drive, contemplate, slink, flail

Using Transitional Words and Phrases

Using transitional phrases between sentences and phrases is essential to making the relationships between ideas clear. Without transitions, sentences often become choppy and do not "flow" well together. Furthermore, because transitions indicate different types of relationships between ideas, writers should use the *appropriate* transitional words and phrases to indicate how ideas relate to each other.

Section I

In the following sentences, circle the appropriate transitions in parentheses to connect ideas and make the sentences convey the relationships between them as clearly as possible.

Example: Baseball practice was not canceled (even though; therefore) rain had flooded the field.

Even though: Baseball practice was not canceled even though rain had flooded the field.

1. The pitcher threw for eight innings (before, while) the coach took him out of the game.

2. One player refused to practice. (Therefore, Whereas) he was forced to sit out in the next game.

3. The coach made the players run (until, before) they were heaving with pain.

4. (Whereas, Because) most batters are either right-handed or-left-handed, Mike can switch hit (whereas; because) he is ambidextrous.

5. The league discourages players from chewing tobacco (because, although) players often serve as role models for youth.

6. The players have many complaints about the coach. (For example, Therefore), they say he has favorite players who do not follow the rules but still get plenty of playing time.

7. The players have many complaints about the coach. (For example, Therefore), they refuse to hustle on the field.

8. (Although, Because) some players and their parents have issues with the coach, the team wins most of the time and will advance to regional competition.

9. (Although, Because) some players and their parents have issues with the coach, the team is holding a meeting after practice to resolve their differences.

10. The assistant coaches will drag the field and put away equipment (since, while) the head coach meets with the players and their parents.

Section II

Now that you have had some practice choosing the correct transitions, connect the following sentences with transitions from the word bank below. You should not use the same transition twice, and you will not use all of them. Additionally, you may find more than one appropriate transition for connecting the ideas between the sentences.

Also	Therefore	Indeed	For instance	Accordingly
Afterwards	Although	Finally	Thus	Furthermore
Because	However	For example	Additionally	Similarly

1. When Joe was little, his little league team won a championship. His coach took the team out for pizza and ice cream.

   _____

   _____

2. Baseball could be made safer for children. Leagues could switch to using wooden bats instead of aluminum bats.

   _____

   _____

3. Sam's coach asked her father to be an assistant coach. Michael's father showed up to practice the next day and helped run the team through exercise drills.

   _____

   _____

4. Betting on little league games should be illegal. Anyone caught doing so should be thrown in jail.

   _____

   _____

5. Groundskeepers came to the ballpark and raked the dirt on the field, trimmed the grass in the outfield, and picked up trash outside the field. They packed up their equipment and went home.

   _____

   _____

6. For young children, baseball should be a fun and positive activity. All players should get to bat and play in the field.

   _____

   _____

7. For older kids, baseball gets more competitive. Playing time is often determined by hitting and fielding ability. Some players spend more time on the bench than they would like.

   _____

   _____

Final Draft

Avoiding Idiomatic Phrases

Idioms are words or phrases whose meanings are specific to a given language and do not translate literally into their intended meaning. Idioms are common in everyday conversation but are often viewed as inappropriate in formal academic writing. In this exercise, identify the intended meaning of the underlined idioms.

Example: *Kurt Vonnegut, the American novelist renowned for his satire and black humor, kicked the bucket in April, 2007.*

kicked the bucket = died

1. David <u>ran to the store</u> to buy only milk and eggs, but he found <u>a steal</u> on Cheerios and bought seven boxes.

_____

_____

2. After getting low midterm grades in all her courses, Geneva had <u>a wake-up call</u> and decided to <u>hit the books.</u>

_____

_____

3. Reminding Jonathan that it's a <u>dog eat dog world</u>, the coach urged him to keep working for a starting position and not to <u>throw in the towel.</u>

_____

_____

4. Thinking he was <u>ahead of the game</u>, Nick relaxed until realizing that the semester was almost over and he still <u>had a lot on his plate.</u>

_____

_____

Now that you have had some practice identifying the meanings of idioms, underline the idioms in each of the following sentences and rewrite the sentence with words or phrases that express more clearly the intended meaning.

1. Joseph was on cloud nine after receiving an "A" on his first composition essay.

_____

_____

2. After procrastinating for days, Barry realized he had to bite the bullet and get his essay written.

_____

_____

3. As freshmen, many students feel like they are in uncharted waters trying to adjust to college life.

_____

_____

_____

4. Often, students procrastinate on major assignments until the end of the semester then realize they are a day late and a dollar short.

_____

_____

_____

5. Joseph and Barry were hungry for barbecue, so they walked to The Little Dooey and went to town on a rack of ribs.

_____

_____

_____

6. At the last minute, Cory and Taylor decided to attend the Egg Bowl, so they hit the road after eating Thanksgiving dinner.

_____

_____

_____

Using Concise and Appropriate Language

Using concise language means making your words count. Unnecessary words and phrases often appear in writing because they are part of the process of wrestling with ideas and getting thoughts on paper. However, as you continue to draft, work to identify words and phrases that add length to a sentence but do not contribute to the overall meaning. To achieve concision, use active verbs, eliminate empty words and phrases, and cut repetition.

In the following exercise, each sentence has one or more unnecessary words or phrases Underline the wordy passages and rewrite each sentence to make it more clear and concise.

Example: The reason why most people drive from place to place is because their destinations exist miles away from where they live.

Most people drive from place to place because their destinations exist miles away from where they live.

1. The gathering of smog happens due to the fact that many cities have a dense population of workers who commute.

   _____

   _____

   _____

2. Some new laws have been enacted by the national government in an attempt to curb pollution problems in large cities.

   _____

   _____

   _____

3. I believe that car companies should try to make more efficient cars because gas costs so much anyway, in my humble opinion.

   _____

   _____

   _____

4. Many car companies have started manufacturing and making electric cars that do not use gas at all or hybrids that use much less fuel than traditional cars.

   _____

   _____

   _____

5. At this point in time, it is hard to find cars that get less than 25 miles per gallon of gas.

_____

_____

_____

6. Despite the fact that new regulations have required car companies to increase vehicle efficiency, many people still object because of the fact that they do not think the government should be able to tell private companies how to make their products.

_____

_____

_____

7. There is still a large market for large utility vehicles that appeal to working-class citizens who might not be able to work in the event that such vehicles were banned for the reason that they do not get good enough gas mileage.

_____

_____

_____

8. These citizens who have jobs but do not make much money cannot afford to buy new cars that have good gas mileage.

_____

_____

_____

9. The cars that can be afforded by people who have lower income are ones that are of older age.

_____

_____

_____

10. So in conclusion, to summarize there is still a demand by working-class citizens who have a right to buy older cars, even in the event that they burn more fuel.

_____

_____

_____

Editing for Concision and Clarity

Inexperienced writers often use "fillers" in their writing. Fillers are empty words or phrases that do not contribute any meaning to the ideas presented. Fillers take up unnecessary space on the page and come in many forms; they can appear at the beginning, middle, or end of a paragraph. They usually consist of familiar words and phrases used in everyday speech to add emphasis or stress. However, in writing, they hinder the reader by obscuring the writer's intended meaning.

Section I

In the following exercise, each sentence contains an underlined word or phrase that is filler. Rewrite each sentence, removing the filler and replacing it with specific details that clarify the meaning intended by the filler.

Example: _Since the dawn of time, people have fought each other over natural resources._

Many wars throughout human history have been fought over natural resources.

1. People like to say that fossil fuels will last forever and that we should keep using oil because it is our primary source of energy.

_____

_____

_____

2. One aspect of the issue people often ignore is the availability of alternative sources of energy.

_____

_____

_____

3. Oil happens to be one of the most expensive and difficult resources to acquire.

_____

_____

_____

4. The fact of the matter is that oil is not an infinite resource, so we should invest in finding new resources and technologies for extracting and using them.

_____

_____

_____

5. It is said that finding new sources of energy will not reduce America's reliance on oil.

_____

_____

_____

Section II

In addition to fillers, redundant words and phrases appear often in student writing. Redundant words or phrases cause a similar problem—taking up space without contributing meaning. These words and phrases are repetitive, using different words to say the same thing and can, in some cases, actually produce contradictory meanings.

In the following sentences, identify and remove the redundant words and phrases, leaving only what is necessary to convey the desired meaning.

Example: *Environmental issues are significantly important in politics today.*

1. Many politicians contend that polluting the earth is immorally wrong.

2. In today's modern society, we should be aware of how our lifestyles affect the environment.

3. Even though scientists present many actual facts about environmental damage, many remain skeptical.

4. Many believe that in the final end of humanity will be caused by humans.

Section III

A final impediment to student writing tends to be the use of phrases that state the obvious. Like fillers, they take up unnecessary space and do not contribute any meaning to the sentence. Often, they are words or phrases that attempt to assert the validity of opinions. However, instead of using these phrases to do so, writers should establish credibility by providing convincing evidence to support their points.

In the following sentences, identify and remove the unnecessary words or phrases.

Example: *I believe that humans are responsible for taking care of the planet.*

1. There is nothing more important than preserving what we have for those who come after us, in my humble opinion.

2. As a matter of fact, if we do not help preserve the environment for our children and grandchildren, they will be left with a desolate, barren planet.

3. To summarize, if we do not do something now, the future for those who will come after us is bleak.

4. In conclusion, if we do not stop destroying our planet, there will be no future for those who come after us.

Grammar:
Getting it Right

Contents

Building Sentences

Parts of Speech

Nouns—Exercise 1: Identifying Nouns

Underline the **nouns** in the following sentences.

1. Shana was closer to the answer than she thought.

2. When Josephine has a party, her parents usually serve pizza.

3. UPS will deliver the package that Claudio sent to Cleveland.

4. The new French restaurant in town, Chez Louis, sometimes serves a delicious dish called Duck a l'Orange.

5. Melba argued with her boyfriend about dancing with another woman at the party.

6. The new television program is about robots that battle crime in the twenty-fifth century.

7. After her graduation from Starkville High School, Wien wants to travel to Europe on a cruise ship.

8. These orange trees should have been watered more often.

9. The captain of the *Santa Cruz* demanded entrance into the private harbor, but the harbormaster refused because the huge liner was much too big for the small port.

10. There is an old joke that a camel is simply a horse designed by a committee.

Nouns—Exercise 2: Identifying Nouns

Underline the **nouns** in the following sentences.

1. The colors of the autumn foliage were so glorious that the sight left Katie and Shawna nearly speechless; nature lovers appreciate this time of year.

2. The foreman told Heinrich that the crew would be lucky if the building's frame was finished before quitting time.

3. Yesterday's newspaper said that The Peerless Bakery will move into new quarters next month.

4. "When Jack and Betty were in high school," said my mother, "teachers never allowed a student to question a teacher's authority."

5. Jun's car has developed several large cracks in its windshield; the girls will have to go to the game in Rachel's car, instead.

6. A car bearing an Illinois license plate slowed down near the accident, but apparently the driver decided that he didn't want to get involved in the scene.

7. Every student in the dorm except Melisande and Cassandra will spend the upcoming vacation with her family.

8. One of the greatest classes I've ever taken is economics because Dr. Shields helped me understand our financial system more clearly.

9. Either Atticus or the neighbor's dog, Crowley, was barking as loudly as he could last night.

10. Each first-year student must pass a physical examination before attending the first day of classes.

Nouns—Exercise 3: Singular and Plural Nouns

For the following nouns, write an "**S**" in the blank if the noun is **singular**, and write a "**P**" in the blank if the noun is **plural**.

1. phone _____

2. nucleus _____

3. ox _____

4. class _____

5. mother-in-law _____

6. examination _____

7. knife _____

8. ex-wife _____

9. watch _____

10. sheep _____

11. dorm _____

12. scarf _____

13. sophomore _____

14. alga _____

15. newspaper _____

16. committee _____

17. hero _____

18. larva _____

19. parenthesis _____

20. axis _____

Nouns—Exercise 4: Singular and Plural Nouns

The nouns underlined below have been changed to a plural form. **If that form is incorrect**, write **the correct plural form** above the noun, and **if the plural is correct**, write a "**C**" above the noun.

1. Many <u>bisons</u> died during the expansion of the American railroad system.

2. Hundreds of <u>traveleres</u> were loaded onto <u>buses</u> headed to Texas after the cruise ship limped into the harbor.

3. The United States has experienced several <u>crises</u> in the wake of the <u>attacks</u> on September 11, 2001.

4. Several <u>squids</u> mysteriously washed onto California <u>beaches</u> last year.

5. After examining all of the <u>datums</u>, the <u>investigators</u> determined that the building caught fire due to faulty wiring in the basement.

6. After examining the <u>contractes</u>, the record company decided to add several <u>addenda</u> to the previously agreed-upon <u>items</u>.

7. Gandalf led the Fellowship of the Ring into Rivendell, the city of the <u>elves</u>.

8. Several <u>specieses</u> of <u>birds</u> have become extinct due to deforestation in the Amazon Basin.

9. The <u>leafs</u> fall off the <u>trees</u> after their <u>colores</u> have faded to a golden brown.

10. My grandmother grows <u>tomatoes</u> and <u>potatos</u> in her gardens every year.

Nouns—Exercise 5: Singular and Plural Nouns

Underline all **nouns** in the following sentences. Write "**S**" above the **singular nouns** and "**P**" above the **plural nouns**.

1. Clarence is one of those men who never does tomorrow what can be put off until next week.

2. My mother is planning the guest list for my wedding.

3. Several students in my class joined the Army or the Navy.

4. The money from the sale was donated to the children's fund for a new playground.

5. Cooking a stir-fry requires large amounts of rice, peppers, broccoli, and other vegetables.

6. At the zoo, I watched three young girls chase their little brother through the monkey house until he fell and skinned his knees.

7. A horde of little country children and one lone donkey were trooping down the road.

8. The team of soccer players went out for pizza even though they had lost the game.

9. Years ago there weren't the same social and economic problems that young people face today.

10. A sundae loaded with syrups, marshmallows, whipped cream topping, nuts, and all the fixings is always too much for Elaine's diet.

Verbs—Exercise 1: Identifying Verbs

Underline the **verbs** in the following sentences. **Note:** Most sentences contain more than one verb.

1. Vivian attends MSU, where she studies biology.

2. My head ached because I drank too much beer.

3. The students found their books at last.

4. When I arrived, everyone went home.

5. My roommate thinks that I am stupid because I make bad grades.

6. I rode my bicycle to campus today.

7. As we approached the car, we noticed that someone had broken the windshield.

8. If I practice the piano every day, I might be able to learn this difficult piece of music.

9. When my turn came, I told the counselor that I had already taken all the required courses.

10. My English teacher failed me because I missed too many classes.

Verbs—Exercise 2: Identifying Verbs

Underline the **verbs** in the following sentences. **Note:** Each sentence contains more than one verb.

1. We generally think of a volcano as a large mountain that belches lava and smoke from a crater at its top, but the important part of a volcano is not the part we can see.

2. Inside every volcano, there is a conduit, or pipe, that brings molten rock to the surface, where it builds the mountain that people can see.

3. The molten rock is known as magma as long as it is under the ground; after the volcano erupts, the rock hardens and is called lava.

4. Few people have seen the birth of a volcano, but Drisco Pulido was standing in his yard when the Mexican volcano Paricutin first made its appearance on February 20, 1943.

5. Pulido, his wife, his son, and a neighbor were all watching as smoke and ash began to rise from a small hole in the middle of a field where Pulido had grown corn for many years.

6. At first, the cone was so small that Pulido could have stepped over it, but by the next day the cone was ten meters high, and, a week later, it was 140 meters high.

7. As the cone continued to grow, everyone in Pulido's little town was forced to move out of the village; when the volcano stopped erupting in 1952, the top of the cone had risen 410 meters above the original level of Pulido's cornfield.

8. Usually a cinder cone like Paricutin doesn't become so large; cinder cones, which are made entirely of lava fragments, seldom get more than three hundred meters high.

9. Composite cones often grow quite large, however: Mount St. Helens, Mount Ranier, and Mount Hood are examples of this type of cone.

10. Neither Mount Ranier nor Mount Hood is as tall as Japan's Mount Fuji or Hawaii's Mauna Loa, which is considered the world's largest active volcano.

Verbs—Exercise 3: Action Verbs

Underline the **action verbs** in the following sentences. **Note:** Some sentences may contain more than one verb.

1. Last summer, my friend Joe visited from Florida.

2. I took him to the beach near my house.

3. He wanted to see what a Mississippi beach looks like.

4. That day, we lay on the beach for two hours.

5. Unfortunately, after two hours, we realized that we had gotten sunburned.

6. We planned to swim and play volleyball.

7. Instead, we sat in the sand most of the day with my friends.

8. I learned that sun tanning endangers sensitive skin like mine.

9. Swimming wards off sunburns, however.

10. The water diffuses UV rays and keeps the skin cool.

Verbs—Exercise 4: Linking Verbs

Underline the **linking verbs** in the following sentences. **Note:** Many sentences contain more than one linking verb. **Do NOT** underline the action verbs.

1. The Beatles were a rock band from Liverpool, England.

2. Though my aunt is a hard worker, she feels that a person needs a break sometimes.

3. This spaghetti tastes like it needs more salt.

4. When I called my mother this afternoon, she sounded sick.

5. When the city inspectors looked at the old West Chester Hotel in 1980, they saw that it appeared unstable.

6. The Statue of Liberty remains one of the United States of America's most iconic images.

7. My brother attempted to prove that he was a better swimmer than I, but my record proved too difficult for him to beat.

8. When I felt the softness of the fabric, I knew it was perfect for my niece's new baby blanket.

9. The horse's leg looked broken, so the veterinarian looked at the X-rays.

10. I turned the leaf over to see if it had turned a different color on the underside.

Verbs—Exercise 5: Helping Verbs

Underline the **main verbs** in each sentence, and **circle** the **helping verbs**. **Note:** Many sentences contain more than one verb phrase.

1. The puppies were playing while we were trying to bathe them.

2. When I was practicing the song, my sister would unplug my guitar.

3. At the same time that Erica is painting the mural, Maxwell will dance a performance piece; it will be a beautiful presentation.

4. The volcano in Washington might erupt again, so we should prepare for that eventuality.

5. We should have gone to see the movie this weekend because it would have been fun to get out of the house.

6. We could run to the store to get some milk, but that would mean we would have to change out of these dirty clothes.

7. Sarah had not been watching television, so she did not know that school had been canceled due to snow.

8. The meeting has been canceled; the school board will reschedule it for next week.

9. Shanice, can you help Danny with his homework since he is having trouble with fractions?

10. May I ask you where you got that necklace? I have been looking for one just like it.

Verbs—Exercise 6: Helping Verbs

Underline the **main verbs** in each sentence, and **circle** the **helping verbs**. **Note:** Some sentences may contain more than one verb phrase.

1. Do you think that we should have gone to visit Grandma with Josefina yesterday?

2. Diane was walking to the mall yesterday when a young man asking for donations for the Red Cross approached her.

3. I am not sure that there is a right or wrong answer to the question that Dr. DeGabriele asked in class yesterday.

4. Does Michaela think that the school will close if it snows overnight, or does she think it will remain open?

5. I have taken so many pictures of my cat Queenie that I can almost fill up an entire photo album.

6. I don't believe that there is any way that we could mess up this painting project any more than we have already done; maybe we should hire a professional.

7. When Renaldo said the line, "The call is coming from inside the house," I knew that it was time for me to jump out of the closet and yell very loudly.

8. Andrew Lloyd Webber, who is known for writing award-winning Broadway musicals such as *Cats* and *Jesus Christ Superstar,* has been accused of musical plagiarism on multiple occasions.

9. I told Donald that, when he finally decides whether or not he will get a tattoo, he should spend the extra money to get it done by a well-respected artist—not one that works out of his house.

10. Japanese comic books, also known as manga, are becoming increasingly popular in the United States, particularly those manga that are made into animations such as *Naruto* and *Bleach.*

Prepositions—Exercise 1: Identifying Prepositions

Underline the **prepositions** in the following sentences. **Note:** Many sentences contain more than one preposition.

1. The boat sank in heavy seas.

2. The story is written in the past tense.

3. After the plane landed in the middle of the open field, the frightened passengers deplaned.

4. Torn copies of *Seventeen* fell from the roof of the building.

5. The path through the trees led to a natural spring.

6. On Christmas morning, the kids awoke early and began searching for their presents under the Christmas tree.

7. Throughout the night, the tower bells rang in celebration over the safe return of the town's soldiers.

8. Despite his fears that he had not been accepted to Mississippi State University, Jerome was the first student in his class to receive an acceptance letter.

9. On the weekends, Hiam teaches several counseling classes at the Jewish Community Center.

10. As a result of suggestions made at the committee meeting, the president of the PTO sent letters asking for help with the fundraisers.

Prepositions—Exercise 2: Identifying Prepositions

Underline the **prepositions** in the following sentences. **Note:** Many sentences contain more than one preposition.

1. According to my GPS, the new restaurant is located near the Cafe on Main.

2. Nyla found her brand new shoes buried among her little brother's toys.

3. Gliding into the room after her brother, Teodora was clenching a rose between her teeth.

4. Several of the town's locals claimed that they had spotted a UFO floating above city hall.

5. We finally found our dog inside the shed, nursing a brand new litter of adorable basset hound puppies.

6. Throughout the evening, the audience cheered as fireworks exploded in the sky.

7. Despite his fear of spiders, Reginald managed to crawl under the house and fix the broken pipe.

8. We had to cross through the back alleys to find our car, which was parked one block from Beale Street.

9. Without our heavy luggage weighing us down, we quickly made our way through the airport.

10. Sophia's mother told her to come home by 11:00, but she snuck in the back door sometime around 1:30.

Prepositions—Exercise 3: Identifying Prepositions

Underline the **prepositions** in the following sentences. **Note:** Many sentences contain more than one preposition.

1. We were surprised to find several birds hidden among the long rows of trees.

2. Beyond the small, aged farmhouse house, a derelict grain silo rose ominously in the distance.

3. The man in the car is my uncle Stephan, who is a building contractor from Milwaukee, Wisconsin.

4. Cory turned the box over to read the microwave instructions before he realized that the box was open, so he spilled the contents all over the floor.

5. Despite the fact that I have told my friends several times that I am allergic to milk, they still believe that I am only lactose intolerant.

6. There are scores of people who believe that there are several "secret societies" such as the Illuminati secretly running the world outside of the public view.

7. According to experts, while drinking through a straw can protect teeth from drinks that can stain teeth, this activity can also cause wrinkles, so it is important to sip lightly.

8. The flock of geese attempted to avoid the huge jetliner that invaded its flight path, but unfortunately several geese were sucked into the engines and killed.

9. After much exploration, researchers found that, except for huge deposits of a common mineral ore, the mountainous region offered no other natural resources.

10. Some theorists believe that if certain types of communicable diseases spread quickly throughout the entire population of a region, then a zombie apocalypse could theoretically occur.

Prepositions—Exercise 4: Prepositions and Homonyms

Underline the prepositions in the following paragraph. Keep in mind that some words are **homonyms** that sound like prepositions but are not being used as such.

James had forgotten that he wanted to go <u>to</u> the store, for he really wanted to get a new CD that came out that day. He tried running <u>after</u> his mother, who was already backing out <u>of</u> the driveway, but he could not catch up to her. Instead, he stood <u>by</u> the mailbox as she drove away. He waited on her there for a few minutes, hoping she would have seen him and would come back to get him. He had to get that CD in time because if everyone <u>but</u> him got it <u>before</u> school the next day, he would be embarrassed. James liked to be <u>on</u> top <u>of</u> things, and this delay was irritating his impatient nature. In order to get to the store, he decided to walk. He left his mother a note <u>on</u> the refrigerator. <u>During</u> the long walk, he thought about how much he needed his own cell phone.

Adjectives—Exercise 1: Identifying Adjectives

Underline all of the **adjectives** in the following sentences. **Note:** There may be more than one adjective in each sentence.

1. Willie never gets discouraged, even when his best ideas fall apart.

2. The poor turtle just lay on his back, pedaling his short, stubby legs.

3. Some of my hard-earned money has gone toward some useless, expensive items.

4. My favorite red backpack has a broken zipper and a large slit in the front pocket.

5. Mr. Borish's old basset hound Mollie paddled ashore and lay on the cool sand.

6. The tall girl who sits in the front row was bragging about buying a new purple bikini.

7. My least favorite part of having a messy roommate is having to pick up his dirty used tissues when he has a cold.

8. My mother's father was a Navy diver during the Second World War, and he and his best friend traveled to several exotic foreign places.

9. My father's old reclining chair was sitting on the curb after he got home from a tiring day at work; my mother had bought him a brand-new leather recliner with oversized cup-holders in the arms.

10. When a raging fire broke out in the engine room of the cruise ship, the electrical systems failed, and the poor passengers were forced to take cold showers and eat stale sandwiches for several long, grueling days.

Adjectives—Exercise 2: Using Correct Articles

Circle the appropriate **article** for each option.

1. He had (a/an) W inscribed on his bracelet.

2. (The/A) strange person showed up at my door last night.

3. (A/an) hostess usually seats people in (a/an) restaurant.

4. It is (a/an) honor.

5. I thought I saw (a/an) unicorn.

6. I am going to be (a/an) RA this semester.

7. Dorian wasn't sure what was (a/the) purpose of the activity.

8. There was (a/an) X drawn in the sand.

9. She played (a/an) xylophone in the marching band.

10. There is (a/an) underground mall in Belgium.

Adverbs—Exercise: Identifying Adverbs

Underline all of the **adverbs** in the following sentences. **Note:** There may be more than one adverb in a sentence.

1. My sister, who is in the choir, sings clearly and very well with a lovely voice.

2. I did not want to go to work this morning because I was very sleepy from staying up late.

3. Our instructor will accept late work only if we have a doctor's excuse.

4. I am finally done with all of my reading.

5. There was some really good cake in the kitchen this morning; it is not there anymore.

6. This fuzzy blue sweater is too thick to wear in this insanely hot weather.

7. The dog is sleeping because he is so tired from running around all day.

8. How quickly can you get me to the airport?

9. If there is even the slightest chance that it will rain, they will probably cancel the ball game.

10. This is really the only time that I will be in my office.

Pronouns—Exercise 1: Identifying Pronouns

Underline the **pronoun(s)** in each of the following sentences.

1. John, Sarah, and I sang a lot of good songs back then.

2. My sister couldn't tell who was the fastest: Barbara, Anne, or herself.

3. Keep what I told you a secret from her and Allie.

4. If you ask Harry or me to do the job, either of us will be glad to do it for you.

5. Nobody knew your story except for you and me.

6. Each soldier in that platoon is responsible for the care and cleaning of his or her own guns and mess kits.

7. Everyone on the team has not been playing as well as he or she can.

8. The doctor himself told me that exercising can increase one's stamina and fitness.

9. Some people like to post profile pictures on Facebook that they have taken of themselves.

10. My cat, Fluffy, likes to wind itself around my friend's legs each time Jennifer comes to our house.

Pronouns—Exercise 2: Personal Pronouns

Underline the **personal pronoun(s)** in each of the following sentences.

1. The lady you met at Sarah's party was just promoted to regional sales manager.

2. My new candle cast a bright circle of light on them.

3. I think Max and Janice are great together; they have been dating for several months.

4. Susan, Scott, and she are going to the movies on Friday night.

5. The boy we saw was short and had red hair; he couldn't be the boy you saw.

6. Although the speaker knew more about the subject than I, we were bored by his repetition of the main points of his lecture.

7. The foreman is a good friend to you and me, and he likes to give us jobs when he can.

8. We will nominate the candidate we like; then, we'll try to get the rest of the student body to vote for our choice.

9. The company manager brought her the briefcase while we were on our lunch hour.

10. We always thought she would be the lead actress because she can turn into almost any character.

Pronouns—Exercise 3: Relative and Indefinite Pronouns

Part 1: Underline the **relative pronoun(s)** in each of the following sentences.

1. The scholarship was supposed to be given to whomever had the highest grades, but the scholarship committee could not determine whose grades were highest.

2. The student who had the shortest name had to give the first presentation.

3. The doctor told me that my blood pressure was normal and that I did not need medication for my high cholesterol.

4. My favorite pen, which is a fine-tipped ballpoint, leaked all over my shirt pocket.

5. I don't know what my mother was thinking when she gave me such an ugly sweater; who would ever wear something so hideous?

Part 2: Underline the **indefinite pronoun(s)** in each of the following sentences.

1. Anyone with a bit of common sense could figure out how to change the oil in his or her car.

2. All of my family has the need to tell each other what to do, even if no one has asked for advice.

3. Most of the dogs in the pound would give anything to go home with somebody.

4. Every pair of shoes that Joe owns is either brown or black.

5. Neither of the students in the front row remembered his or her homework today, but nobody else forgot his or her assignments.

Part 3: Underline the **intensive or reflexive pronoun(s)** in each of the following sentences.

1. The conductor has to remind herself to take her baton to every concert so that all of the musicians can see the directions she gives.

2. The President himself gave the commencement speech for the graduation ceremony at my university.

3. The children in the class found themselves quite bored by their teacher's lesson on multiplication.

4. I realized when I got home that I had forgotten to put my key to the house back on my key ring; this meant that when I left this morning, I had locked myself out!

5. When my brother and I visited our great-aunt in Ireland, she insisted that we make ourselves at home and let her know if we needed anything to make our stay more comfortable.

Part 4: Underline the **possessive pronoun(s)** in each of the following sentences.

1. She took my favorite pair of rain boots with her to Seattle in case the weather was rainy during her trip.

2. This book is mine; yours is on the bookshelf in the living room, but from the location of your bookmark, it is clear that you have not completed your reading for our class tomorrow.

3. The students had given up three days of their school vacation to write a paper for their composition course, but they quickly decided that writing papers had lost its appeal.

4. My cell phone beeped incessantly once its battery life was reduced to fifteen percent, which caused it to lose its remaining battery life even more quickly.

5. Many new homeowners are afraid to leave their houses on vacation in case something bad happens to their homes.

Pronouns—Exercise 4: Possessive Pronouns

Underline the **possessive pronouns** in each of the following sentences. **Note:** There may be more than one pronoun in each sentence.

1. Jeanine is sure that these seats are ours.

2. Leon rested on the couch that evening and played *World of Warcraft* on his new computer.

3. I'm not sure that this is the best way to raise money for our campaign.

4. I am sure that there are several people who will support me in my endeavor.

5. I can always tell my husband's computer from mine because his has scratches all over it, and mine looks like new.

6. While Jerome doesn't think that his grandmother was actually one of The Supremes, he still gets his friends to ask for her autograph when they visit her house.

7. This cell phone isn't yours; your phone doesn't have a picture of my girlfriend on the background, does it?

8. The dog spent the entire afternoon chasing its own tail while we tried to clean our apartment.

9. Since this is the first Christmas since they had their baby, Michael and Josephine will celebrate at their house.

10. Though Bettina and Bethany are twins, they have never shared the same style; they both have styles that are all their own.

Pronouns—Exercise 5: Reflexive Pronouns

Underline the **reflexive pronoun** in each of the following sentences, and **draw an arrow** to its **antecedent**.

1. We couldn't believe it ourselves.

2. I don't think there was any way that I could have embarrassed myself any more than I had that morning.

3. After a long day at work, Taylor decided to treat himself to a cold beer and a large pepperoni pizza.

4. After we arrived at the hotel, we showered and made ourselves at home.

5. In spite of the fact that we kept shutting it down, the laptop kept turning itself back on until the battery ran down.

6. J.D. was surprised to find that, ultimately, he had only hurt himself when he decided to get revenge on his ex-girlfriend.

7. The teacher told the students to read quietly to themselves while she checked over their homework.

8. Marianna told Donnell that there was no way that she would ride that roller coaster, but she eventually found herself screaming next to him on the Texas Giant.

9. We spent hours searching frantically for our cat only to find that it had gotten itself wedged between the washer and the dryer.

10. After spending two years working on a very difficult graduate degree, Carla decided that the best way to reward herself for a job well done was to buy herself a brand new MacBook Pro.

Conjunctions—Exercise: Identifying Conjunctions

Underline the **conjunctions** in the following sentences. **Note:** There may be more than one conjunction in each sentence.

1. There was no way we could have finished the project before morning, but Jessica insisted that we try anyway.

2. Boone decided that he would wait for the next bus, for walking across campus would make him arrive late for his final exam.

3. My cat Dora liked to sleep on the back of my couch, but I didn't like it because she shed so much.

4. On Sundays, my husband and I like to go to the Veranda and order their delicious club sandwiches.

5. I don't want to have to go to the doctor's office this afternoon, but if I don't go today, I won't get in to see her again until March.

6. We had to eat fast food before the concert in order to arrive on time, so we stopped at a burger chain.

7. Ted was very firm and stood up to Chris, so the rest of the members of the group treated him with great respect for the rest of the semester.

8. We wouldn't get to see a Broadway play, yet we still decided to go to New York this summer.

9. Jordan usually likes to watch sitcoms, but she recently discovered *The Walking Dead* and loved it.

10. Several students petitioned the university to continue employing Dr. Gaffigan, but the board voted, and they decided to force the aging professor to retire.

Interjections—Exercise: Using Interjections

Rewrite each sentence, **adding** an appropriate interjection **from the list below** and making sure to **punctuate** properly. **Note:** There are multiple options for each sentence.

ah	eureka	oof	thanks	well
alas	hallelujah	oops	there	whoa
bam	hurray	shh	uh-oh	yes
boom	oh	surprise	um	yuck
eh				

1. Just when I thought I had fixed the door, it fell.

_____

_____

_____

2. I found it!

_____

_____

_____

3. The baby wobbled on his legs, standing for the first time, and then hit the floor with a grin.

_____

_____

_____

4. I really needed a new copy of this book!

_____

_____

_____

5. I am not sure about that idea.

_____

_____

_____

Types of Phrases

Prepositional Phrases—Exercise 1: Identifying Prepositional Phrases

Underline the **prepositional phrases** in the following sentences.

1. Antonio was hoping to meet his girlfriend in Acapulco.

2. Pancho always works in his yard on Sunday.

3. According to Amanda, we will open presents after we eat the cake.

4. Although I wanted to see *The Lion King* on Broadway, I could not get tickets to the show.

5. A novel by Jenny Brooks won the National Book Award; she accepted the award in an extravagant ceremony in New York City.

6. The first draft of our paragraphs was due yesterday, but we begged our teacher for an extension.

7. Taylor carefully plants bulbs in the fall and roses in the spring, watering them thoroughly after planting.

8. We were walking toward Howell Hall when we noticed a small puppy hidden among the bushes outside of Giles Hall.

9. Because she teaches at Mississippi State University and also takes classes for her master's degree, Ms. Lashley rarely has time to go to dinner with her friends.

10. My roommate constantly reads novels about princesses hidden inside towers, about knights slashing through hordes of monsters, and about dragons hovering above ancient towers.

Prepositional Phrases—Exercise 2: Identifying Prepositional Phrases

Underline the **prepositional phrases** in the following paragraph.

The one person in my family who has had the most influence on me throughout my life would have to be my great-grandmother, MaLiza. She is ninety-six years old, but she is highly intelligent and no-nonsense even though she never attended school. She is one of the most highly respected women in her town, working hard to ensure that her family and friends never go without the necessities of life and sending us soup and cornbread when we feel under the weather. Although she spends a lot of time making sure that her family is safe and healthy, Grandma MaLiza always finds time to take care of herself and her dogs, Poco and Bongo. She has even taught both of her dogs to perform tricks and entertains the children of the neighborhood with her dogs' antics. Besides the usual standby tricks such as "Sit" and "Stay," she has taught her dogs to jump over each other and to weave between her legs on command. Grandma MaLiza and her dogs are popular in the neighborhood, but to me, she is just my sweet great-grandmother, who slips peppermints in my pockets and calls me every weekend to ask me how my week was. I cannot imagine a better way to end a long week of studying for classes and scurrying around campus than hearing her crackling, faded voice humming into the phone as we say goodbye, saying, "You will always be my baby."

Infinitive Phrases—Exercise 1: Identifying Infinitive Phrases

Underline the **infinitive phrases** in the following sentences.

1. Do I have enough money to take the trip down to Florida?

2. I was excited to go to the concert.

3. To be in a movie is Rachel's dream job.

4. Mr. and Mrs. Smith are going to travel to Kentucky for the weekend.

5. To be a doctor is William's goal in life.

6. The teacher was asked to speak for three class periods in a row.

7. Did you have time to get your hair cut?

8. Our plan is to travel in the summer to Mexico.

9. Try to proofread your essay before you turn in your final draft.

10. Would you like to swim if it is pretty outside?

Infinitive Phrases—Exercise 2: Identifying Infinitive Phrases

Underline the **infinitive phrases** in the following sentences.

1. To be famous has been Sherry's ambition since she was a little girl.

2. Mallory was excited to get a good grade in her biology class.

3. Does Joey or Kaitlyn have enough gas to take us to the beach?

4. To be the best friend I can be is very hard sometimes.

5. The filly playing out in the field wanted to eat the apple.

6. Fred tried to obtain his boating license during the week.

7. It was hard to follow what the woman in the wreck was saying.

8. To move to Tennessee is Susan and Bill's goal this year.

9. I will be able to play soccer this afternoon at the intramural fields.

10. To be happy is sometimes harder than it seems.

Appositive Phrases—Exercise 1: Identifying Appositive Phrases

Underline the **appositive phrases** in the following sentences.

1. C. S. Lewis, one of the most well-known fantasy authors, also wrote several religious works, such as *The Great Divorce* and *Mere Christianity.*

2. Yasmina was excited to tell her coworkers that her daughter, a student at Armstrong Elementary, made all A's this semester.

3. The Apple TV, a neat device which allows users to connect their Apple devices to their television sets, is known as a digital media receiver.

4. The first video gaming system, the Magnavox Odyssey, was released in 1972 and featured over twenty-five different games.

5. *Gone With the Wind,* one of the highest grossing movies of all time, was about a love affair between Scarlett O'Hara, a spoiled debutante, and Rhett Butler, a skilled blockade runner.

6. After our trip to Gatlinburg, TN, we drove through Cade's Cove, a historic town nestled in a lush green valley deep within the Great Smoky Mountains.

7. I have the worst time keeping my terrier, Remus, from scratching at my couch cushions in an attempt to burrow under them.

8. Have you seen *Zombieland,* a hilarious zombie movie in which a shy man travels across the United States to find the last Twinkie in existence?

9. While there have been thousands of different car models manufactured since the invention of the automobile over a hundred years ago, few are as recognizable as the iconic Chevrolet Bel Air, the '57 Chevy.

10. One of the most feared fish in the sea, the great white shark, is often a scapegoat for many shark attacks, the real blame for which often rests on its much more voracious cousin, the tiger shark.

Appositive Phrases—Exercise 2: Combining Sentences to Create Appositive Phrases

Combine the following pairs of sentences using an **appositive phrase**.

1. Fong will come to our class next week to tell us about the many different types of Asian cuisine. Fong is a student from Korea.

   _____

   _____

   _____

2. My grandfather, Jack, was a frogman in the Mediterranean Sea during World War II. Frogmen were Navy soldiers trained as combat divers.

   _____

   _____

   _____

3. Dian Fossey was an activist and scientist who studied gorillas in Africa for eighteen years. Dian Fossey was found murdered in her cabin in 1985.

   _____

   _____

   _____

4. The cougar is found on all three American continents. The cougar is a cat that is closely related to the common house cat.

   _____

   _____

   _____

5. The Beatles formed in Liverpool, England in 1960. The Beatles are one of the most well-known bands in the history of Rock and Roll music.

   _____

   _____

   _____

6. My father travels once a month overseas to other countries to work. My father is an off-shore oil driller.

_____

_____

_____

7. Turquoise is a decorative stone that has been used in jewelry, weaponry, and art for thousands of years. Turquoise is often found in arid climates such as Sinai and the southwestern region of the United States.

_____

_____

_____

8. Seth McFarlane is simultaneously acclaimed as a daring, innovative artist and criticized as a low-brow, subversive chauvinist. Seth McFarlane is the creator of *Family Guy* and *American Dad.*

_____

_____

_____

9. Harry Potter faced and survived many dire, dangerous challenges and ultimately defeated the evil Lord Voldemort. Harry Potter was known as "The Boy Who Lived." Lord Voldemort was known as "He-Who-Must-Not-Be-Named."

_____

_____

_____

10. Author William Faulkner created the fictional Yoknapatawpha County and situated most of his novels and short stories there. William Faulkner was born in New Albany, Mississippi.

_____

_____

_____

Types of Clauses

Independent and Dependent Clauses—Exercise 1: Identifying Independent and Dependent Clauses

Label each of the following clauses as either **independent (IC) or dependent (DC)** in the blank provided.

_____   1.   *The Simpsons* is one of the most beloved and longest-running television series of all time.

_____   2.   Because she was late for her own wedding.

_____   3.   After we found out that my brother had been in a serious accident on the way home from football practice.

_____   4.   J.K. Rowling spent several years determining the rules that govern Harry Potter's magical world.

_____   5.   If only there were some way that we could travel back into the past and visit some of the greatest minds the world has ever known.

_____   6.   In the middle of the night, I heard what sounded like a wolf howling in the field behind my house.

_____   7.   So that we could have enough money to pay for college and not have to work while taking classes.

_____   8.   Until there were enough volunteers to rebuild the destroyed community.

_____   9.   Once when Jasmine was a young girl growing up in a small neighborhood in Lincoln, Nebraska.

_____   10. Several years ago, a museum in Jackson hosted an exhibition which displayed artifacts from Russian history.

Independent and Dependent Clauses—Exercise 2: Identifying Independent and Dependent Clauses

Label each of the following clauses as either **independent (IC)** or **dependent (DC)** in the blank provided.

_____ 1. When removing wallpaper from a bathroom.

_____ 2. You should always add water to an iron to get steam.

_____ 3. Opening a water bottle usually takes two hands.

_____ 4. While closing the door softly so that the baby would not wake up.

_____ 5. If only the keyboard for the computer in the lab in the library would work.

_____ 6. Although it wouldn't work until I banged it against the desk repeatedly.

_____ 7. I was still thrown out of the library for disturbing the peace.

_____ 8. Even my mother agrees that it is acceptable etiquette to eat macaroni and cheese from the microwaveable cup.

_____ 9. When Jace insisted on throwing away empty soda bottles in the recycling bin.

_____ 10. I hate breaking a plastic fork while eating my frozen dinner.

Independent and Dependent Clauses—Exercise 3: Identifying Independent and Dependent Clauses

Label each of the following clauses as either **independent (IC) or dependent (DC)** in the blank provided.

_____   1. Sticky notes all over my computer help me remember important tasks.

_____   2. Into the scary dark cave opening beneath the trees we went.

_____   3. When I wake up each morning.

_____   4. There is no need for an alarm clock.

_____   5. Since all of the seats on the shuttle that ran from Montgomery Hall to the commuter parking lot near the Sanderson Center were covered in something sticky.

_____   6. That we were going to have to run to class to be on time.

_____   7. Before opening the bottle of soda that Michael had dropped down the stairs.

_____   8. As if the only reason to go to the library is to meet someone for coffee.

_____   9. Now that I have my own shiny new car in which to drive around.

_____   10. Unless I meet with a classmate to get the notes from the last lecture.

Independent and Dependent Clauses—Exercise 4: Identifying Clauses Within a Sentence

Underline the **dependent clauses** in the following sentences **once** and **underline** the **independent clauses twice**. **Note:** Not all sentences will contain dependent clauses.

1. When you get home for spring break, we will take a vacation to the mountains.

2. Even though there were several thousand people in costume at the animé convention, both my sister and I won awards for best costumes.

3. Dante had to limp home in the rain after he broke his ankle skateboarding.

4. Ms. Gassaway teaches English as a second language at the university, so she spends a lot of time planning lessons in order to help non-native speakers learn English.

5. Provided that she makes all high grades during her first year in college, Miko's parents promised to take her on a cruise to Europe this summer.

6. As a small child, my brother wouldn't eat vegetables; as a result, my parents believe to this day that his growth was stunted.

7. I don't think that I will have many problems making money now that I have a degree in education.

8. Rather than break a promise to his daughter, Michael spent all the money he had in order to buy her a new puppy.

9. There are millions of people who believe that we haven't landed on the moon even though there is plenty of evidence that we have.

10. Last Friday, Leila and Dionne drove to Memphis for a weekend getaway, and they went to see *Les Miserables* at The Orpheum.

Independent and Dependent Clauses—Exercise 5: Creating Complete Sentences

Turn the following dependent clauses into **complete sentences** by adding an **independent clause**. Remember to **punctuate** correctly.

1. whereas some dogs never bark at strangers

   _____

   _____

   _____

2. even if the taxi to the airport arrives on time

   _____

   _____

   _____

3. as if there were any way that Alisha would spend the night playing video games rather than studying

   _____

   _____

   _____

4. unless you can find another person who would be willing to give a speech at the last minute

   _____

   _____

   _____

5. whenever there was a play, an opera, or a concert at Thalia Mara Hall in Jackson, MS

   _____

   _____

   _____

6. where the street comes to the Mississippi River and bends sharply to the left

   _____

   _____

   _____

7. so that Sultana would be able to finish her project discussing the effects of erosion on riverside property value

_____

_____

_____

8. as we were waiting in line to buy tickets to Beyoncé's concert at the end of March

_____

_____

_____

9. even though there was plenty of room for everyone hoping to listen to the President's "State of the Union Address"

_____

_____

_____

10. In order to ensure that Nikola was able to meet her birth mother as soon as she arrived at her hotel

_____

_____

_____

Relative Clauses—Exercise 1: Identifying Relative Clauses

Underline the **relative clauses** and **circle** the **relative pronouns** in each of the following sentences. **Note**: There may be more than one relative clause in each sentence.

1. My brother, who has a lisp, was teased a lot in school.

2. The coffee Jesse drinks, which is a Hawaiian Kona blend, always tastes burned to me.

3. The cat that is curled up on the top of the couch had to have surgery when it was a kitten.

4. The vending machine that is in the basement of this building shredded my dollar bill.

5. The chair that Kate was sitting in broke, which caused her to sit on the floor for the rest of class.

6. The bulletin board, which is usually plastered with colorful flyers and brochures, is completely bare.

7. The paint that Jerry's roommate bought for the living room is the color of pea soup.

8. The student who writes the best essay for the contest will win a cash prize.

9. The lottery winners can donate a portion of their winnings to whomever they would like without a tax penalty.

10. Jackie, whose father wants her to work for his company this summer, surprised her family by announcing that she intends to live in Peru over the summer vacation.

Relative Clauses—Exercise 2: Correctly Using Relative Pronouns

Circle the **relative pronoun** in the parentheses that shows the relationship between the ideas in the independent and dependent clauses linked together. **Note**: There may be more than one set of relative pronouns from which to choose.

1. Morgan's mother, (that, who) loves to watch soap operas during the day, was very upset that the cable was not working.

2. Matt hates to do Calculus homework, (that, which) makes his decision to be a mechanical engineer quite puzzling.

3. Sadie has a new kitten (that, who) likes to chase its own tail and sleep on top of the clean laundry.

4. My new cell phone, (which, that) has the newest operating system pre-installed, runs twice as fast as my old phone, but the battery lasts only half as long.

5. Brandon's golden retriever, (whom, which) we like to call "The Orange Tornado," left a path of destruction in the living room again when he chased the cat through the room.

6. The peanut butter and jelly sandwich (that, what) Kelly brought for lunch was squashed so badly by the books in her backpack (which, that) she had to eat it with a spoon.

7. The bottle of Sprite, (which, who) Caitlyn bought to settle her stomach, had so much carbonation it sprayed the entire third row when she opened it, (which, that) made her feel even worse.

8. The window in my bedroom allows me to see (whomever, whoever) is walking up the sidewalk to our door.

9. The backpack (that, who) José bought had fifteen different pockets (that, what) he could use for all of his school supplies and books.

10. Keith, (who, whose) parents came to see him during homecoming weekend, had to spend six hours cleaning his room to keep his mom from yelling at him for making such a horrible mess.

Relative Clauses—Exercise 3: Correctly Using Relative Pronouns

Write a **relative pronoun** in the blank that shows the relationship between the ideas in the independent and dependent clauses linked together.

1. Leo's dad, _____ company sells parts to manufacturers overseas, travels all over the world.

2. The editors of my textbook, _____ they are, must have wanted to torture students.

3. The announcements for Abigail's wedding, _____ will take place in June, were finally mailed last week.

4. The problem _____ Reed was having with his roommate could not be resolved by their resident advisor, so he had to ask for a room transfer.

5. My favorite instructor, _____ always cancels classes on Fridays, was fired for incompetence.

6. The new MP3 player, _____ also plays videos, costs $250.

7. The first hundred people _____ come to the store today will receive a free gift and a book of coupons worth fifty dollars.

8. The laptop my brother bought me, _____ has the only copy of my ten page paper, just caught on fire.

9. The trees around the Drill Field, _____ have lovely foliage in the fall, make my allergies go crazy in the spring.

10. The students _____ parents send them care packages are the envy of their friends.

Relative Clauses—Exercise 4: Combining Sentences Using Relative Clauses

Combine the following pairs of sentences into a complex sentence using a relative clause.

1. Leslie's mom does not work during the summer. Leslie's mom is a teacher at the local elementary school.

   _____

   _____

   _____

2. Chase won a scholarship for his outstanding GPA. His GPA was a 4.0.

   _____

   _____

   _____

3. It is difficult to find shoes that are my favorite color. My favorite color is coral pink.

   _____

   _____

   _____

4. I think there is only one valid reason for a person to jump out of a plane. A person can jump out of a plane if it is on fire and about to crash.

   _____

   _____

   _____

5. My roommate received a notice that his car had been towed. My roommate parked in the President's parking space.

   _____

   _____

   _____

6. Clarissa learned a valuable lesson yesterday. She took a big swallow of milk without smelling it first.

   _____

   _____

   _____

7. Bobby wants to be a comic book writer. He grew up enacting scenes from his favorite comic series with his brother.

_____

_____

_____

8. My class in art history is cancelled for tomorrow. Art history is helpful for students planning to work in a museum.

_____

_____

_____

9. The car hit the fire hydrant. The car is still speeding down the street.

_____

_____

_____

10. The movie is about two people who travel backwards in time. I want to see the movie.

_____

_____

_____

Relative Clauses—Exercise 5: Punctuating Relative Clauses

Correct the **punctuation** for the relative clauses in each sentence. If the punctuation is correct, write "**C**" in the blank next to the sentence.

_____ 1. My dog, who weighs eighty pounds, likes to pull me around the neighborhood on my roller-skates.

_____ 2. My favorite book which is *Pride and Prejudice* was made into a movie several times.

_____ 3. The sign, that is on the doors of the elevator, warns people that the elevator is broken.

_____ 4. I gave twenty dollars to my little brother who used the money to buy a new video game instead of buying Mom a birthday gift.

_____ 5. The mashed potatoes that my mom makes are better than Grandma's.

_____ 6. The purpose of the doorstop which is to hold the door open cannot be fulfilled if the dog keeps burying it in the backyard.

_____ 7. I went to the store for milk but came home with ten pounds of Snickers which is my favorite candy bar.

_____ 8. The robot in the movie shot the hero in the arm which is probably the best place to get shot.

_____ 9. The only student wearing brown who sits in the back row is famous for acing every test without studying.

_____ 10. The only student wearing red who is sitting in the back row is famous for sleeping through every class.

Simple Sentences—Exercise 1: Combining Subjects and Verbs

Construct a **simple sentence** with each subject and verb pair provided below.

1. Subject: boy Verb: ran

_____

_____

_____

2. Subject: cats and dogs Verb: are

_____

_____

_____

3. Subject: college students Verb: study

_____

_____

_____

4. Subject: Earth Verb: rotates

_____

_____

_____

5. Subject: my professor Verb: instructs

_____

_____

_____

Simple Sentences—Exercise 2: Creating Simple Sentences from Subjects

In the exercise below, the nouns have been provided, but not the verbs. **Construct** a simple sentence with an **appropriate verb** for each.

1. Subject: men

   _____

   _____

   _____

2. Subject: moose

   _____

   _____

   _____

3. Subject: the senator and his wife

   _____

   _____

   _____

4. Subject: the boy with the balloons

   _____

   _____

   _____

5. Subject: literature

   _____

   _____

   _____

6. Subject: the pot of rice

   _____

   _____

   _____

7. Subject: the stapler

_____

_____

_____

8. Subject: the Escalade in the parking lot

_____

_____

_____

9. Subject: bottled water

_____

_____

_____

10. Subject: Jacob's little brother

_____

_____

_____

Simple Sentences—Exercise 3: Creating Simple Sentences from Verbs

In the following space provided, **construct** simple sentences with **appropriate subjects**.

1. Verb: have followed

_____

_____

_____

2. Verb: paint

_____

_____

_____

3. Verb: will be allowed

_____

_____

_____

4. Verb: taste and sample

_____

_____

_____

5. Verb: is writing

_____

_____

_____

6. Verb: had swung

_____

_____

_____

7. Verb: is giving

_____

_____

_____

_____

8. Verb: will pass

_____

_____

_____

9. Verb: opened

_____

_____

_____

10. Verb: holds

_____

_____

_____

Compound Sentences—Exercise 1: Combining Sentences Using Coordinating Conjunctions

Using an appropriate coordinating conjunction (for, and, nor, but, or, yet, so), **combine** the two sentences in each exercise **to form a compound sentence**.

1. My father bought a boat after attending a local boat show. My mother made him return it after learning how much it cost.

   _____

   _____

   _____

2. I hate breaking glasses right after removing them from the dishwasher. It seems like such a waste of water and soap.

   _____

   _____

   _____

3. Molly was driving fifteen miles an hour over the speed limit in a school zone. She received a ticket from the police officer following her.

   _____

   _____

   _____

4. The big screen televisions at the store went on sale for half off. My parents bought two of them.

   _____

   _____

   _____

5. Tonight I will study for my French exam on Tuesday. I will wash the piles of dirty laundry from my closet.

   _____

   _____

   _____

6. James's parents told him that he could have a new laptop for his birthday in September. He would have to work at the family business during the summer to earn it.

_____

_____

_____

7. The car crash may have been caused by the driver of the red car not yielding to the driver of the blue car. The car crash may have been caused by the driver of the blue car not using a turn signal when changing lanes.

_____

_____

_____

8. The frozen yogurt Jonathan ordered came with sprinkles. It did not have any other toppings like caramel syrup or cherries.

_____

_____

_____

9. I can never afford the clothes in those fancy magazines. I look at the magazines anyway.

_____

_____

_____

10. Stephano never goes to the grocery store without his debit card. He does not go without a shopping list.

_____

_____

_____

Compound Sentences—Exercise 2: Choosing Coordinating Conjunctions

Circle the **coordinating conjunction** (for, and, nor, but, or, yet, so) in parentheses that best communicates the relationship between the two independent clauses.

1. I planted sixteen tomato plants in the spring, (but, so) only four of them survived through the summer.

2. The mechanic told Jackie that her car was going to be expensive to repair, (or, for) the head gasket on her engine was warped.

3. I told my brother that he could have my old Playstation, (or, and) our mother could take it to the local thrift store as a donation.

4. I always turn the lights off when I leave a room, (so, yet) my electric bill is always much higher than it should be.

5. Once a week, I eat at my favorite local pizza restaurant, (and, yet) I always order the same pizza: pepperoni with jalapeños and pineapple.

6. I always wear my seatbelt in a moving car, (for, so) I never get a ticket for failing to buckle up.

7. I hate watching horror movies that give me nightmares, (or, so) I always rent romantic comedies on Halloween.

8. Neither of my roommates knows how to wash dishes (or, nor) offers to vacuum the apartment.

9. I love to eat chocolate cake and ice cream, (but, so) I hate to exercise and get sweaty.

10. The worst part about summer is having to mow my five-acre lawn, (for, and) we only have a push-mower.

Compound Sentences—Exercise 3: Creating Compound Sentences

Using the coordinating conjunction (for, and, nor, but, or, yet, so) in parenthesis after each sentence, **create** an appropriate new independent clause **to form a compound sentence**.

1. I hate eating brussel sprouts. (but)

_____

_____

_____

2. My dog keeps escaping from my backyard. (so)

_____

_____

_____

3. My laptop has broken three times in the last two months. (yet)

_____

_____

_____

4. Jesse's favorite hat is an olive green color. (so)

_____

_____

_____

5. Faith's dad went to the grocery store. (or)

_____

_____

_____

6. Each Thursday night, I get all dressed up. (and)

_____

_____

_____

7. Erin's mother is very upset. (for)

_____

_____

_____

8. There is no food left in the pantry. (nor)

_____

_____

_____

9. I went for a walk with my best friend to Eckie's Pond. (and)

_____

_____

_____

10. I enjoy having new clothes to wear. (but)

_____

_____

_____

Compound Sentences—Exercise 4: Using Transitions

Insert a **transitional word or phrase** that appropriately demonstrates the relationship between the two clauses into the blank.

1. Jake started his exercise regimen with fifty pushups and one hundred sit-ups; _____, he ran five miles around the track.

2. I used teeth whitening strips twice a day for six months; _____, my teeth lightened five shades.

3. The dog knocked my mom's favorite lamp off of the table; _____, she banished him to the backyard.

4. I eat mostly salads and vegetables; _____, I gained five pounds last week.

5. My best friend considered having a frozen meal for dinner; _____, she made spaghetti and meatballs from scratch.

6. Amy's boyfriend took four years to propose to her; _____, he popped the question two weeks ago and presented her with a five-carat diamond.

7. The little boy pulled on Samantha's pigtails; _____, he pulled so hard that a handful of hair came out!

8. The tennis shoes that Carrie bought for Casey were three sizes too big; _____, they were the wrong color.

9. The magazine subscription my parents gave me was a great gift; _____, I wish they had bought me a new car.

10. Zoe's house is too far away for everyone to walk there after the party; _____, she has only a one bedroom apartment.

Compound Sentences—Exercise 5: Combining Sentences Using Transitions

Rewrite each of the following pairs of sentences into **a single compound sentence** using a **transitional word or phrase**. Remember to **punctuate** your sentence correctly.

1. It's not surprising that first-year student typically gain weight. New college students often eat lots of unhealthy fast food.

   _____

   _____

   _____

2. Jessica tries to make her jewelry match all of her outfits. She always wears amethyst earrings with her purple sweater.

   _____

   _____

   _____

3. Megan dropped her phone in a puddle. She has to buy a new one.

   _____

   _____

   _____

4. Aubrey's brother backed her new car into their neighbor's mailbox. Their father refuses to let him drive anymore.

   _____

   _____

   _____

5. Jelly doughnuts are my favorite. I don't eat them because they're so fattening.

   _____

   _____

   _____

6. Many people think that all new college students are irresponsible. Most new students are very careful to complete all of their homework and attend all of their classes.

   _____

   _____

   _____

7. My brother got a part-time job so that he could afford a Playstation 3. I got a job so that I could afford groceries.

_____

_____

_____

8. The photographer tried to get the baby to smile for the picture by shaking a rattle. She made cooing noises and smiled at the infant.

_____

_____

_____

9. I realized that I had left my lights on in my car overnight. My car battery was dead.

_____

_____

_____

10. The mechanic told me my alternator was malfunctioning. I needed an oil change and new spark plugs.

_____

_____

_____

Name _____

Compound Sentences—Exercise 6: Combining Sentences Using Transitions

Rewrite each of the following pairs of sentences into **a single compound sentence** using a **transitional word or phrase**. Remember to **punctuate** your sentence correctly.

1. Planting potatoes takes a lot of hard digging and weed pulling. Carrots also require a large amount of soil preparation.

   _____

   _____

   _____

2. The printer in the library prints on both sides of the page. The printer my roommate has prints on only one side at a time.

   _____

   _____

   _____

3. I have missed two classes this week already. I would skip my class on Friday.

   _____

   _____

   _____

4. My father was supposed to bring home a case of Dr. Pepper. He brought home Dr. Thunder.

   _____

   _____

   _____

5. Maggie starts her chocolate chip cookie recipe by beating butter and sugar together. She adds the eggs and flour.

   _____

   _____

   _____

6. For dinner, Alison is chopping vegetables for the salad. Jason is stirring the spaghetti sauce.

   _____

   _____

7. The batteries on the remote control are dead. We are stuck watching the Food Network for a while.

_____

_____

_____

8. Cynthia and Austin, who love carbs and dairy, are having a dinner party on Thursday. They will provide cheese and crackers as snacks.

_____

_____

_____

9. I can't go to the movies tonight because I have a test tomorrow. Nothing good is playing in theaters right now.

_____

_____

_____

10. The ducks keep trying to steal bread from the small children on the shore. The swans wait patiently on the pond.

_____

_____

_____

Compound Sentences—Exercise 7: Creating Sentences Using Transitions

Using the **transitional word or phrase** in parentheses after each sentence, **create** an appropriate new independent clause to **form a compound sentence**.

1. The coffee in the pot has coffee grounds floating around the bottom. (still)

    _____

    _____

    _____

    _____

2. Jordan is always making home-cooked meals. (in contrast)

    _____

    _____

    _____

    _____

3. The bright blue colors of recycling bins can be somewhat distracting. (on the other hand)

    _____

    _____

    _____

    _____

4. New college students often feel lonely during their first semester at college. (however)

    _____

    _____

    _____

    _____

5. A first-year student will learn several important things in his or her first semester. (for example)

    _____

    _____

    _____

    _____

6. Learning a new hobby can be enjoyable as well as educational. (of course)

_____

_____

_____

_____

7. The Writing Center can offer students assistance with improving their papers. (therefore)

_____

_____

_____

_____

8. The Student Union features many restaurants for students' convenience. (in addition)

_____

_____

_____

_____

9. Papers that are submitted after the deadline lose ten percent of the grade per day. (consequently)

_____

_____

_____

_____

10. The parking ticket Michael received for leaving his truck parked in a handicapped space is very expensive. (in fact)

_____

_____

_____

_____

Complex Sentence—Exercise 1: Choosing Subordinating Conjunctions

Circle the **subordinating conjunction** in the parentheses that best communicates the relationship between the two independent clauses.

1. (Although, Because) I studied for a week for my calculus exam, I received only forty-seven points out of one hundred.

2. Karl decided to let Ted and Barney close the restaurant for him (since, even though) he needed to leave early and believed they would take good care of his last customers.

3. (After, While) my brother wrecked his car, he had to walk to school and work.

4. (As if, Because) I wanted to take piano lessons, I purchased an inexpensive keyboard on which to practice.

5. Lily's father agreed to let her borrow his Ferrari to go to the dance (provided that, unless) she obey the speed limit at all times, wear her seatbelt, and detail the car the next day.

6. (Whether, Before) Robin could purchase a new pair of shoes, she had to donate at least two pairs of her old shoes to charity.

7. Randy was forced to resign from his job (once, in order that) he shredded very important documents and spilled coffee all over his boss.

8. (Unless, While) we manage to get all of the stains out of the carpet, my roommate will find out that we spilled a bright red slushy on his side of the room.

9. (Even if, As if) we only stop for gas twice on our way to Texas, it will take us nine and a half hours to get to Houston.

10. Jerry was very worried (that, if) he would not get a tuition waiver next semester (that, if) he failed his math class.

Complex Sentence—Exercise 2: Combining Sentences
Using Subordinating Conjunctions

Rewrite each of the following pairs of sentences into a **single complex sentence** using a **subordinating conjunction**. Remember to **punctuate** your sentence correctly.

1. Matthew changed the oil in his car. He planned to rotate his tires.

   _____

   _____

   _____

2. Alyssa wanted to take a trip to Italy. Chloe wanted to go on vacation in Croatia.

   _____

   _____

   _____

3. Noah asked his sister to distract their mom. He wrapped presents for Mother's Day.

   _____

   _____

   _____

4. The street ended abruptly past the white house. The bridge had started to collapse.

   _____

   _____

   _____

5. Brandon wanted to ride on a train. He learned about the impact trains have had on history.

   _____

   _____

   _____

6. Dylan knew that he would need an umbrella. The storm clouds went away.

   _____

   _____

   _____

7. Anna wanted to open her own bakery. She could support her family.

_____

_____

_____

8. Victoria talked to her grandmother very loudly. She had lost most of her hearing.

_____

_____

_____

9. Nathan goes out on a date. He first asks his sister to make sure that his clothes and hair look nice.

_____

_____

_____

10. Lauren wanted to figure out what major would be best for her. She took six classes in different subject areas during her first semester.

_____

_____

_____

Complex Sentence—Exercise 3: Combining Sentences Using Subordinating Conjunctions

Rewrite each of the following pairs of sentences into a **single complex sentence** using a **subordinating conjunction**. Remember to **punctuate** your sentence correctly.

1. She did not want to break up with her boyfriend. Mia knew she could not keep dating him because he made her crazy.

   _____

   _____

   _____

2. Benjamin loved to watch scary movies. He couldn't stand being home alone after watching *The Texas Chainsaw Massacre.*

   _____

   _____

   _____

3. Lisa was opening her front door. She suddenly became aware that neighborhood children were toilet-papering the tree in her front yard.

   _____

   _____

   _____

4. I told Rick several times to pick up his dirty clothes. They are still in a smelly heap on the floor.

   _____

   _____

   _____

5. James came home from school. He made grilled cheese sandwiches for a snack.

   _____

   _____

   _____

6. The children in the neighborhood thought Mrs. Prynn was a witch. She had a wart on her nose, a black cat, and a huge herb garden.

   _____

   _____

7. Ryan is going to get a ticket for leaving his car in staff parking. He moves it before the parking personnel see it.

_____

_____

_____

8. I have not been to see a movie in theaters. I started attending college, which demands all of my time now.

_____

_____

_____

9. Alexander decided that he wanted to become an astronaut. He toured the NASA facilities in Huntsville, Alabama.

_____

_____

_____

10. William works twenty hours a week. He still can't make more than $200.

_____

_____

_____

Complex Sentence—Exercise 4: Combining Sentences Using Subordinating Conjunctions

Rewrite each of the following pairs of sentences into **a single complex sentence** using a **subordinating conjunction**. Remember to **punctuate** your sentence correctly.

1. Haley flung her hair dryer at her boyfriend's head. He told her that her jeans made her look fat.

2. Tyler tried to work extra hours this month. He can afford to buy his girlfriend a necklace for her birthday.

3. Elephants were being killed by the thousands. Hunters wanted to get ivory from their tusks.

4. Jamie had always pictured himself becoming a social worker. His mother had always wanted him to become a surgeon.

5. Caleb was able to run fifteen miles without stopping to rest. He decided to sign up for the Seattle marathon next year.

6. Hunter dreaded telling his father that he had changed his major from Pharmacology to English. His father had always supported all of Hunter's decisions.

7. Allison's little brother likes to eat at the same restaurants as the MSU football players. They are his role models.

_____

_____

_____

8. Morgan told all of her friends that she was going on a cruise to Alaska over spring break. She was really stuck at home babysitting her annoying little sister all week.

_____

_____

_____

9. I am going to ring this doorbell. Someone comes to the door and gives me Halloween candy.

_____

_____

_____

10. Rachel got a new haircut. She got gum stuck in her hair.

_____

_____

_____

Complex Sentence—Exercise 5: Creating Complex Sentences

Using the subordinating conjunction in parentheses after each sentence, **create** an appropriate new independent clause to **form a complex sentence**.

1. Gabriel was sure that he had gotten an A on his midterm. (Although)

_____

_____

_____

2. Jasmine decided to take courses during the summer. (In order to)

_____

_____

_____

3. Alexandra's mom told her that the family would be visiting Kentucky over fall break. (When)

_____

_____

_____

4. Megan washed the dishes that had piled up in the apartment. (While)

_____

_____

_____

5. Many new students find that they are homesick. (After)

_____

_____

_____

6. Jordan had to go to his instructor's office hours. (Because)

_____

_____

_____

7. Elijah found it difficult to watch the movie clip in his film class. (As)

_____

_____

_____

8. Cameron knew that he was going to be in trouble with his girlfriend. (Unless)

_____

_____

_____

9. Sydney completed all of her homework for the next week. (So that)

_____

_____

_____

10. Savanna intended to get a summer job in Starkville. (Wherever)

_____

_____

_____

End Punctuation—Exercise: Choosing the Correct End Punctuation

For each sentence below, **fill in** the blank provided with the correct **end punctuation** (a period, a question mark, or an exclamation mark) that best completes the idea or emotion of the sentence.

1. I am going to scream if I have to see one more spider_____

2. None of these questions should be difficult to answer if you have had time to study_____

3. Considering the recent amount of littering, what would your best solution be_____

4. Oh, how this thunder needs to stop so I can sleep_____

5. Miguel, you were the one who apparently did that when everyone else was asleep_____

6. Julia's sister just learned she won $17.1 million from the lottery _____

7. Do you know how to request books from another library_____

8. After you finish grocery shopping, what do you want to do_____

9. When I got out of class, I walked back to my car and found that it had been towed_____

10. Sarah, you should be careful driving on campus tonight because there will be a lot of traffic for the game_____

Commas—Exercise 1: Dates and Addresses

Correct any comma errors in the following sentences by **inserting** a comma where needed and **crossing out** any unnecessary commas. If there are no comma errors to correct, write "**C**" in the blank.

1. _____ James took his first trip to Phoenix Arizona in July, 2010.

2. _____ Catherine learned that St. Patrick's Day always falls on March, 17 no matter what day of the week it is.

3. _____ Elvis Presley was born in Tupelo Mississippi on January 8 1935 in a two-room house.

4. _____ After driving for two and a half hours, we finally made it to our destination: Memphis Tennessee.

5. _____ Jeremy's new address will be 1234 Sunnybrook Lane Starkville, Mississippi once he moves in on September 1 2014.

6. _____ Grace had always wanted to get married in Las Vegas Nevada to save money on a fancy wedding, but as soon as she told her mother she was engaged, her mom set a wedding date: June 7 2013.

7. _____ After opening all of our presents on December, 25, my family likes to sit around the tree and drink cocoa and enjoy our new gifts.

8. _____ On Tuesday, April 9, 2013, Joshua backed into a new Mercedes parked in front of his house at 1626 Ivy League Lane Starkville Mississippi and caused the police to come out to the scene of the wreck to write up a report.

9. _____ The Museum of Modern Art in New York City New York is located at 11 West 53rd Street New York, New York.

10. _____ After my first visit to Cozumel, Mexico, I knew that I wanted to spend my next vacation there, so I booked an entire two weeks at the hotel on the beach for June 2014.

Commas—Exercise 2: Introductory Elements and Direct Address

Correct any comma errors in the following sentences by **inserting** a comma where needed and **crossing out** any unnecessary commas. If there are no comma errors to correct, write "**C**" in the blank.

1. _____ During my last trip to the library I got so many books that the librarian offered to help me carry all of them to my car.

2. _____ With all due respect sir you cannot park your car in the handicapped spot unless you have a handicap sticker.

3. _____ Cody, will you water my plants while I am out of the office next week?

4. _____ Yes I can water your plants, but I will not be able to pick up your mail for you.

5. _____ Well Stephanie tried to get tickets to the concert for the whole group, but they were already sold out.

6. _____ Ma'am I'm afraid you dropped this twenty dollar bill on your way out of the store.

7. _____ Sarah Louise Smith you get back into bed this instant!

8. _____ Brittney will go to her mother's house for Thanksgiving, but she is going to her dad's house for Christmas this year.

9. _____ In, the middle of the long speech he was giving my professor lost his train of thought, so we never learned who he ultimately thought was the most important person in literature.

10. _____ At the beginning of the summer I like to take a trip to the beach, to work on my tan so that I'm not embarrassed to wear shorts.

Commas—Exercise 3: Introductory Elements

Circle the option that describes the best way to punctuate each sentence.

1. Therefore it is very useful to study all of the dates for the history exam to receive bonus points.

   a. No comma   b. Therefore, it

2. I would like to introduce my boyfriend to my parents this weekend.

   a. No comma   b. I, would

3. Next we will be going to the State Capitol for the sixth graders' field trip.

   a. No comma   b. Next, we

4. Each day summer is getting closer and closer.

   a. No comma   b. day, summer

5. However not everyone gets to enjoy his or her summer; some people must go to school then as well.

   a. No comma   b. However, not

6. Consequently some instructors give just as much work in summer classes as in full-length semesters.

   a. No comma   b. Consequently, some

7. Some fun places to visit while in Nashville are the Grand Ole Opry and Broadway Street.

   a. No comma   b. visit, while

8. One might consider also staying at the Opryland Hotel for his or her vacation there.

   a. No comma   b. One, might

9. Furthermore the shopping and the music and Nashville make up the core of the city.

   a. No comma   b. Furthermore, the

10. Today is going to be the day I find out if I have to take summer classes or if I get to go to Nashville.

    a. No comma   b. Today, is

Commas—Exercise 4: Items in a Series and Direct Quotation

Correct any **comma errors** in the following sentences by **inserting** a comma where needed and **crossing out** any unnecessary commas. If there are no comma errors to correct, write "**C**" in the blank.

1. _____ Ted really enjoys watching horror movies football games and golf.

2. _____ Staci eats a lot of different sandwiches, but her favorites are grilled cheese roast beef and peanut butter and jelly.

3. _____ Karrie has been helping, Howard, Andy and Jared, with their project for their biology class.

4. _____ Jumping rope jogging and swimming are all good examples of aerobic exercise.

5. _____ Clarissa's favorite actors are Gerard Butler Neil Patrick Harris and Ryan Gosling.

6. _____ My high school teacher used to shout at the class "If you don't learn how to factor polynomial equations, you will flunk this class!"

7. _____ My roommate told me "If you don't start putting your food containers in the trash, you'll have to move out."

8. _____ This morning, my professor announced "There will be a quiz at the beginning of class on Tuesday."

9. _____ Mark Twain once said, "It is better to remain silent and be thought a fool than to open one's mouth and remove all doubt."

10. _____ As I walked across campus yesterday, I met a guy who said "If you can give me a ride to Wal-Mart, I will pay you fifty dollars."

Hyphens—Exercise: Using Hyphens Correctly

In each of the following sentences, **circle** the appropriate option in parentheses.

1. Hannah's (mean looking, mean-looking) cat always frightens me when I get home late at night.

2. We got some (much needed, much-needed) rain today; the nap I enjoyed instead of mowing the lawn was also (much needed, much-needed).

3. Sarah's older brother turns (thirty two, thirty-two) next month, and he wants to celebrate by going on a (camping trip, camping-trip) with their parents.

4. Tasha's (ex-husband, ex-husband) has been calling her constantly all (summer long, summer-long).

5. Your (work shirts, work-shirts) fell on the floor last night—you are going to have to (repress, re-press) all of them!

6. Did you really think that representative was going to be (reelected, re-elected)?

7. I really didn't know anything about my (sister in law, sister-in-law) except for what I had heard by (word of mouth, word-of-mouth).

8. Don't (overdo, over-do) it!

9. Chaz wants to become a (dog training expert, dog-training expert).

10. After Andrea (recovered, re-covered) from her fall, she (recovered, re-covered) the hole in the floor so no one else would trip there.

Avoiding Construction Problems

Fused Sentences—Exercise 1: Identifying and Correcting Fused Sentences

Some of the sentences below are fused sentences, and some are correct. **Correct the punctuation for fused sentences**; **write "C"** in the blank next to sentences that are **correct**.

1. _____ I love English tests they can be hard sometimes.

2. _____ We opened the closet, and inside there were several large ugly spiders.

3. _____ Eben runs much faster than Joe but Joe is a stronger swimmer than Eben.

4. _____ We got out of the car we were amazed to see a woman who was swimming in the icy water.

5. _____ Devon disliked water skiing so we rode jet skis instead.

6. _____ John worked hard yet he failed to win honors.

7. _____ You weren't here when Haifa called you I told her that you would call her later.

8. _____ Wendy and Keisha are good friends however, they fight sometimes.

9. _____ Yesterday I tried to build a snowman in my yard but the snow was too muddy.

10. _____ We gave Michael the rest of the pizza Shea told him to give some to his roommate, but Michael ate it all.

Fused Sentences—Exercise 2: Correcting Fused Sentences

Each of these sentences is fused. Use the space given to **correct these sentences** using one of the following strategies. **Use each strategy** at least once.

Options for Correcting Fused Sentences

- Create two separate sentences.
- Add a semicolon and a transitional word or phrase.
- Add a comma and a coordinating conjunction.
- Add a semicolon.
- Add a subordinating conjunction to form a complex sentence.

1. My favorite sport is golf my sister prefers soccer.

   _____

   _____

   _____

2. Though Jesse wasn't wearing any shoes he sprinted toward the ice cream truck he wanted a chocolate cone.

   _____

   _____

   _____

3. The money from the bake sale has been donated to the library we hope to buy a few books for the children's section.

   _____

   _____

   _____

4. Mom came outside and saw Derrick preparing to jump off the roof into a pile of hay after she yelled at him, he climbed back down and was grounded for a week.

   _____

   _____

   _____

5. It was a sunny day the whole family drove to the beach after work.

   _____

   _____

   _____

6. My mother Joyce swam in the 1972 Olympics she was sick.

_____

_____

_____

7. It is cold outside some people are still wearing t-shirts.

_____

_____

_____

8. Some people refuse to buy hybrid cars they think that they are not necessary they can help people save a lot of money in gas.

_____

_____

_____

9. The troops marched past the soldier's casket they saluted him one last time as an illustration of respect.

_____

_____

_____

10. We were near a police station our new car was damaged by vandals we had insurance we were able to get it fixed.

_____

_____

_____

Fused Sentences—Exercise 3: Correcting Fused Sentences

Correct each of the following **fused sentences**; use **two different strategies** for each.

1. Downing his opponent was difficult Jerome was a strong wrestler.

   A. _____

   _____

   B. _____

   _____

2. The quarterback threw a perfect pass the receiver dropped the ball on the ten yard line.

   A. _____

   _____

   B. _____

   _____

3. The wool blanket was scratchy however the down comforter was soft and feathery.

   A. _____

   _____

   B. _____

   _____

4. I don't know what you think you're doing that book is mine.

   A. _____

   _____

   B. _____

   _____

5. History is often thought of as a boring subject the past can be very interesting.

   A. _____

   _____

   B. _____

   _____

6. The couple married and moved to another city they divorced a year later.

   A. _____

   _____

   B. _____

   _____

7. In the pond swam a number of swans some of them flew away some of them stayed behind.

   A. _____

   _____

   B. _____

   _____

8. Roberto and José went to the movies they saw Iron Man 3 Roberto loved it José said it wasn't any good.

   A. _____

   _____

   B. _____

   _____

9. Several students in my graduating class have joined the army only two have had to go to Afghanistan.

   A. _____

   _____

   B. _____

   _____

10. People think that Robert Frost's "The Road Not Taken" is only about a person who made a good decision about his or her life they have missed the point of the poem.

   A. _____

   _____

   B. _____

   _____

Fused Sentences—Exercise 4: Identifying and Correcting Fused Sentences

In the following paragraph, there are several **fused sentences** and several **correct sentences**. **Underline** the sentences that are **correct**, and **correct the fused sentences**.

After growing tired of his work as a druggist, Arthur J. Grimsky decided to become a candidate for the post of Representative from the Third District. He believed that he could win the primary election easily in fact, he doubted if anyone would dare to run against him. Because he had become good friends with his customers, acquaintances, and business associates in the local Chamber of Commerce, he knew he would have no problem winning the election. After he made his decision, he proceeded to file as a candidate in the primary election of his party. His candidacy was endorsed by the Chamber of Commerce, the local Labor Council, and the Women's civic league this made him believe that his campaign would certainly be successful even if other candidates entered the race. When the deadline for filing had passed, Grimsky found himself opposed by only one man: Horace Lertch, the bartender at the Wilkins Hotel. Lertch was a pleasant fellow, who was well liked in the community however, he was neither very intelligent nor very well educated. This convinced Grimsky that nobody would seriously consider voting for Lertch as a United States Congressman. Nevertheless, Grimsky made careful plans for his campaign he began to speak to groups of citizens throughout the district. Whenever he spoke, Grimsky used the biggest words he knew and spoke disparagingly of the ignorance of his opponent this made a very unpleasant impression on the voters, although he did not realize what he was doing. Lertch, meanwhile, stayed behind his bar, talked to his friends, and asked them to tell other people that he would try to be an honest and hardworking representative. Lertch's inactivity made Grimsky more confident than ever consequently Grimsky began to act as if he had already won the election. Grimsky's pride and arrogance completely alienated most of his supporters, and on election day, the voters chose Lertch, who had succeeded in letting Grimsky defeat himself.

Comma Splices—Exercise 1: Identifying Comma Splices

Some of the following sentences have comma splices and some do not. **Revise sentences with comma splices** on the lines provided. **Write "C"** on the lines if the sentence is **correct**.

1. Many domestic cars cost less, however, many foreign cars have better gas mileage.

_____

_____

_____

2. Because all of the food was cold, the restaurant was bad.

_____

_____

_____

3. We spent all of our money, therefore, we will be staying in tonight.

_____

_____

_____

4. Becky's skills are perfect for the new job; we intend to hire her.

_____

_____

_____

5. The basketball team had a losing season, the coach was fired.

_____

_____

_____

6. The horse was retired from competition, her leg injury wouldn't heal.

_____

_____

_____

7. I have a good idea for a paper, I will start on it today.

_____

_____

_____

8. He called the girl many times, she would not answer.

_____

_____

_____

9. He had gone out with her last Friday, but he didn't know what was wrong.

_____

_____

_____

10. The principal arrived, the students became quiet immediately.

_____

_____

_____

Common Splices—Exercise 2: Correcting Comma Splices

Correct the **comma splices** in each of the following sentences by **rewriting them** on the provided lines.

1. Each person has his or her own car, they are all very fast.

_____

_____

_____

2. Randy ran on the track, then he went to the gym to lift weights.

_____

_____

_____

3. Whitney loves horses, she rides them every day after classes.

_____

_____

_____

4. The people in the mall were coming and going very fast, it was Black Friday.

_____

_____

_____

5. Taylor Swift is a very famous singer, she does not fit into a single genre.

_____

_____

_____

6. Smartphones are great tools for organization, many people would not know how to live without them.

_____

_____

_____

7. New York is an iconic city in the United States, thousands of tourists flock there every year.

   _____

   _____

   _____

8. Harry Potter is a hit book series, it has movie adaptations as well.

   _____

   _____

   _____

9. Though Jessica is very busy, she still takes time to teach us how to quilt and sew, she is a very good teacher.

   _____

   _____

   _____

10. Mississippi State University is a very friendly campus, there are many clubs and activities in which to become involved.

    _____

    _____

    _____

Comma Splices—Exercise 3: Identifying and Correcting Comma Splices

Some of the following sentences have comma splices and some do not. **Correct each comma splice** when necessary by **rewriting** the sentence, and **write "C"** on the lines if the sentence is correct.

1. The three branches of the government are the legislative, executive, and judicial, the executive is the most public of the three.

   _____

   _____

   _____

2. Everything was taken down in order to make room for the new hospital, the bricks were used as a walkway in the courtyard.

   _____

   _____

   _____

3. The flood destroyed the house and all of its contents, the homeowners were devastated.

   _____

   _____

   _____

4. The town was deserted after the war, the only thing left was the rubble.

   _____

   _____

   _____

5. The advertising company spent long hours on the campaign, the client proofread the ads thoroughly.

   _____

   _____

   _____

6. Many people choose to save money by buying a house, others prefer the flexibility of renting an apartment.

   _____

   _____

7. The rain finally stopped coming down, the sun started to peek out from behind the clouds.

_____

_____

_____

8. Many people use caffeine to help them stay alert and active, the main sources of caffeine are coffee and soda drinks.

_____

_____

_____

9. Many students are interested in the field of nursing, schooling often takes an extra year or two to complete after high school.

_____

_____

_____

10. Many Americans have become too dependent on caffeine, they often have to drink 2-4 high caffeine drinks a day content to avoid a mental crash.

_____

_____

_____

Run-On Sentences— Exercise 4: Correcting Fused Sentences and Comma Splices

Decide whether the sentence is a fused sentence or comma splice. Then put an "**F**" (fused sentence) or "**CS**" (comma splice) in the space beside the sentence. Then **revise** the sentence on the lines provided.

1. Blue is my favorite color I do not like red.

_____

_____

_____

2. Many people do not go to college, they go to trade school or get a job.

_____

_____

_____

3. Lots of people go back to college, they need a diploma to get a better job or a promotion.

_____

_____

_____

4. Being happy in your chosen career path is crucial to being good at your job people who are unhappy often do not do as well or even quit.

_____

_____

_____

5. Washington, D.C. is a unique place to visit, the capitol is a very beautiful building.

_____

_____

_____

6. The sun always rises in the east, the sun sets in the west.

_____

_____

7. Even though I felt terrible today, I went to take my test I felt prepared.

_____

_____

_____

8. The test was in my history class, the subject was states' rights.

_____

_____

_____

9. The teacher explained the project guidelines I carefully listened.

_____

_____

_____

10. Elizabeth won the grand prize trip to Hawaii at the raffle she wanted to go to the airport right away.

_____

_____

_____

Mixed Construction—Exercise 1: Correcting Mixed Construction

The following sentences contain mixed constructions. **Revise** them using **logical structures**. **Note:** You may use more than one sentence for your revision.

1. Although the weather was nice, why did he wear a thick coat today?

_____

_____

_____

_____

2. Because I could not get to the store is the reason I do not have a notebook for class.

_____

_____

_____

_____

3. In my favorite movie there is a good relationship because I think it is important to have respect for each other.

_____

_____

_____

_____

4. Due to the all of the controversy over the election is why there are so many news reports about it.

_____

_____

_____

_____

5. Depending on the way you play this video game depends on if you want to be evil or good in the end.

_____

_____

_____

_____

Mixed Construction—Exercise 2: Correcting Mixed Construction

Read the following sentences, checking for mixed construction problems. If the sentence is correct, write "C" on the lines. If the sentence contains a mixed construction, **revise** it.

Note: You may use more than one sentence in your revision.

1. The only thing I have in common with my brother is to like the same kinds of movies.

_____

_____

_____

2. For all of the readings we had for class this week, we were supposed to write a journal entry.

_____

_____

_____

3. If the main reason you are going to the tanning bed is to look good at the beach, why are you planning on laying out every day when you get there?

_____

_____

_____

4. When we all went to Bulldog Bash together is the most fun I had all semester.

_____

_____

_____

5. If there is going to be free pizza at the meeting, maybe we should go.

_____

_____

_____

Fragments—Exercise 1: Identifying Fragments

Read each of the following items. Some of them are fragments; others are complete sentences. If the item is a **fragment**, write "**F**" in the blank. If it is a complete sentence, write "**S**" in the blank.

_____   1. Has red lights that blink slowly off and on during the night.

_____   2. This instrument shows planes where to avoid flying.

_____   3. The poster on the bulletin board that advertised the upcoming school play.

_____   4. Flashing your lights at someone can warn them of road hazards.

_____   5. The coffee I bought from the fast food restaurant after stopping to get a snack.

_____   6. The hat Jared wore on the float trip.

_____   7. It fell into the water and floated away.

_____   8. Refilling the freon for your car's air conditioning is easy to do.

_____   9. The cell phone tower beside the road on my way home from school.

_____ 10. Carrying all those heavy books to classes, even in a sturdy backpack with lots of cushioning.

Fragments—Exercise 2: Identifying Fragments

Read each of the following items. Some of them are fragments; others are complete sentences. If the item is a fragment, write "**F**" in the blank. If it is a complete sentence, write "**S**" in the blank.

_____ 1. Jason's card reader in his laptop stopped working when he spilled his can of soda on it.

_____ 2. The blinds in the bedroom on the north end of the house.

_____ 3. Even though I got an A in all my classes this semester.

_____ 4. Although I put two dollars in the vending machine that usually works fine.

_____ 5. Satisfying my chocolate craving was not possible.

_____ 6. The water bottle that has been rolling around in the floorboard of my car all semester.

_____ 7. The smell coming from the Chinese food containers under my roommate's bed.

_____ 8. Testing the smoke alarms every three months is an important part of home maintenance.

_____ 9. Jumping off the roof of the shed onto the trampoline in the yard while his friends looked on.

_____ 10. The concert that we all attended last week in Tupelo at the BancorpSouth Center.

Fragments—Exercise 3: Correcting Fragments

Each of the following items contains a fragment. Make each fragment into a **complete sentence** by supplying the missing subject, verb, and/or complete thought.

1. Earning minimum wage at his job.

_____

_____

_____

2. Is always losing his car keys.

_____

_____

_____

3. Broke into three pieces and couldn't be glued back together.

_____

_____

_____

4. In honor of my mother's birthday.

_____

_____

_____

5. Opened a new jar of peanut butter even though the old one was still half full.

_____

_____

_____

6. The dog that lives in the house next to mine.

_____

_____

_____

7. The website that has all my favorite memes.

_____

_____

_____

8. With a smile on his face.

_____

_____

_____

9. The carwash down the street from Kellie's house with the rentable pressure washer.

_____

_____

_____

10. After working all day on a computer at work.

_____

_____

_____

Fragments—Exercise 4: Correcting Fragments

Each of the following items contains a fragment. Make each fragment into a **complete sentence** by supplying the missing subject, verb, and/or complete thought.

1. Worrying about the state of her checking account.

   _____

   _____

   _____

2. Checking into a hotel for spring break.

   _____

   _____

   _____

3. Tried to turn into the crowded parking lot of the restaurant.

   _____

   _____

   _____

4. To get into a student club.

   _____

   _____

   _____

5. Because of working out in the Sanderson Center on a regular basis.

   _____

   _____

   _____

6. To open her own business making cupcakes and cookies.

   _____

   _____

   _____

7. Since buying a new car from pushy salespeople at the dealership.

_____

_____

_____

8. Would offer me a job that pays $100 an hour.

_____

_____

_____

9. Whoever put a dollar bill in the vending machine.

_____

_____

_____

10. Whether the car in front of me came to a complete stop for the red light.

_____

_____

_____

Fragments—Exercise 5: Correcting Fragments

Each of the following items contains a fragment. Make each fragment into a **complete sentence** by supplying the missing subject, verb, and/or complete thought.

1. Whenever I go home to visit my family.

   _____

   _____

   _____

2. Before leaving my house each morning.

   _____

   _____

   _____

3. Once Sherrie can afford to buy a new television.

   _____

   _____

   _____

4. Provided that my roommate has not eaten the last of the eggs.

   _____

   _____

   _____

5. Unless Zach is able to devote several hours to his paper.

   _____

   _____

   _____

6. While Sierra waited for the mechanic to fix the dents in her bumper.

   _____

   _____

   _____

7. Rather than tell his parents what really happened to his mother's favorite lamp.

8. Since Jackie's little brother learned how to drive.

9. Where to find the best-tasting burgers in town.

10. Which means that Jamal will not be going home for Thanksgiving.

Subject/Verb Agreement—Exercise 1: Choosing Correct Verbs

These sentences are examples of structures that often lead to errors of subject-verb agreement. **Circle** the correct verb from within the parentheses. In each sentence, the subject of the verb is printed in bold type.

1. It is strange that the **wisdom** we should gain from past mistakes (is, are) usually ignored.

2. The **value** of many of my college courses, I am sure, (remains, remain) to be judged and understood long after I have graduated.

3. In view of all this uncertainty, (doesn't, don't) **it** seem unwise to begin specializing early in our education?

4. Neither rebellious **youth** nor the **uncertainty** of the times (accounts, account) for some of these strange fads.

5. I can see that a thoughtful **reading** of many poems and novels (teaches, teach) a person much about life.

6. Not **one** of the undergraduates who work on our school paper (regrets, regret) the extra time it requires.

7. There (is, are), in addition to newswriting, many other promising **fields** that I might explore.

8. In that country military **service**, not business or the industries, (has, have) a priority on a young person's future.

9. The **competition** from experienced staff members, some of whom are seniors, (works, work) to my disadvantage.

10. (Has, Have) every **one** of these planes been inspected recently?

11. In newscasting, for example, a **life** of travel, of excitement, and of seeing fascinating people and places (is, are) possible.

12. There already (exists, exist) on this campus five men's honorary **fraternities**.

13. At Shady Beach we need not worry because the **lifeguard** or **one** of his assistants (is, are) always on duty.

14. Included in the schedule of events at the picnic (was, were) a three-legged **race**, a sack **race**, and a pie-eating **contest**.

15. As most people know, an enormous **amount** of insecticides (has, have) been exported to tropical countries from America.

Subject/Verb Agreement—Exercise 2: Choosing Correct Verbs

These sentences are examples of structures that often lead to errors of **subject-verb agreement**. **Circle** the correct verb in parentheses.

1. Since the weather is so beautiful today, (doesn't, don't) it seem like a great time for a picnic?

2. The number of different activity courses offered by our physical education department (is, are) extremely large.

3. Seen hastening from the scene of the crime (was, were) a young man and two women dressed in coveralls.

4. (Has, Have) everyone in the office been notified of the change in the operating hours?

5. The printed bulletin announced that there (is, are) only a few days left before the contest ends and the winner is selected.

6. Sitting beside the two girls (was, were) an old gentleman in a gray coat and two children eating peanut butter sandwiches.

7. Not included in the itinerary for the next day (is, are) the trip to Wesser Falls and the tour of the area museum.

8. The sophisticated nature of the control systems for the rockets (requires, require) the use of a high-power computer.

9. The fascinating story of the settlement of those two western states by pioneers from the East always (provides, provide) enjoyment to those attending the lectures.

10. On the battered clipboard (was, were) a notice of the next inspection and several forms for the inspectors to sign.

11. Fifty dollars (is, are) a very fine price for such a terrific looking pair of shoes.

12. After he won the contest, a number of friends and relatives (was, were) quite eager to help him invest the money.

13. The number of people trying to write novels and short stories (has, have) increased in recent years.

14. Joan owns two huge dogs, neither of which (is, are) worth anything as a watchdog.

15. No one except a few jokers and would-be comedians (has, have) answered my call for people to participate in my study of UFOs.

Subject/Verb Agreement—Exercise 3: Identifying Verb Errors

Correct all the errors in **verb usage** in the following sentences. **Strike through** incorrect verbs and **write** the correct verb form above it. If a sentence is correct, **write "C"** in the space.

_____ 1. If it weren't he who borrowed your car, who do you think it could have been?

_____ 2. Some of us who knows Jared well are pleased at his weight loss.

_____ 3. Only one of the houses that were sold has a garage.

_____ 4. The family eat together every evening.

_____ 5. Neither the sofa nor the chairs needs recovering.

_____ 6. The top two teams in each division gets to go to the playoffs.

_____ 7. All of our exported wheat is not enough for all of the people who is starving.

_____ 8. The similarity in their clothes is just one of those things that make my roommates seem like one person.

_____ 9. The style of clothes that my roommates wear are now very popular.

_____ 10. He is one of the many students who plays basketball well.

_____ 11. Some of the statistics released by the state shows that Memphis has a high murder rate.

_____ 12. All of the students on the sidewalk is wearing shorts and sandals.

_____ 13. The responsibility for the mix-up in the doctors' offices are theirs, not mine.

_____ 14. Everybody take his or her own car to the movies and go to the restaurant afterward.

_____ 15. One of my classmates call me frequently.

_____ 16. Most of the robbers uses masks to cover their faces during home invasions.

_____ 17. Some of the carpet were soaked when the water heater leaked.

_____ 18. Some of the chocolates were melted when they were left in the car.

_____ 19. Both Jamie and Sam studies hard, but their toughest subject, mathematics, give them trouble.

_____ 20. Neither blue ink nor pencil are acceptable for use on the exam.

Subject/Verb Agreement—Exercise 4: Writing Sentences Using Correct Subject/Verb Agreement

Using the singular subjects provided below, complete the sentences by **adding a predicate.** Make sure that the verb agrees with the noun. **Write** all sentences in the **present** tense.

1. My dog _____

_____

2. The student _____

_____

3. The child _____

_____

4. During the second set, the drummer _____

_____

5. The cow _____

_____

6. The college that my sister attends _____

_____

7. His room _____

_____

8. She _____

_____

9. The baby _____

_____

10. My sofa _____

_____

Now **rewrite** the sentences you have written, **making subjects and verbs plural.**

Subject/Verb Agreement—Exercise 5: Agreement

In the following sentences, subjects agree with verbs, and pronouns agree with antecedents. **Make** the change described **in parentheses** after each sentence, and then **revise** the sentence to maintain agreement.

Example: *The student attends weekly conferences with her teacher.*

(Change <u>The student</u> to <u>Students</u>.)

Students attend weekly conferences with their teacher.

1. He who does poorly in school often loses respect for himself. (Change He to People.)

    _____

    _____

    _____

2. Teenagers who collect baseball cards often devote much money and time to their hobby. (Change <u>Teenagers</u> to <u>A teenager</u>.)

    _____

    _____

    _____

3. The dancer who fails to practice risks injuring herself. (Change The dancer to Dancers.)

    _____

    _____

    _____

4. The computers were purchased because of their simplicity. (Change <u>The computers</u> to <u>The computer</u>.)

    _____

    _____

    _____

5. Their exams over, the seniors celebrate by throwing a party. (Change seniors to senior.)

    _____

    _____

    _____

6. The photographs show the beauty of the landscape, but their dim light obscures details. (Change photographs to photograph.)

_____

_____

_____

7. All workers have some complaint about their jobs. (Change All workers to Each worker.)

_____

_____

_____

8. Even though the disarmament conferences have resulted in little change, the government continues to attend them. (Change conferences to conference.)

_____

_____

_____

9. Judith is the one who always makes the decisions, and the rest of us resent her authority. (Change Judith to Judith and Bill.)

_____

_____

_____

10. Since we don't know what's behind it, the locked door seems more mysterious than it probably is. (Change door to doors.)

_____

_____

_____

Pronoun/Antecedent Agreement—Exercise 1: Identification

Circle each **pronoun** in the following sentences, and then underline the **antecedent** of the pronoun(s) in each sentence.

1. Everyone can get his or her name on the mailing list.

2. None of the puppies were bought; they stayed at the house.

3. A person should insure his or her car and house.

4. The study group had its weekly study session tonight.

5. The family has its car in the parking lot next door.

6. Everybody has his or her own secrets.

7. The students in the class of 2013 wore their rings to the graduation ceremony.

8. Jack's mom and brother took their vacations together.

9. Either Mary or Ellen broke her arm.

10. All are invited to the gala; they just need to call and make a reservation.

Pronoun/Antecedent Agreement—Exercise 2: Compound Antecedents

Circle the correct **pronoun(s)** in parentheses in each of the following compound sentences. **Underline** the **antecedent** for the pronoun(s).

1. My mom and sister are very particular about (her, their) hair.

2. Neither the dog nor the cat could find (its, their) food.

3. Alaska and Hawaii both have (its, their) own customs that differ from the rest of the United States.

4. Molly and Brian planned (his or her, their) trip to the Maldives.

5. Fish cost more than (their, its) owners wish.

6. Maryland and Virginia have (their, its) claims to Washington, D.C.

7. Did George or Billy choose (his, their) phone today?

8. Neither the glue nor paper maintained (its, their) shape.

9. Do fruits or vegetables last longer in (its, their) container or loose in a crisper drawer?

10. The ship's passengers and its crew had (its, their) lunch on board.

Pronoun/Antecedent Agreement—Exercise 3: Collective Nouns

Circle the correct **pronoun(s)** in the parentheses for the following collective nouns.

1. The group starts (its, their) tour in New York City.

2. The moose travel all across (its, their) homeland in the wintertime.

3. All of the students in the class returned (his or her, their) books to the library.

4. Every one of the actresses must know (her, their) lines.

5. Some of the silver in the cabinet has lost (its, their) luster.

6. People need to visit (his or her, their) doctors at least once a year.

7. The team received (its, their) trophy for having the most wins in a season.

8. The deer jumped to (its, their) feet when they saw hunters.

9. The class had (its, their) schedule changed for next week.

10. The committee voted on (its, their) guidelines for their new members.

Pronoun/Antecedent Agreement—Exercise 4: Indefinite Pronouns

Circle the correct **pronoun(s)** in the parentheses.

1. Some of the girls had (their, her) hair curled for the dance.

2. All of the audience liked (their, its) seats.

3. Most of the dogs are ready for (his or her, their) owners to come and get them.

4. Everybody must have a passport before going on (their, his or her) trip to another country.

5. Neither of the two problems showed (their, its) answer easily.

6. Many famous people have (their, his or her) houses in Beverly Hills or New York City.

7. Somebody dropped (his or her, their) money on the way out.

8. Everyone must face (his or her, their) own obstacles in life.

9. One of the flight attendants broke (her, their) heel on the flight.

10. Both of the teachers changed (her, their) clothes after school for the parade.

Pronoun/Antecedent Agreement—Exercise 5: Compound Pronouns

Read each of the following sentences carefully. If the sentence contains an error in **pronoun/antecedent agreement**, **strike through** the incorrect pronoun(s) and **write** the correct pronoun in the blank before the sentence. If the sentence is correct, **write "C"** in the blank. There may be more than one error in pronoun/antecedent agreement.

_____ 1. Either Rick or Michael broke his guitar strings on stage last night.

_____ 2. Neither Patricia nor Alice had their test given back in class this week.

_____ 3. Bonnie and Clyde made their fortune by robbing banks.

_____ 4. Both lions and tigers show its teeth as a warning to innocent prey.

_____ 5. Either Bob or Tyler is expected to do their job for the church on Saturday.

_____ 6. Neither of the two girls was ready for her audition.

_____ 7. Either Lizzie or Callie is going to take her test online.

_____ 8. Both Lisa and Rachel got married this past year.

_____ 9. Harry and Ginny named their boys after people who had helped them defeat Lord Voldemort.

_____ 10. Because they didn't order their books early enough, neither Jessie nor Percy received them in time to write his paper.

Pronoun Case—Exercise 1: Choosing the Correct Pronoun

Circle the correct **pronoun(s)** in parentheses for each of the sentences below.

1. Several of (us, we) drove to Memphis yesterday to see the Harlem Globetrotters demonstrate their amazing skills.

2. Savannah and (they, them) were late to the party last night because they drove fifteen miles past the right exit before they realized it.

3. There is no one in our class who is as good at complex mathematical equations as (she, her).

4. Though I have studied both of the Xbox controllers from every angle, I still can't figure out which one is (my, mine) and which one is (your, yours).

5. Joanna's parents firmly believe that one as smart as (she, her) should be passing all of her classes.

6. Just a few more weeks of eating only dried noodles to save money and that vintage sea foam green Vespa will be (my, mine).

7. The dean's staff members were surprised to discover that it was (them, they) who clogged all of the toilets in McCain Hall, and not one of the fraternities.

8. (We, Us) engineering students met every day for two weeks before our big final and were happy to discover that all of (we, us) had passed.

9. Neither Danny nor (I, me) have time to go to Jackson this weekend, but since it is my mother's birthday, we really need to go see (she, her).

10. While my mother was never really sure whether or not the locket was ever really (her, hers), she cherished it simply because it was closely connected to her favorite author's birthplace, so it meant a lot when she gave it to (I, me).

Pronoun Case—Exercise 2: Choosing the Correct Pronoun

Circle the correct **pronoun(s)** for each of the sentences below.

1. It was certainly not (him, he) dancing that ridiculous dance.

2. As for Danielle and (him, he), they will not be attending the ball this weekend.

3. There are few people who are as good at working on computers as (him, he).

4. Between you and (me, I), I don't think that Alexandra is going to pass this exam.

5. It doesn't appear to (I, me) that the person who took this picture is (he, him).

6. When Dr. Richmond retired, several of his co workers threw a retirement party for (him, he).

7. It was very important to (I, me) that everyone to understand the reasons for my dropping (me, my) calculus class.

8. Jessamine and (me, I) attempted to sneak up on my father while he was working in his office, but he caught (we, us).

9. After Jonathan had graded the students' exams, it became clear to (he, him) that August and (her, she) had cheated off of each other's papers.

10. It will either be you or (I, me) who will receive that scholarship, since the other candidates have none of the experience that (we, us) have.

Pronoun Case—Exercise 3: Correctly Identifying Pronoun Case

Review each of the underlined **pronouns** in the following sentences. If the case of the pronoun is correct, **write "C"** in the blank. If the case is incorrect, **strike through** the pronoun and **write** the correct pronoun above it.

_____ 1. Jeremiah does not think that <u>we</u> were invited to Vince's party this weekend.

_____ 2. <u>Our</u> working together as a team and developing smart studying habits helped us all to pass the exam with flying colors.

_____ 3. Once we had eaten the large Thanksgiving dinner that she had prepared, Grandmother gave all of the leftovers to <u>we</u> grandchildren.

_____ 4. Donovan and <u>she</u> woke up early so that they would have time to fix breakfast before heading off to their classes.

_____ 5. Danté decided to go for his masters degree after Dr. Dodds and <u>him</u> talked it over for a few hours.

_____ 6. After reading our uncle's will, we found out that he had left all of his farmland to my brother and <u>me</u>.

_____ 7. There is no way that Sylvia's mother will understand <u>she</u> needing to take a break from studying during spring break.

_____ 8. <u>We</u> freshmen need to work especially hard at the beginning of our college careers so that we can establish good study habits.

_____ 9. After several years scraping together cash and working hard to earn the money, my husband and <u>me</u> were able to afford that new car we so desperately needed.

_____ 10. I am sure that the department will have no problems with <u>we</u> studying together as a team as long as we don't cheat or copy off of each other's papers.

Pronoun Case—Exercise 4: Who and Whom

Circle the correct form of **who or whom** in parentheses for each of the sentences below.

1. I have no idea (who, whom) won the Oscar for Best Supporting Actress this year.

2. (Who, Whom) do you believe might have stolen Rani's computer off of her desk?

3. To (who, whom) do you think that I should give these flowers?

4. I think you should ask Anise, (who, whom) probably knows more about complex differential equations than anyone else I know.

5. People (who, whom) believe that the city of Atlantis is populated by mermaids perplex me.

6. (Who, Whom) can we go to find out the answer to this question?

7. It turns out that the first person (who, whom) we interviewed was the best person for the job.

8. Anyone (who, whom) wants to go to England this spring should sign up on the bulletin board outside the main office.

9. The recipient of the scholarship was (who, whom)?

10. For this scavenger hunt, it is important that we find a partner (who, whom) knows a lot about the history of the university.

Past Tense Verbs—Exercise 1: Changing Present Tense to Past Tense

Revise the sentences below by **changing** the present tense verbs in each of the following sentences **to past tense**.

1. The deer cross the road in a large group.

   _____

   _____

   _____

2. The batteries for the remote control to the new sound system die.

   _____

   _____

   _____

3. Jessica's nieces wash their hands for the length of time it takes to sing "Twinkle, Twinkle, Little Star."

   _____

   _____

   _____

4. The new secretary answers the phone with the wrong company name.

   _____

   _____

   _____

5. The sun bleaches the fabric on the lawn furniture until it fades to a dull yellow.

   _____

   _____

   _____

6. She calculates the amount of sales tax for her new dress.

   _____

   _____

   _____

7. Will claims the jackpot on the lottery ticket he bought yesterday.

_____

_____

_____

8. The collie perfectly completes the complicated obstacle course in the competition.

_____

_____

_____

9. The ninety-seven-year-old grandmother bolts her front door.

_____

_____

_____

10. The semi-truck driver brakes swiftly to avoid the car that pulls out in front of him.

_____

_____

_____

Past Tense Verbs—Exercise 2: Changing Present Tense to Past Tense

● **Revise** the following sentences to **change** the present tense verbs in each of the following sentences to past tense. **Note:** Watch for irregular verbs.

1. The construction workers cover the manhole with a large piece of plywood.

   _____

   _____

   _____

2. The maids clean the hotel room after check-out time.

   _____

   _____

   _____

3. The dogs bite into their juicy piece of steak.

   _____

   _____

   _____

4. The wind blows so hard that I fall off my bicycle.

   _____

   _____

   _____

5. Cornelia buys three new dresses and a set of luggage for her vacation.

   _____

   _____

   _____

6. Lucian hears loud music in the hallway of his apartment.

   _____

   _____

   _____

7. Shawn rides with Travis to work to save money on fuel.

_____

_____

_____

8. We draw straws to decide who must pay for the pizza.

_____

_____

_____

9. The twin sisters compare notes from their chemistry class.

_____

_____

_____

10. The cuddly kitten brushes against the ankles of her owner and meows for attention.

_____

_____

_____

Past Tense Verbs—Exercise 3: Irregular Past Tense

Revise the following sentences to **change** the present tense verbs in each of the following sentences to past tense. Watch for irregular verbs. **Note**: There are multiple verbs in each sentence.

1. The fire roars in the stone fireplace of the ski lodge while we drink our cocoa.

   _____

   _____

   _____

2. I go to the store for more flour while she begins mixing the other ingredients for cake.

   _____

   _____

   _____

3. The Olympic swimmer dives into the pool after his coach blows his whistle.

   _____

   _____

   _____

4. The businessman shakes hands with everyone who sits at the table with him during the meeting.

   _____

   _____

   _____

5. While the popsicles freeze, we eat an entire bowl of watermelon and drink a whole pitcher of punch.

   _____

   _____

   _____

6. The brothers sleep in bunk beds so they fight with each other all night.

   _____

   _____

   _____

7. My grandmother fixes my favorite meal every Thanksgiving, but she makes me do the dishes.

_____

_____

_____

8. Haylie hammers nails into the wall for her pictures, but she swings the hammer too hard.

_____

_____

_____

9. My sister forgives her boyfriend, yet he still buys her flowers to apologize for wrecking her car.

_____

_____

_____

10. We ring the doorbell of the scary house before we realize that we are at the wrong house.

_____

_____

Past Tense Verbs—Exercise 4: Irregular Past Tense

Revise the following sentences to **change** the present tense verbs in each to past tense. Watch for irregular verbs. **Note**: There may be more than one verb in each sentence.

1. My grandfather rises at six every morning to feed all of the animals on the farm.

_____

_____

_____

2. I lie on the sofa for a quick catnap and feel completely refreshed afterward.

_____

_____

_____

3. The cat springs into action when the mouse runs across the room.

_____

_____

_____

4. I raise my hand every time the teacher asks a question about verbs.

_____

_____

_____

5. Sarah lays her outfit for tomorrow across the back of the chair.

_____

_____

_____

6. John sets his coffee cup on the desk while he writes a note for the secretary.

_____

_____

_____

7. The printer heats up so much that it begins smoking.

_____

_____

_____

8. We hurry through the mall and catch up with Eddie and Michael.

_____

_____

_____

9. Brian swears that he can build a full-size rocket in the backyard.

_____

_____

_____

10. Anthony forgets to eat when he gets involved with his science projects.

_____

_____

_____

Past Tense Verbs—Exercise 5: Editing for Errors in Past Tense

Edit the following sentences for errors in the use of the verb "**to be.**" **Strike through** any underlined **verbs** that are **incorrect**, and **write** the **correct forms above** them. If all of the verb forms in a sentence are correct, write "**C**" in the blank provided.

_____   1. Paul and Mark were best friends during their first-year student year, but they was worst enemies after they found out they was dating the same girl.

_____   2. The chessboard David's grandfather gave his brothers were placed in the donation pile until David rescued it.

_____   3. Josh and Nick was going to the movies on Friday, but they were unable to go when their teacher assigned them two chapters of calculus homework.

_____   4. Ryan were forced to stay on campus while his roommates were able to go to Cozumel for spring break.

_____   5. The wireless mouse I use on all my computers were acting funny; I found out that my brother was putting peanut butter in the battery compartment.

_____   6. The candles was burning all evening until the wicks finally was smothered by the melted wax.

_____   7. The coffee table my uncle built for me was made out of oak and mahogany.

_____   8. The painting was hanging on the wall in the living room last week, but the nails holding it up was so rusty that the painting fell down.

_____   9. Douglas were given a choice between eating a soup or salad with his meal; he was having a hard time deciding which one he wanted until he smelled the soups.

_____   10. The water goblets my mother used for Thanksgiving was broken when the cat ran across the table and knocked everyone's glass onto the floor.

Past Tense Verbs—Exercise 6: Past Participles

Circle the correct form of the past participle in parentheses in each of the following sentences.

1. I had (broke, broken) the school record for number of naps in class before I was (gave, given) my midterm grade: an F.

2. I have (laid, lain) my reading glasses down somewhere, but I can't seem to remember where.

3. The diving team has (swum, swam) in pools across the country.

4. Patrick has (took, taken) driver's education four times, but he still has not (drove, driven) a car anywhere but the parking lot.

5. Maria has (wrote, written) a ten-page paper in less than four hours for her history course, but she was not (gave, given) a passing grade on it.

6. Kimberly was (shook, shaken) up after her fender bender, but she was okay because she had (wore, worn) her seatbelt.

7. The sun had (sank, sunk) behind the horizon before we had (saw, seen) any news about the eclipse that day.

8. Maggie's sister has (grew, grown) a foot in the last year, perhaps because she has (ate, eaten) all of her vegetables at every meal.

9. The pictures Elizabeth had (drew, drawn) for my mother were her most prized possessions.

10. I was skeptical when Laura informed us that she had (fell, fallen) in love after she had (known, knew) her new boyfriend for only a week.

Illogical Shifts—Exercise 1: Shifts in Person

Correct any shifts in **person** in the following sentences. If the sentence is correct, write "C" in the blank.

_____ 1. I really enjoy reading books because they make you feel as if you were in a fantasy world.

_____ 2. Students who come to college seeking a degree often do not realize how many hours you have to put in to make good grades.

_____ 3. The hostages were told that they would have to undergo several hours of questioning before they could return home to their families.

_____ 4. Anyone could make it through that obstacle course if you train hard enough.

_____ 5. Many hopeful teachers believe that they will not have to carry their work home after a long day's work, but they are mistaken.

_____ 6. Daniele's breakfast was delicious; you could tell that she worked really hard on it.

_____ 7. Actresses like Zooey Deschanel are often known for their vibrant, offbeat personalities.

_____ 8. In order for a person to succeed in many fields, you have to work hard and treat your co-workers with respect.

_____ 9. You can land a good job after college if you work hard and make good grades.

_____ 10. I think that a person can easily train to run track if you put your mind to it.

Illogical Shifts—Exercise 2: Shifts in Tense

For the following paragraph, **underline** any **illogical shifts in tense**, and **write** the correct form of the verb above the illogical shift.

    My first visit to the circus, ten years ago, was a thrilling experience. I loved the smell of roasting peanuts, the tastes of the delicious pink and yellow lemonades, the sound of crackling popcorn, and the sight of the funny old clown. I am so excited that I want to see everything at once: the roaring lions, the clumsy elephants, and the seals that act as if they are human. Then there is the fat lady, who must have weighed at least five hundred pounds, or the thin man, who looks as if someone could push him over using only one little finger. The freaks were really a pitiful sight, but I gazed in admiration at the strong man, who was the image of Atlas. Thinking about it now makes me want food: hot dogs, lemonade, and funnel cakes. Somehow, at the circus they taste so much better than when I bought them in the corner store. To top off that perfect afternoon, there is a ride on the Ferris wheel. Everyone was so happy that all troubles are forgotten the minute one walks into the circus grounds. The band keeps playing a cheery tune in order to keep everyone in a joyous mood, but when I was a child, no band is necessary to keep my spirits up when the circus tents are near.

Illogical Shifts—Exercise 3: Recognizing Shifts

The following paragraph contains **shifts in tense and person**; **underline** any of these illogical shifts, and **write** the correct form above the mistake.

When his wife died in 1632, Shah Jahan, the emperor of the Moguls, builds the magnificent Taj Mahal in her honor. Similarly, after Marc Antony and Cleopatra became lovers, he presents her with Cyprus, Phoenicia, and Coele-Syria. Since the average present-day lover owns far less real estate than Marc Antony, they have to give more modest gifts. Richard Burton, however, gives to Elizabeth Taylor several love tokens that would have impressed even Cleopatra. For example, he gave her a $1,050,000 gem that he purchases from Cartier. Though people cannot often give such lavish gifts to their lovers, you shouldn't get too discouraged. Today's modern lover, of course, cannot afford an incredibly expensive item, but they can give more modest gifts. Most people are perfectly happy with a box of candy or a few roses, so you can show your affection in a more cost-effective manner. A lover can write a handwritten note that expressed the depth of their affection. Of course, the best way that lovers was able to show how much they care is to simply tell your love every day how much they mean to you.

Apostrophes—Exercise 1: Using Apostrophes Correctly

Mark through any unneeded or misplaced **apostrophes** and/or add apostrophes where needed. If the sentence is correct, put "**C**" in the blank.

_____   1. Carol and Cory's favorite football teams are rivals.

_____   2. Back in the 1990's, there were a lot of sitcoms on TV.

_____   3. It's not right to steal.

_____   4. If you are going to borrow Dennis's jacket, you should ask him first.

_____   5. James and Ashley's band played at the party last Friday night.

_____   6. Who took the key's to Jennifer's car?

_____   7. Every puppy rescued from the shelter comes with it's shots.

_____   8. We are all having dinner over at the Bradley's house.

_____   9. Are'nt you going to come to the movies with us?

_____ 10. NPR's report on GMO's was very informative.

Apostrophes—Exercise 2: Using Apostrophes Correctly

Mark through any unneeded or misplaced **apostrophe**s and add apostrophes where needed. If the sentence is correct, put "**C**" in the blank.

_____   1. You should give at least two week's notice before leaving your job.

_____   2. Take it; it's your's.

_____   3. The children's play hour is coming up soon, so the class is getting restless.

_____   4. The security guard on duty keep's an eye on the building at night.

_____   5. I am going to get A's and Bs this semester.

_____   6. Janet's and Jacob's dinner date was at a very nice restaurant.

_____   7. Tyrese's car is in the shop today.

_____   8. Womens' right to equal pay is an important ethical issue.

_____   9. The people in the photo look like they're having a good time.

_____ 10. Rap music was around in the 80's, but it really took off in the 90's.

Commonly Confused Words—Exercise 1: Choosing the Correct Word

For each of the following sentences, **circle** the **word in parentheses** that best fits the meaning of the sentence.

1. (Its, It's) no surprise that Emily is dating Nick, for they have many interests in common.

2. (Whose, Who's) car is parked next to the motorcycle in the parking lot?

3. Adrian also has to stop (buy, by) the shoe store, so he and Nathan are riding together.

4. After breaking his mother's favorite lamp, Carter suffered from a guilty (conscience, conscious).

5. Alice's horse broke (its, it's) leg when it jumped over the fence and landed in a hole.

6. Amelia went (threw, through) the roadblock with no problems, but Grace was held up for almost fifteen minutes while the officers checked her registration.

7. Andrea was sure that her team would not (loose, lose), so she bragged about them all week.

8. Andrew used to loan money to his friends in high school, but he was a lot more trusting (then, than) I.

9. Brooke loves the (weather, whether) in Mississippi, but she often misses Oklahoma.

10. Caleb and Jack announced that (their, they're, there) will be a concert by their band in Friday night.

Commonly Confused Words—Exercise 2: Choosing the Correct Word

For each of the following sentences, **circle** the **word in parentheses** that best fits the meaning of the sentence.

1. Cassie was trying to decide (weather, whether) it would rain or not; if it rained, she would need her galoshes.

2. Charlotte is a better dancer (then, than) Miley is, but she rarely goes to parties.

3. Chloe had (know, no) idea that her family had planned a surprise party for her birthday this year.

4. Cooper tried to (raise, rise) his arm above his head after Ethan punched him in the shoulder, but he had a difficult time accomplishing this task.

5. Do you know (whose, who's) the person in charge of taking the tickets for the play tonight?

6. During long classes, students especially appreciate a (brake, break) to get a drink and use the restroom.

7. Dylan desperately wanted to be (apart, a part) of his older sister's band, but he didn't know how to play any instruments.

8. Ellie was (use, used) to the way that the living room was arranged before Carrie moved all the furniture.

9. Emma seems to go to the store (everyday, every day) for something she forgot to buy the last time she was there.

10. Everyone (accept, except) Ashley showed up to the Oliver's birthday party.

Commonly Confused Words—Exercise 3: Choosing the Correct Word

For each of the following sentences, **circle** the **word in parentheses** that best fits the meaning of the sentence.

1. Gabriel believes that the hardest thing for a person to experience would be to lose would be his or her (sight, cite).

2. I love mechanical pencils because I never seem to run out of (lead, led).

3. I told Isabella to meet me (hear, here) for coffee an hour ago, but she still hasn't arrived.

4. I was surprised to see that it was (all ready, already) three o'clock because the day had seemed so long.

5. If we had to deal with noisy neighbors on a regular basis, I'd be (quiet, quite) angry.

6. It is very difficult to (find, fine) a pair of jeans that fit a person just right.

7. Jackie was (suppose, supposed) to take the trash down to the curb before Friday, but she forgot.

8. Jacob tried to (affect, effect) the outcome of the lottery by putting his name on all the tickets.

9. Jennifer didn't really mind that her sister had worn her dress, but she was mad on (principal, principle) because her sister had not asked permission first.

10. Julia was happy to model for her family, but she felt very self-(conscience, conscious) in her dress when she went to the dance.

Commonly Confused Words—Exercise 4: Choosing the Correct Word

For each of the following sentences, **circle** the **word in parentheses** that best fits the meaning of the sentence.

1. Julie had just gotten a (knew, new) pair of earrings for her birthday, so she decided to get her ears pierced again.

2. Kayla was certain that she had (passed, past) her history course, but she wasn't sure about Biology.

3. Leah decided not to let her (passed, past) mistakes stand in the way of her doing well in college.

4. Liam was happy to (accept, except) a ride to the store from his classmate Noah.

5. Lily and Ella wear the same size shoe, so I bought several pairs for those (to, too, two).

6. Logan had to wear a hardhat before he was allowed to enter the construction (cite, site).

7. Lucas ended up wrecking his brother's car after his soda bottle slipped behind the (brake, break) pedal, preventing him from stopping the car.

8. Luckily, the people who live in the apartment above us are pretty (quiet, quite).

9. Madeline almost (threw, through) a fit when she realized that the mechanic had charged her twice as much for labor as he'd quoted.

10. Many of the most popular baby names today (where, were, we're) in fashion thirty or forty years ago.

Commonly Confused Words—Exercise 5: Choosing the Correct Word

For each of the following sentences, **circle** the **word in parentheses** that best fits the meaning of the sentence.

1. Mason got into a lot of trouble when he failed to (cite, site) his paper's sources properly.

2. Mia decided that she was (to, too, two) tired to go with her friends for ice cream.

3. My brother and I know that (where, were, we're) in trouble with Mom when she uses our middle names.

4. My father always swore that he would give anything to get a little (peace, piece) and quiet around the house.

5. Nathan planned to go (buy, by) a pair of shoes at the store after class.

6. No one could have guessed the (affect, effect) that the car payments would have on Steve's budget.

7. Olivia had to pay a large (fine, find) when the highway patrol officer caught her speeding on MS-82.

8. On the weekends, Ava likes to (lie, lay) in her bed all day watching movies.

9. One way to know (you're, your) lucky is to talk to someone from an impoverished country.

10. Rachel was trying to sneak into the kitchen quietly so that no one would notice that she was taking the last (peace, piece) of cake.

Commonly Confused Words—Exercise 6: Choosing the Correct Word

For each of the following sentences, **circle** the **word in parentheses** that best fits the meaning of the sentence.

1. Rebecca likes to (use, used) a lemon scented furniture polish because she thinks it makes her house smell fresh.

2. Riley will (sit, set) in his deer stand for six hours and not see a single deer.

3. Sam and Brandon have a class with (their, they're, there) other roommate, but they don't study together.

4. Samantha needed a new way (to, too, two) get to work since the construction was blocking her way.

5. Sitting in the back of the classroom can make it difficult for students to (hear, here) their teacher.

6. Sometimes students don't (know, no) that they can use the Writing Center free of charge, but they can.

7. Sometimes you want to go (where, were, we're) everybody knows your name: Basic Composition class.

8. Sophie just (knew, new) that her boyfriend was going to pop the question over Christmas break, but she really didn't want him to.

9. The best way to find out (you're, your) midterm grade is to look on Blackboard.

10. The moving speech Owen delivered (lead, led) the crowd to believe he would be the best person for the job.

Commonly Confused Words—Exercise 7: Choosing the Correct Word

For each of the following sentences, **circle** the **word in parentheses** that best fits the meaning of the sentence.

1. The puppies (lie, lay) their toys on the ground while they munch on their dog treats.

2. The sun will (raise, rise) above the tallest building in Starkville before ten o'clock this morning.

3. There are many things that set Daniel (apart, a part) from his twin, but the biggest difference between them is their hair color.

4. This year, we had to use our (everyday, every day) plates and bowls for Thanksgiving dinner because Mom had forgotten where she put the good china.

5. Thomas likes to (sit, set) the thermostat to 80 degrees in the summer to save on the electric bill.

6. Valerie was excited because her front tooth was (loose, lose).

7. We were (all ready, already) to go to the movies until Ethan spilled his soft drink on everyone in the car.

8. When students get in trouble in high school, they must go see the (principal, principle).

9. Xander and Katy told us that (their, they're, there) going to Romania this summer.

10. Xavier and Tina had (suppose, supposed) that their new dog will take a long time to be housebroken.

Adjectives/Adverb Usage—Exercise 1: Choosing the Right Modifier

Correct all of the errors in **adverb or adjective use** in the following sentences by **crossing out** errors and writing your corrections **above** the errors.

1. The student speaker did very good at graduation.

2. The deer in the yard ran off quick when we opened the door.

3. My mother makes the best gumbo; I learned from her that you have to stir the roux constant and patient until you get the right color.

4. The man looked angry at his fresh made lunch splattered on the floor.

5. The President's speechwriters must be real good.

6. In the relay race, the red team ran quicker than the blue team but lost when Terrance dropped the baton.

7. I would rather climb the mountain then ride up the lift; I need the ground under my feet.

8. I have read much magazines about hairstyles.

9. That dog sure loves his chew toys!

10. The every day costs of housing, electricity, groceries, and gas are just too much for families with minimum-wage incomes.

11. I am looking for a more small version of the phone I used to own.

12. Serena has seen too much dogs running through the streets; it has caused her many stress.

13. This is an all together positive idea.

14. If the show goes well, we won't have to think bad of our efforts.

15. I read only books when my teacher promotes how exciting they can be.

16. My dog Pickle plays with her new and green chew toy everyday.

17. I was shocked to find out the news when I was so unprepared.

18. There are not fun things to do in this town; I'm no surprised.

19. This is a quickly way to do this than what we have been told.

20. Her schedule doesn't allow her to get to school more quicker than I would hope.

Adjective/Adverb Usage—Exercise 2: Eliminating Double Negatives

Read each sentence below. If the sentence uses a **double negative**, **rewrite** it in correct form on the provided lines. If the sentence is already correct, label it as correct by putting a "**C**" on the lines.

1. I don't know nothing about working on cars.

   _____

   _____

   _____

   _____

2. We don't need no help with this project.

   _____

   _____

   _____

   _____

3. There are no more chocolates left for the group to share.

   _____

   _____

   _____

   _____

4. With only so much effort, one cannot find a good job.

   _____

   _____

   _____

   _____

5. I don't feel good about taking no test today.

   _____

   _____

   _____

   _____

6. Basketball isn't nobody's favorite sport in our family.

_____

_____

_____

7. If you want to go out tonight, don't try nothing funny.

_____

_____

_____

8. We don't have much time left to get out of this traffic and into the arena.

_____

_____

_____

9. Perhaps a better gift for him would be something he actually likes.

_____

_____

_____

_____

10. When you are finished eating, don't leave no plates or silverware on the table.

_____

_____

_____

_____

Capitalization—Exercise 1: Correcting Capitalization Errors

Correct any **capitalization** errors in each of the following sentences. If there are no capitalization errors in the sentence, write "**C**" in the blank.

_____   1. The president of the company, edward jones, gave his secretary a big raise.

_____   2. My brother learned to speak english by repeating things aunt karen said.

_____   3. Jeremy's uncle gave him the keys to a brand new mustang for his birthday.

_____   4. I gave dad a new set of golf clubs for father's day.

_____   5. The mississippi river is the longest in north america.

_____   6. St. patrick's day comes on the 17th of march every year, but thanksgiving day can occur on different dates in november each year.

_____   7. When Trey sliced open his finger, he had to use four band-aids and an entire roll of gauze in order to get the bleeding to stop.

_____   8. Daphne's parents took her to Mount Rushmore during the christmas holidays.

_____   9. Last semester, Laynie took american government, but this semester she's going to take a biology course.

_____   10. Many artists from the South are meeting at a conference in Memphis; the conference center is south of the interstate.

Capitalization—Exercise 2: Correcting Capitalization Errors

Correct any **capitalization** errors in each of the following sentences. If there are no capitalization errors in the sentence, write "**C**" in the blank.

_____ 1. Mississippi State University has many fun clubs for students to join, including the Association of Student Social Workers, Bulldog Ice Hockey, and Mickey's Movie Club.

_____ 2. My roommate drinks a pot of earl gray tea once a day, but I prefer to buy coffee from Starbucks.

_____ 3. My high school prepared me for many things that I have experienced at Mississippi State University.

_____ 4. The holiday my sister enjoys the most happens in the early spring and involves hearts, flowers, and roses.

_____ 5. The street where Angela lives was home to a famous author in the eighteenth century.

_____ 6. When the two brothers opened their restaurant, they hired a new chef from france.

_____ 7. Given his enjoyment of theater, one would expect Grant to buy tickets to A streetcar named desire, but he refuses to attend the play.

_____ 8. My mother will only buy towels from the better homes and garden collection because she insists that these towels last longer and absorb water better.

_____ 9. After driving his new ford around the parking garage, tim decided that he would prefer to park on the street; after all, beale street was not very crowded.

_____ 10. My uncle, who lives in a neighborhood with a lot of crime, is likely to get robbed because he just purchased a new sony high-definition television worth two thousand dollars.

Developing Effective Sentences

Transitional Words and Phrases—Exercise: Choosing the Correct Transitional Word or Phrase

Circle the appropriate **transitional word or phrase** from the options given in the parentheses. **Note**: There may be more than one set of options in each group of sentences.

1. (Until, Although) several people told him that the project would fail, Dion insisted that he could get one of Leonardo Da Vinci's designs to work.

2. Harold scoured his house, searching frantically for his car keys. (Meanwhile, Although), Melina shut off her alarm and began to dress for work.

3. Danae applied for several positions immediately after college. (Also, Nevertheless), it was over a year before she found a job.

4. I am sure that there is no way that you can make up for breaking my PlayStation controller. If you buy me a new one, (also, however), I will think about it.

5. My brother is accomplished in many different forms of art. (However, For instance), he sculpts marvelous statues, paints breathtaking landscapes, and photographs astounding images.

6. When people fall into the trap of the "slippery slope" fallacy, they believe that other people must accept their views about a particular topic. (Otherwise, However), the world will spiral out of control and descend into chaos.

7. Some students wait until the last minute to complete assignments, hoping that their grades will not suffer. (After, Similarly), other students often don't plan ahead and find that they do not have time to complete assignments satisfactorily.

8. Darrell and I decided that sitting at the house with our stomachs rumbling was no way to spend a Friday night. (Therefore, First), we decided to walk across the Drill Field to get some dinner at the Union.

9. Joanna and Micah went to the movies to see the new Denzel Washington movie. (Afterward, Tomorrow), they went to Coldstone Creamery to eat yogurt and talk about their classes.

10. During his first year Stephen received several speeding tickets and parking fines. His parents (subsequently, furthermore) decided to take his car and force him to ride the bus for the entire semester. (As a result, Lastly), Stephen learned to become a more responsible driver.

Varied Sentence Structure and Combination—
Exercise 1: Beginning with a Phrase

Revise the following sentences, placing the **appropriate phrases** at the beginning in order to **improve emphasis**.

1. Each of the teachers has dropped one assignment for this class in the past.

   _____

   _____

   _____

2. Each one of us packed a large bottle to ensure that we had enough water for our hike.

   _____

   _____

   _____

3. Cheryl benefitted greatly from her tutoring sessions, adhering closely to the advice of her tutor.

   _____

   _____

   _____

4. We read five novels about racism during the Civil Rights Movement throughout the semester.

   _____

   _____

   _____

5. The Carpathia, which first appeared as a dot on the horizon, seemed like a miraculous vision to the frozen Titanic survivors.

   _____

   _____

   _____

6. It is important to have all of your ingredients at room temperature before beginning to bake the perfect cake.

   _____

   _____

   _____

7. There are some chocolate chips for these cookies on top of the small freezer in the pantry.

_____

_____

_____

8. John Grisham, a Mississippi State University graduate, became famous for authoring popular crime and suspense novels.

_____

_____

_____

9. I chose to wear comfortable shoes under my graduation gown instead of strappy high heels.

_____

_____

_____

10. You can quickly get to the park by cutting through several neighborhoods using the directions I gave you.

_____

_____

_____

Varied Sentence Structure and Combination—
Exercise 2: Shifting Emphasis

Revise the following sentences according the **bracketed instructions** at the end of each sentence.

1. The paper was given a failing grade by the teacher because it did not meet the requirements of the assignment. [Revise for active voice.]

   _____

   _____

   _____

2. Steven's wife went to the store to buy muffins even though he was making breakfast. [Revise order of ideas.]

   _____

   _____

   _____

3. D-Day is known as one of the bloodiest operations of World War II, and it occurred on June 6, 1944. [Revise to emphasize the most important detail.]

   _____

   _____

   _____

4. The funding of the school is very crucial in developing an award-winning football program. [Revise for stronger verbs.]

   _____

   _____

   _____

5. During her tenure as a professor, she was also the director of the graduate program. [Revise for stronger verbs.]

   _____

   _____

   _____

6. In order to make a good grade in this class, you must do your homework, check your syllabus daily, and read the e-mails from your instructor. [Revise for order of importance.]

_____

_____

_____

7. Much of our pop culture is influenced by Monty Python's comedy even though students may not have heard of this comedy troupe. [Revise order of ideas.]

_____

_____

_____

8. Samuel Clemens wrote under the name of Mark Twain and produced some of America's greatest literature. [Revise to emphasize the most important detail.]

_____

_____

_____

9. Rachel was surprised by her husband when he brought her flowers after her horrible week. [Revise for active voice.]

_____

_____

_____

10. Eating fast food, texting, and applying makeup while driving are known to cause accidents for distracted drivers. [Revise for order of importance.]

_____

_____

_____

Varied Sentence Structure and Combination— Exercise 3: Revising for Varied Sentences

Revise the following paragraph, making sure to use a **variety of sentence structures**.

In order to make baked chicken, first you have to preheat the oven by setting it to 350 degrees. Second, cut up the vegetables. Then, add seasoning to your chicken. Put water in a pan and add the chicken. Cover the chicken with aluminum foil. Next, place the chicken in the oven for approximately one hour and ten minutes. Cook the chicken until it's tender. Then, fill a small pot with water. Set the stove to high. Place the pot on the heated burner. Bring the water to a boil. Add the rice. Cook the rice for fifteen minutes. Take the cooked chicken from the oven. Dice the chicken into one-inch cubes. Mix a can of cream of chicken soup with the diced chicken. Place the chicken mixture back into the oven and bake until bubbly. Drain the rice. Add some butter and salt to the rice to taste. Take the chicken mixture from the oven. Spoon the rice onto plates. Top the rice with chicken mixture. Finally, you can eat the delicious meal that you prepared!

304

Varied Sentence Structure and Combining Sentences— Exercise 4: Combining Sentences Effectively

Combine the following groups of sentences on the lines provided, trying to get **one sentence per group** without sacrificing the meaning. Notice that the sentences could be combined to form one paragraph.

- Walter Payton grew up in Columbia, Mississippi.
- Walter Payton is a football player.
- He is probably one of the most famous in the world.

_____

_____

_____

- Jim Brown had the former record.
- His record was 12,312 yards gained by rushing.
- Walter Payton broke Jim Brown's record.
- He broke this record on October 2, 1984.
- Everyone in the stands at the game cheered Payton.

_____

_____

_____

_____

- Walter's brother was a football star.
- His name was Eddie.
- Walter was in high school.
- Walter preferred music.
- Walter ran track.
- Walter played in the band.

_____

_____

_____

_____

- Eddie and Walter watched football games.
- They watched them on television.
- Eddie and Walter went outside.

- Eddie and Walter practiced plays.
- They saw the plays on T.V.
- They practiced their own versions of these plays.

_____

_____

_____

_____

- Walter was a track star.
- Walter started playing football on a team.
- He was sixteen.
- He had never played football before.
- He was a natural athlete.
- He could play anything well.

_____

_____

_____

_____

- Walter graduated high school.
- Kansas State University offered Walter a scholarship.
- Walter turned it down.
- Walter wanted to go to Jackson State.
- Walter wanted to play football with his brother.
- His brother played for Jackson State.

_____

_____

_____

_____

- Walter got a nickname.
- Walter's nickname was "Sweetness."
- Walter was at Jackson State.
- Walter's moves were "sweet."
- People thought his name should be "Toughness."

_____

_____

_____

Varied Sentence Structure and Combination—
Exercise 5: Combining Sentences Effectively

Combine the following groups of sentences on the lines provided, trying to get **one sentence per group** without sacrificing the meaning. Notice that the sentences could be combined to form one paragraph.

- Many civilians see wartime battles as glorious.
- Also, many civilians see the battles as patriotic.
- Many civilians think battles are surrounded by an aura of honor and integrity.

_____

_____

_____

- Numerous adjectives are used to portray the necessity of fighting and dying for a cause.
- These adjectives are often idealistic.
- What cause is more necessary than the protection of one's own country, town, and family?
- What about one's way of life?

_____

_____

_____

- Soldiers travel far from home.
- They travel across oceans and continents.
- While they are far from home, these soldiers battle enemies.
- These enemies are seen as threatening the ideals the soldiers hold dear.
- These soldiers are brave.
- The ideals are precious to the soldiers.

_____

_____

_____

- The sacrifices of military service are often described as worthy.
- They are also described as just.
- Sometimes people see the sacrifices of soldiers as almost beautiful.
- Some people hold a romantic view of sacrificed soldiers.

_____

_____

_____

- However, there are aspects of war that the general public does not know.
- Only veterans know these aspects of war.
- Only veterans know the brutality, the gruesomeness, the chaos, and the disgust of war.
- They are also the only ones who have an awareness of killing and of watching others die that one experiences at war.
- The soldier's awareness of killing and watching others die is stark.

_____

_____

_____

Varied Sentence Structure and Combination—
Exercise 6: Combining Sentences Effectively

Combine the following groups of sentences on the lines provided, trying to get **one sentence per group** without sacrificing the meaning. Notice that the sentences could be combined to form one paragraph.

- Direct plagiarism is copying a source.
- Direct plagiarism is copying word for word.
- Direct plagiarism occurs without indicating when material is quoted.
- The student does not credit the author.

_____

_____

_____

_____

- A writer should indicate where borrowing begins.
- A writer should indicate where borrowing ends.
- A writer should indicate these clearly.
- Not indicating clearly a source clearly is plagiarism.

_____

_____

_____

_____

- It is important to learn a citation style.
- MLA is a citation style.
- A writer will sometimes cite a source once.
- The reader assumes the previous sentence has been paraphrased.
- The reader assumes the previous paragraph has been paraphrased.
- Most of the essay is a paraphrase of this one source.

_____

_____

_____

_____

- The writer has failed to indicate his borrowings.
- The writer has failed to indicate clearly.
- Paraphrases should be indicated.
- Summaries should be indicated.
- They should be indicated by surrounding them with citation.

_____

_____

_____

- They should be indicated at the beginning with the author's name.
- They should be indicated at the end with a parenthetical reference.
- The writer must indicate when a paraphrase begins, ends, or is interrupted.
- The writer must indicate when a summary begins ends, or is interrupted.
- The writer must indicate when a quotation begins, ends, or is interrupted.

_____

_____

_____

- Mosaic Plagiarism is common.
- It is a type of plagiarism.
- The writer does not copy the source directly.
- The writer changes a few words in each sentence.
- The writer reworks a paragraph.
- The writer makes slight changes.
- The writer does not credit the author.

_____

_____

_____

- The sentences are not quotations.
- The paragraphs are not quotations.
- The sentences are close to quotation.
- They should be quoted directly.
- The source should be cited.
- The source should be cited if the sentence has changed.
- The changes are enough to qualify as a paraphrase.

_____

_____

_____

Effective Punctuation—Exercise 1: Correct Comma Placement

In the following paragraph, **place commas** in the correct positions.

Music is an important tool in the social world as it touches people in many ways. Music is a way for people to express their emotions share them with the masses and move people. But lately artists in the music industry are not known for their talent but rather their image and indiscretions. And the music is no longer the main focus. For example pop and rap music has become image-obsessed industry that does not concern itself with the quality of musical talent eliminating the focus on the actual music. Mainstream music is no longer about emotional responses but instead money reputation which is often sexual and popularity. For example pop stars and rap artists are known for their police records, their latest relationships and affairs, or their paparazzi photographs. Music needs to get back to just that the music and leave all of the fame and fortune to be had only with the quality of music.

Effective Punctuation—Exercise 2: Semicolons

In each of the following sentences, **place** a **semicolon** in the correct position. **Note:** Some sentences will need more than one semicolon.

1. My cat is not very graceful she often falls off of the couch.

2. Clowns are scary their faces are just so weird.

3. Dr. Freeling is a tough but fun teacher he often brings in funny news stories to discuss in class.

4. While Simon's European history class was in Europe, they traveled to London, England Madrid, Spain and Vienna, Italy.

5. Diane thinks that this year's homecoming will be sometime in September Todd thinks it will be in August.

6. Some students believe that the best way to study for an exam is to start early others believe that cramming the night before helps the information to remain fresh on their minds.

7. However they choose to study, students must make sure to take the time to prepare for an exam otherwise, they will find themselves in a bind on exam day.

8. When Sharece goes home for the weekend, she often gets into long conversations with her mother Sherece and her mother consider themselves to be best friends.

9. The classic horror movie *Poltergeist,* in which a family is haunted by an evil entity, is touted as being one of the scariest movies of all time the most famous line from the movie occurs when the five-year old Carol-Anne turns to her family and says, "They're here."

10. Some of the most famous people who were born in Mississippi were William Faulkner, a prominent Southern novelist Medgar Evers, an important leader in the Civil Rights Movement and Oprah Winfrey, an extremely famous entrepreneur and former talk show host.

Effective Punctuation—Exercise 3: Colons and Commas

In each of the following sentences, **place** either **colons or commas** in the correct position as needed. **Note**: Some sentences will need more than one semicolon.

1. A good club sandwich must have a few key ingredients honey mustard, dill pickles, bacon, and lots of cheese.

2. I wonder what Margaret Thatcher meant when she said "Europe was created by history. America was created by philosophy."

3. Stephen King had this to say about inspiration and the writing process "Amateurs sit and wait for inspiration, the rest of us just get up and go to work."

4. Remember the best ways to pass your Basic Composition class complete your assignments and visit the Writing Center for help.

5. There were three reasons why Robbie didn't do well on his finals he overslept, he didn't study, and he went to a party the night before.

6. When we packed for our trip, we took three things a GPS, a power adaptor, and an inflatable mattress.

7. Blockbuster action movies must have certain elements big explosions, lots of car chases, and a very attractive leading man or woman.

8. The club's new membership included the following students Moseley, Mandi, Whitney, and Jessica.

9. It is important for students to keep in mind that there are many different ways to keep up with their busy schedules special apps on their phones, e-mail reminders, and even simple calendars.

10. There were three reasons I decided to visit my hometown for the weekend there was a festival in town, my best friend was visiting her parents, and my Aunt Joanna had given birth to a new baby boy.

Effective Punctuation—Exercise 4: Effective Punctuation Placement

Put the **appropriate punctuation** in place to correct the following sentences. If a sentence is already correct, put a "**C**" in the blank provided.

_____ 1. Most of the time, basketball players are healthy and fit however sometimes they get injured.

_____ 2. The sounds of the football games reach a very far distance even as far as my house.

_____ 3. In Starkville, for example, the cheers the yells and the whistles blowing are all common things I can hear.

_____ 4. There is no telling how much time we spent at the museum I think we stayed there for four hours.

_____ 5. The loud sound of cars honking was heard however I had my earphones in.

_____ 6. Because we cannot hear as well as dogs, they hear crazy stuff such as far off noises the skid of tires and the whisper of the wind.

_____ 7. Many people don't like certain things about Mississippi State's football games such as the cowbells and loud fans.

_____ 8. There are many different types of classes that are offered in the summer Creative Writing British Literature and Southern Literature and Film are just a few of the options.

_____ 9. There is no way we can tell the future however we can use the past to make a good guess.

_____ 10. Because I studied for the exam for two days I received a good grade.

Effective Parallelism—Exercise 1: Expression in Sentences

Reword each sentence to express emphasis and importance through parallelism.

1. I love *The Help* because it's clever, set in my home state of Mississippi, and historical.

_____

_____

_____

_____

2. Walking on campus on a normal day is often tedious, but it's fun and exciting when I walk on campus on a snowy day.

_____

_____

_____

_____

3. People sometimes forget that forgetting happens to other people sometimes.

_____

_____

_____

_____

4. Last year, I made significant visits to the record store, the health clinic, and my sister's.

_____

_____

_____

5. In times of trouble, call me, but don't call when the time is too troubling.

_____

_____

_____

6. Bradley Cooper, tutoring, and napping are my favorite interests.

_____

_____

_____

_____

7. Take your time, and you'll do better; rushing often wastes time.

_____

_____

_____

_____

8. How long before we see the faults of our past before our future faults aren't seen?

_____

_____

_____

_____

9. Try taking medicine and time to feel better; impatience should be left alone.

_____

_____

_____

_____

10. The last thing he did before the day ended was exercise; eating junk food was also something else he did.

_____

_____

_____

_____

Effective Parallelism—Exercise 2: Expression in a Paragraph

Rewrite the paragraph on the lines provided in order to better express **emphasis and importance** through **parallelism**.

Sometimes, we forget what is most important to our success. We also forget what's least important to our lives. Happiness may be fleeting at times. It isn't always an everyday occurrence. However, it's worth striving and persevering for. By the time we have the advantage of hindsight, we have almost lost the time to act. If there is one good piece of advice to give, it almost always comes from experience. It can also come from taking an objective step back to see life as it is. This journey we take together often feels lonely. It is not a lonely endeavor. It is a challenge to overcome loneliness and fear.

_____

_____

_____

_____

_____

_____

_____

_____

_____

_____

_____

_____

_____

_____

_____

_____

_____

_____

_____

_____

Considering Voice and Style

Punctuation and Style—Exercise 1: Parentheses and Emphasis

Revise the following sentences, using **parentheses** to deemphasize the least important details or to make "asides" (side comments).

1. New-release video games are getting increasingly expensive with every increasingly expensive new set of consoles that comes out.

2. Carrie bought such varied ingredients for special recipes while she was at the grocery store including baker's chocolate, maple syrup, crab legs, turnips, and radishes that she thought the cashier would find her strange.

3. After a long weekend of babysitting two toddlers and their energetic Chihuahua, Shae was of course completely exhausted.

4. We are going to read *Slaughterhouse Five,* my favorite novel, for class this semester.

5. Mississippi State University takes pride in its Southeastern Conference, or SEC, football team.

6. I have to get ready to present my unfinished project to my sociology class next week.

_____

_____

_____

7. After almost three decades, the Chernobyl nuclear disaster that happened on April 26, 1986, still casts an ominous shadow over the Ukraine.

_____

_____

_____

8. Chad told me not to tell anyone this, so keep it quiet, but he and Kendall are planning a surprise party for all of the graduates.

_____

_____

_____

9. How could anyone expect me to break my back getting up from this lawn chair just do to yard work on such a nice day?

_____

_____

_____

10. Because I missed the opening game for the second time in a row, I am making plans for next year's season opener immediately.

_____

_____

_____

Punctuation and Style—Exercise 2: Colons, Dashes, and Emphasis

Revise the following sentences, using **colons or dashes** appropriately to introduce or to set off important information.

1. The pile of laundry, dirty, smelly, and gigantic as it was, would have intimidated even the most experienced of housekeepers.

   _____

   _____

   _____

2. James just left for his audition, and he looked very nervous on his way out because his eyes were wide, and he was clenching his fists.

   _____

   _____

   _____

3. Mariah, crouching and looking away, slowly approached her newly adopted pit bull terrier, a previously abused and malnourished rescue, so that the poor animal would not be frightened of her.

   _____

   _____

   _____

4. As to your request for all of my grandmother's secret recipes, I have only one word for you, and that is no.

   _____

   _____

   _____

5. Because I find their constant chattering obnoxious and distracting, I will not sit near those girls in the back of the classroom after today.

   _____

   _____

   _____

6. Several of the boys on the team, John, Charles, and Darius, were caught attempting to sneak out of practice to get pizza from across the street.

_____

_____

_____

7. Aside from the educational and cultural benefits, there are several other reasons you might want to attend this event, such as free entry, the free food, and the free music.

_____

_____

_____

8. I will not and I cannot put up with her perpetual harassment anymore.

_____

_____

_____

9. The work of Salvador Dali, with its warped and strange yet smooth images of distorted objects, animals, and people, is probably the most widely known and recognizable artwork of the Surrealist movement.

_____

_____

_____

10. There is one food item that I will never give up, one that keeps me from becoming a vegetarian, and that food item is bacon.

_____

_____

_____

Punctuation and Style: Exercise 3—Revising Punctuation

Combine the following sentences using **colons, dashes, or parentheses** to set off ideas that can be emphasized or deemphasized. The punctuation you choose to use constitutes a style choice, so **explain in the space given** why you think you have made the best (available) choice for each sentence.

1. The giraffe could not reach the leaves on the tree. The giraffe was not fully grown yet.

_____

_____

_____

_____

_____

2. Having already gone to car shop twice in the last month, John prepared himself for the words of the mechanic. John tried to prepare himself, anyway.

_____

_____

_____

_____

3. I do not want to go to the movies tonight for one reason only. All of the movies playing are romantic comedies.

_____

_____

_____

_____

_____

_____

4. You might have to explore to find them, but Starkville hosts a great variety of ethnic restaurants. There are restaurants serving Italian, Greek, Mexican, Chinese, Japanese, Thai, and even Peruvian cuisines.

_____

_____

_____

_____

_____

_____

5. All of my office mates raved about Teisha's cheesecake for weeks. It was too rich for me.

_____

_____

_____

_____

_____

_____

Using Exact Language/Concision—Exercise1: Eliminating Wordiness and Vague Language

Rewrite each of the following sentences, **adding** specific details in place of the bolded vague language and **rephrasing** bolded wordy phrases for concision.

1. **The men** stood in their uniforms in front of **a building** in Washington, D.C.

   _____

   _____

   _____

2. **It is my opinion that** people should remain aware of other drivers on the road when going about their daily activities.

   _____

   _____

   _____

3. **A large number of people** enjoy reading a book to help them unwind at the end of a long day's work.

   _____

   _____

   _____

4. **An animal** darted across the road and leapt over the center divider between the north and southbound lanes of I-55.

   _____

   _____

   _____

5. She ended up missing six days of class **on account of the fact that** her mother was in the hospital.

   _____

   _____

   _____

6. There are several **things** you should consider when planning a budget, including bills, future plans, and income.

_____

_____

_____

7. **Subsequent to** the President's visit to the local school, students decided to take more of an interest in social programs.

_____

_____

_____

8. They have decided to cancel this year's Easter Egg hunt **due to the fact** that only two children showed up last year.

_____

_____

_____

9. **It is a fact that** though platinum is a more expensive metal than white gold, many people cannot tell the difference between the two.

_____

_____

_____

10. **At the present time,** the car industry is in a downturn, but analysts believe it will eventually recover.

_____

_____

_____

Using Exact Language/Concision—Exercise 2: Eliminating Wordiness and Vague Language in a Paragraph

The following paragraph contains **wordy and vague language**. In the space provided, **rewrite** the paragraph, concisely **rephrasing** wordy language and **adding** specific details in place of vague language.

It is my opinion that Indiana Jones's antics share similarities with those of pseudo-archeologists in their interest in the supernatural or the occult. In every single one of his movies, "Indy" sets off on a treacherous, dangerous quest to recover an ancient, antique artifact, such as the Ark of the Covenant, the Holy Grail, or even alien skulls. At the present time, pseudo-archeology commonly deals with big ideas such as ancient aliens, Atlantean civilizations, or psychic archaeology, among others. To include an example, in *Indiana Jones and the Kingdom of the Crystal Skull,* Indiana comes across and uses psychic archeology to uncover an ancient alien spaceship disguised as a building in the Amazon rainforest. Consequently, this idea is not unique to movies, as the idea of aliens visiting ancient man was first thought up by a pseudo-archaeologist named Erich Von Daniken in his book *Chariots of the Gods.* In his very popular book, Daniken discusses the concept that ancient man was visited by extraterrestrials. In fact, psychic archaeology has been a thing since the 1930s. Despite the fact that the films show psychic archeology as a success, Indiana Jones's supernatural escapades fit better into the realm of cult archaeology.

_____

_____

_____

_____

_____

_____

_____

_____

_____

_____

_____

_____

_____

_____

_____

Avoiding Awkward Phrasing—Exercise 1: Identifying Awkward Phrasing

In the following paragraph, **underline** wording that you think reads awkwardly. Be prepared to **discuss** why you find the writing awkward. (**Hint**: Read out loud to help identify awkward phrasing.)

When I used to go to piano lessons once a week, I was always nervous. Never really being all that good at reading music did not help at all with my nervousness or help me to relax in order to play the music well. On top of all that, I was a slouching kid who just would never sit up straight like one is supposed to do when one is sitting on the piano bench. Not to mention my small hands could not even reach the keys I needed to most of the time. The worst thing about piano lessons was being corrected constantly. Just when I thought I was doing something right, my instructor would tell me to stop leaning over the keys so that I could try to see what was on the score in front of me. Then a lecture on posture would be given by her as always, and I would have to start all over again, messing up some more. To this very day and the current time in my life, I will always remember that piano teacher. I wish I could play better, but I do not miss taking those classes.

Avoiding Awkward Phrasing—Exercise 2: Revising Awkward Phrasing

Revise the following sentences, **eliminating** awkward phrasing.

1. With all of the loudness and noise at the party, there was not a talking-friendly room to have a conversation in.

   _____

   _____

   _____

2. If you go out on the lake when it's clear out at nighttime, you can get to see a lot of stars.

   _____

   _____

   _____

3. Derek wondered how he was ever going to get up out of bed still having time for breakfast.

   _____

   _____

   _____

4. All of the girls on the softball team got in trouble after they smashed up the boys' drink cooler that they had taken from them in the first place, and the coach said that theirs was not very sportsmanlike behavior.

   _____

   _____

5. All we have to do to become better at getting the answers right is to practice the formulas over and over again and pay careful attention to figuring up the calculations we make.

_____

_____

_____

6. Every step a player takes in this video game could be full of pitfalls, and you might end up getting in trouble when one falls into such a trap.

_____

_____

_____

7. Due to the fact that there might be problems, for every big event there should be someone who will have a sewing kit, safety pins, tape, and a first-aid kit.

_____

_____

_____

8. Every aspect of today's society is changed from what it used to be.

_____

_____

_____

9. The boy who fell down in the well was a story that we heard every time my grandpa came over to visit.

_____

_____

_____

10. Happiness is when you are with the person who is a best friend to you and always respects you as a person.

_____

_____

_____

Using Appropriate Voice and Avoiding Clichés—Exercise 1: Identifying "To Be" Verbs

Underline any forms of the verb **"to be"** in the following sentences. **Note**: There may be more than one "be" verb in each sentence.

1. I was given a new car for my birthday.

2. Jackson was told that his paper needed a large amount of revision, so he was forced to spend hours working on adding and deleting sentences to his essay.

3. Natalie was chosen by the scholarship committee as the recipient for the award.

4. Jennifer was drawn by the artist with a large nose and small eyes even though both her nose and eyes were a normal size.

5. We were overheard talking about the football game by the librarian in the study room.

6. Several cars were damaged by hail during last night's thunderstorm.

7. Mint and basil are grown by many gardeners who like to use herbs in cooking.

8. The popsicles were frozen by the third-graders.

9. The two pizzas were eaten by Jack's three roommates in less than ten minutes.

10. The homeless men in the shelter were fed by the kind people in the soup kitchen.

Using Appropriate Voice and Avoiding Clichés— Exercise 2: Eliminating Passive Voice

Rewrite each of the following sentences using **active voice**.

1. The girls were driven to their piano lessons by their father.

   _____

   _____

2. The dogs were given table scraps by their owner as a special treat.

   _____

   _____

3. Several battles were fought by both armies before a peace treaty was signed.

   _____

   _____

4. The students were caught by their teacher passing notes in class.

_____

_____

5. Aaron and Jayden were bitten by mosquitoes during their camping trip in Tennessee.

_____

_____

6. The keys to her new car were hidden by Paige in a secret pocket in her purse.

_____

_____

7. The Christmas lights were kept by Sean's mom in the attic in the garage.

_____

_____

8. Kylie and Amanda were seen wearing white after Labor Day by Adrian.

_____

_____

9. Riley and Jenna were sold a defective microwave by the salesman in the store.

_____

_____

10. Michelle and Leah were spoken to by their advisor about applying to a master's program.

_____

_____

Using Appropriate Voice and Avoiding Cliché—
Exercise 3: Eliminating Passive Voice

Rewrite each of the following sentences using **active voice**.

1. The horses were ridden by the two boys for several hours through the forest.

   _____

   _____

   _____

2. The apples were sold by the farmer in a wooden stand on the side of the road.

   _____

   _____

   _____

3. The two hot cherry pies were stolen out of Mrs. Harris's window by local teenagers.

   _____

   _____

   _____

4. The weekend was spent by Kyle and Madeline working on their final project for class.

   _____

   _____

   _____

5. The books were read to the class of third graders by Faith and Lillian.

   _____

   _____

   _____

6. The children were made to play inside during recess by their teachers because it was raining.

   _____

   _____

   _____

7. The bands were paid by the restaurant to play for one hour each during the dinner hours.

_____

_____

_____

8. The guitar and saxophone were left to Gabriella by her grandfather.

_____

_____

_____

9. The can of spray paint was shaken very thoroughly by Katelyn.

_____

_____

_____

_____

10. The witnesses were sworn in by the deputy.

_____

_____

_____

Using Appropriate Voice and Avoiding Cliché—
Exercise 4: Identifying and Replacing Clichés

Circle any clichés in each of the following sentences, and **rewrite** the sentences to get rid of the cliché(s).

1. I had to slave over my paper, but it was all in a day's work.

   _____

   _____

   _____

2. It was about time for the old dishwasher to bite the dust.

   _____

   _____

   _____

3. Alyssa acted as if she were born with a silver spoon in her mouth.

   _____

   _____

   _____

4. Avery encountered a problem with her science project, so she had to go back to the drawing board.

   _____

   _____

   _____

5. Audrey seems like everyone's worst nightmare, but her bark is worse than her bite.

   _____

   _____

   _____

6. Cody tried to help me organize the glass ornaments on the tree, but he was all thumbs.

   _____

   _____

   _____

7. Brayden learned the hard way that a parking ticket on campus costs an arm and a leg.

_____

_____

_____

8. Seth was neat as a pin, but Sebastian had decided to throw in the towel when it came to housekeeping.

_____

_____

_____

9. Jaden had to think outside of the box to come up with a good topic for his paper, which is easier said than done.

_____

_____

_____

10. Vanessa found it hard to believe that her sister let the cat out of the bag about their mother's surprise party.

_____

_____

_____

Using Appropriate Voice and Avoiding Cliché—
Exercise 5: Identifying and Replacing Clichés

Circle any clichés in each of the following sentences, and **rewrite** the sentences to get rid of the cliché(s).

1. Ariana told her mother the long and short of her experiences at college to prove for all intents and purposes that Ariana wanted to stay in college until the fat lady sings.

   _____

   _____

   _____

2. To the best of her knowledge, Bailey had never stayed up until the cows came home.

   _____

   _____

   _____

3. Jada knew that she had been barking up the wrong tree when she thought she could have a meaningful relationship with Patrick since they were always at loggerheads.

   _____

   _____

   _____

4. Danielle's cell phone was dead as a doornail because she had been texting on it time and time again.

   _____

   _____

   _____

5. In this day and age, it goes without saying that you have to take the bull by the horns to get results.

   _____

   _____

   _____

6. Ever since she was knee-high to a grasshopper, Tanya's family has tried to keep up with the Joneses.

   _____

   _____

7. I made a three-course dinner that will knock your socks off.

_____

_____

_____

8. Brooklyn's parents had to lay down the law when her sister was caught red-handed sneaking out of the house on a dark and stormy night.

_____

_____

_____

9. Melanie had to bite her tongue when her sister told her to count her blessings after a semi-truck rear-ended her.

_____

_____

_____

10. Last but not least, Avery killed two birds with one stone when she bought a bicycle to use to commute to campus so that she could save on a parking pass and get more exercise.

_____

_____

_____

Contractions—Exercise: Identifying and Replacing Contractions

Mark through the **contraction(s)** in the following sentences and **write** the appropriate wording above the marked-through contractions.

1. I don't know why some people can't do their laundry in a fashionable manner.

2. Shelly couldn't help but notice the large sign that was advertising the salon on the billboard.

3. She'll be coming in tomorrow to get her nails done as well as having her hair cut.

4. It's going to rain for the rest of the weekend.

5. It'll be a great time to stay in and get caught up on my favorite TV series or read the rest of my book.

6. We'd better go soon, or we're going to miss our plane to Colorado.

7. Aren't your parents coming to see you this weekend, or is it the next?

8. I've already planned a trip for this weekend, but I can reschedule it if necessary.

9. Shouldn't you be studying for your exams that are tomorrow?

10. She's already done the work; all she needs to do is type it in report form to give to her boss.

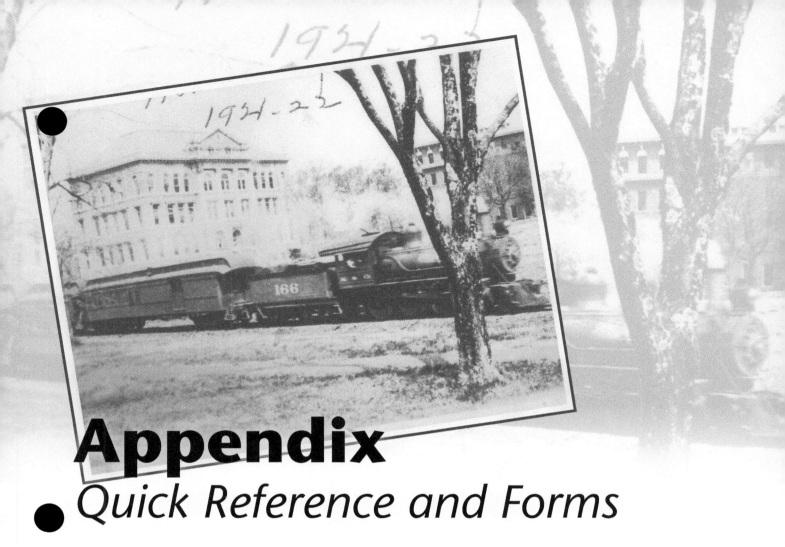

Appendix
Quick Reference and Forms

Commonly Confused Words

To determine proper usage for the commonly confused words below, consult a good college dictionary and jot down the definitions and usage advice.

a part / apart
a while / awhile
accept / except
advice / advise
affect / effect
aggravate / irritate
all / all of
all ready / already
all together / altogether
alliterate / illiterate
allude / elude
allusion / illusion
allusive / elusive / illusive
among / between
amount / number
anxious / eager
any body / anybody
any more / anymore
any one / anyone
as / than
assure / ensure / insure
attain / obtain
autobiography / biography
back seat / backseat
back up / backup
back yard / backyard

ball / bawl
bare / bear
because / since
break up / breakup
bring / take
can / may
capital / capitol
click / clique
complement / compliment
compose / comprise
conscience / conscious
defuse / diffuse
dependant / dependent
device / devise
differ from / differ with
different from / different than
discreet / discrete
disinterested / uninterested
eminent / imminent
empathy / sympathy
especially / specially
every body / everybody
every day / everyday
every one / everyone
faint / feint
farther / further
fewer / less
for / fore / four
formally / formerly

foul / fowl
good / well
granite / granted
heal / heel
hear / here
imply / infer
in / in to / into
instance / instants
its / it's
jam / jamb
kind of / sort of / type of
later / latter
live / stay
loose / lose
may be / maybe
moral / morale
on / upon
patience / patients
peak / peek / pique
pedal / peddle / petal
phenomena / phenomenon
poser / poseur
precede / proceed
precedence / precedents
principal / principle
quiet / quite
rain / reign
real / reel
respectfully / respectively

shone / shown
some body / somebody
some time / sometimes
suit / suite
than / then
their / there / they're
threw / through
throne / thrown
to / too / two
try and / try to
vain / vane / vein
vary / very
verses / versus
wail / whale
wait for / wait on
wander / wonder
waver / waiver
weak / week
weather / whether
wet / whet
who's / whose
your / you're

Common Mistakes

The words below are commonly misused in formal writing. Using a dictionary and/or textbook, determine the correct usage.

a lot
alright
can not
conversate
could care less
could of, should of, would of
fixing to
lite
nohow
suppose to
thru
tonite
use to
xmas

Combining Sentences

When connecting ideas and actions within a single sentence, you have several methods available to you; three are demonstrated below. All the methods are correct, but you should use a combination of them in your writing in order to create sentence variety. As you read the examples below, consider the word(s) used to combine sentences, focusing on the precise meaning expressed in each case. As you write, consult the list provided with each method to help you select appropriate words and phrases. This should result in a clear and precise expression of ideas.

Simple sentences

Jason has a test today.

Jason spent last night studying.

Jason played video games until 2:00 a.m.

Alice loves to work with young children.

Alice volunteers at the local preschool.

Alice is a civil engineering major.

Compound Sentences Using Coordinating Conjunctions

Independent Clause, **coordinating conjunction** Independent Clause

Coordinating Conjunctions (FANBOYS)

for (cause)

and (addition)

nor (alternative)

but (contrast)

or (alternative)

yet (contrast)

so (effect)

Examples:

Jason has a test today, **so** he spent last night studying.

Jason has a test today, **but** he played video games until 2:00 a.m.

Alice loves to work with young children, **yet** she is a civil engineering major.

Alice volunteers at the local preschool, **for** she loves to work with young children.

Compound Sentences Using Transitional Words and Phrases

Independent Clause; **transitional word/phrase,** Independent Clause

Common Transitional Words and Phrases

Addition/Example:	Cause/Effect:	Comparison/Contrast:	Time:
again	accordingly	however	afterward
also	as a result	in comparison	at last
besides	consequently	in contrast	finally
for example	hence	instead	meanwhile
further	otherwise	likewise	next
furthermore	therefore	nevertheless	now
in addition	thus	nonetheless	simultaneously
in fact		on the contrary	then
moreover		otherwise	thereafter
still		rather	
too			

Examples:

Jason has a test today; **therefore,** he spent last night studying.

Jason has a test today; **nevertheless,** he played video games until 2:00 a.m.

Alice loves to work with young children; **however,** she is a civil engineering major.

Alice loves to work with young children; **in fact,** she volunteers at the local preschool.

Complex Sentences Using Subordinating Conjunctions

Subordinating Conjunction Independent Clause, Independent Clause.

OR

Independent Clause **Subordinating Conjunction** Independent Clause.

Common Subordinating Conjunctions

Cause/Effect:	Condition:	Concession:	Space/Time:
because	if	although	after
due to	provided	as if	as long as
since	unless	despite	at
so that	whenever	even though	before
	with	except for	in
	without	in spite of	on
		though	since
			until
			when
			while

Examples:

After Jason spent last night studying, he played video games until 2:00 a.m.

Jason spent last night studying **because** he has a test today.

Since Alice loves to work with young children, she volunteers at the local preschool.

Alice loves to work with children **although** she is a civil engineering major.

Common Proofreading Abbreviations

a/a: adjective/adverb error

awk: awkward phrasing

cap: capitalize this letter

cs: comma splice

cit: missing or incorrect source citation

coh: lack of coherence

con: lack of concision

dm: dangling modifier

dev: inadequate development

frag: sentence fragment

fs: fused sentence

hyph: missing or misused hyphen

log: faulty logic

ital: italicize

mm: misplaced modifier

p/a: pronoun/antecedent agreement error

pc: incorrect pronoun case

pov: shift in point of view

pr: error in pronoun reference

rep: unnecessary repetition

ro: run-on sentence

slang: omit slang expression

sp: spelling error

s/v: subject/verb agreement error

t: incorrect tense

trans: missing transitional word, phrase, or sentence

t shift: inappropriate shift in tense

unity: irrelevant idea

var: lack of sentence variety

vb: error in verb form

w: wordy

wc: ineffective word choice

ww: wrong word(s)

??: illegible or meaning unclear

//: lack of parallelism

no ¶: no new paragraph needed

par, ¶: start new paragraph

¶ coh: paragraph not coherent

¶ dev: paragraph not developed

¶ un: paragraph not unified

Common Editing Symbols

Symbol	Meaning	Example
ℓ	Delete	My grandmother is very very old.
∧	Insert word	We are going shopping at mall.
#	Insert space	The book fell out of his bag.
/	Make lower case	The state of Mississippi is known for its famous Magnolia tree.
≡	Make capital	Mississippi State university has a large campus.
◯	Make all capital	The university offers m.a programs.
◯	Move as shown	a variety of
∼	Transpose letters or words	There are many students?
ds[	Use double space	There aren't any students in the classroom.
◡	Omit space	Class starts at 9 a. m.
¶	New paragraph	The state of Mississippi is heavily agricultural.

Writing Conference Form

Name: _____ EN 0103 / _____

Appointment Date: _____ Appointment Time: _____

The following sections will allow you to think about particular components of your essay and develop questions to ask during the conference. Prior to meeting with your instructor, develop a list of *specific questions*. **Write all questions and concerns in the spaces provided below; bring this form to the conference.** Be sure to arrive early. During the conference, take detailed notes as your instructor provides feedback. Most importantly, note that your instructor *will not edit your paper;* thus, you should be prepared to receive open feedback and apply your instructor's suggestions as you revise.

Prior to the conference, formulate questions and concerns in the spaces below:

Grammar Concerns

Content Concerns

MLA Style Concerns

| |
| |

Instructor's Review:

	Yes	No
The student arrived at or before the scheduled appointment time.	○	○
The student prepared specific questions for the conference.	○	○
The student brought all materials relevant to the essay.	○	○
The student took detailed notes during the conference.	○	○

Instructor's Additional Comments:

| |
| |

Conference Grade:_____/_____

Writing Conference Form

Name: _____ EN 0103 / _____

Appointment Date: _____ Appointment Time: _____

The following sections will allow you to think about particular components of your essay and develop questions to ask during the conference. Prior to meeting with your instructor, develop a list of *specific questions*. **Write all questions and concerns in the spaces provided below; bring this form to the conference.** Be sure to arrive early. During the conference, take detailed notes as your instructor provides feedback. Most importantly, note that your instructor *will not edit your paper;* thus, you should be prepared to receive open feedback and apply your instructor's suggestions as you revise.

　　Prior to the conference, formulate questions and concerns in the spaces below:

Grammar Concerns

Content Concerns

MLA Style Concerns

Instructor's Review:

	Yes	No
The student arrived at or before the scheduled appointment time.	◯	◯
The student prepared specific questions for the conference.	◯	◯
The student brought all materials relevant to the essay.	◯	◯
The student took detailed notes during the conference.	◯	◯

Instructor's Additional Comments:

Conference Grade:_____/_____

Paragraph Grading Form

EN 0103/ _____

Name: _____ Date: _____

Assignment: _____ Score: _____/30 points

Points for this assignment are based on the following criteria:

Topic Sentence:

- Expresses an idea that is narrow enough to be developed in a single paragraph
- States clearly and specifically what the paragraph is about

Development & Support:

- Provides primary points that support the topic sentence
- Includes specific details/evidence to support each primary point

Concluding Statement:

- Ends with one or two sentences that summarize and restate the main idea of the topic sentence

Coherence & Organization:

- Follows the assigned rhetorical strategy
- Arranges primary points and supporting details in a logical way
- Demonstrates a logical progression of points, showing how one idea connects to another
- Moves smoothly between sentences

Transitions:

- Uses transitional words/phrases to move clearly and smoothly between ideas
- Uses transitional words/phrases to indicate the relationship between general and specific ideas

Unity:

- Remains focused on the main idea expressed by the topic sentence

Grammar/Correctness:

- Follows the standard rules of grammar, syntax, and mechanics
- Demonstrates knowledge of MLA format

Grammatical Errors (Grouped by Level of Severity)

Category 1—Compromises both the writer's credibility and the reader's comprehension:

____ Mixed Construction   ____ Capitalization Error (severe)

____ Subject/Verb Agreement Error   ____ Article Missing / Misused

____ Comma Splice   ____ Word Omission

____ Fused Sentence   ____ Wrong Word (severe)

____ Fragment   ____ Apostrophe Missing / Misused

____ Comma Omission (compound sentence)   ____ Double Negative

____ Missing End Sentence Punctuation   ____ Verb Error (wrong form)

____ Failure to Form a Plural   ____ Pronoun Case Error

____ Failure to Form the Past Tense   ____ Misspelled Word (severe)

Category 2—Creates ambiguity or confusion but does not indicate an ignorance of standard usage:

____ Pronoun/Antecedent Agreement Error   ____ Shift in Person or Number

____ Pronoun Reference Error   ____ Shift in Tense or Mood

____ Misused Semicolon   ____ Shift in Subject or Voice

____ Comma Omission (words in a series)   ____ Shift in Direct / Indirect Quotations

____ Comma Omission (non-essential elements)   ____ Misplaced / Dangling Modifier

Category 3—Registers as incorrect but does not seriously distract or confuse the reader:

____ Lack of Parallelism   ____ Awkward Phrasing / Idiom

____ Lack of Exactness / Concision   ____ Failure to Spell out Numbers

____ Lack of Variety   ____ Lack of Possessive before a Gerund

____ Comma Omission (introductory phrase/clause)

Additional Comments:

MSU Honor Code:

On my honor, as a Mississippi State University student, I have neither given nor received unauthorized assistance on this academic work.

_____   _____

Signature   Date

Paragraph Grading Form

EN 0103/ _____

Name: _____   Date: _____

Assignment: _____   Score: _____/30 points

Points for this assignment are based on the following criteria:

Topic Sentence:

- Expresses an idea that is narrow enough to be developed in a single paragraph
- States clearly and specifically what the paragraph is about

Development & Support:

- Provides primary points that support the topic sentence
- Includes specific details/evidence to support each primary point

Concluding Statement:

- Ends with one or two sentences that summarize and restate the main idea of the topic sentence

Coherence & Organization:

- Follows the assigned rhetorical strategy
- Arranges primary points and supporting details in a logical way
- Demonstrates a logical progression of points, showing how one idea connects to another
- Moves smoothly between sentences

Transitions:

- Uses transitional words/phrases to move clearly and smoothly between ideas
- Uses transitional words/phrases to indicate the relationship between general and specific ideas

Unity:

- Remains focused on the main idea expressed by the topic sentence

Grammar/Correctness:

- Follows the standard rules of grammar, syntax, and mechanics
- Demonstrates knowledge of MLA format

Grammatical Errors (Grouped by Level of Severity)

Category 1—Compromises both the writer's credibility and the reader's comprehension:

_____ Mixed Construction   _____ Capitalization Error (severe)

_____ Subject/Verb Agreement Error   _____ Article Missing / Misused

_____ Comma Splice   _____ Word Omission

_____ Fused Sentence   _____ Wrong Word (severe)

_____ Fragment   _____ Apostrophe Missing / Misused

_____ Comma Omission (compound sentence)   _____ Double Negative

____ Missing End Sentence Punctuation	____ Verb Error (wrong form)
____ Failure to Form a Plural	____ Pronoun Case Error
____ Failure to Form the Past Tense	____ Misspelled Word (severe)

Category 2—Creates ambiguity or confusion but does not indicate an ignorance of standard usage:

____ Pronoun/Antecedent Agreement Error	____ Shift in Person or Number
____ Pronoun Reference Error	____ Shift in Tense or Mood
____ Misused Semicolon	____ Shift in Subject or Voice
____ Comma Omission (words in a series)	____ Shift in Direct / Indirect Quotations
____ Comma Omission (non-essential elements)	____ Misplaced / Dangling Modifier

Category 3—Registers as incorrect but does not seriously distract or confuse the reader:

____ Lack of Parallelism	____ Awkward Phrasing / Idiom
____ Lack of Exactness / Concision	____ Failure to Spell out Numbers
____ Lack of Variety	____ Lack of Possessive before a Gerund
____ Comma Omission (introductory phrase/clause)	

Additional Comments:

MSU Honor Code:

On my honor, as a Mississippi State University student, I have neither given nor received unauthorized assistance on this academic work.

_____   _____

Signature   Date

Paragraph Grading Form

EN 0103/ _____

Name: _____ Date: _____

Assignment: _____ Score: _____/30 points

Points for this assignment are based on the following criteria:

Topic Sentence:

- Expresses an idea that is narrow enough to be developed in a single paragraph
- States clearly and specifically what the paragraph is about

Development & Support:

- Provides primary points that support the topic sentence
- Includes specific details/evidence to support each primary point

Concluding Statement:

- Ends with one or two sentences that summarize and restate the main idea of the topic sentence

Coherence & Organization:

- Follows the assigned rhetorical strategy
- Arranges primary points and supporting details in a logical way
- Demonstrates a logical progression of points, showing how one idea connects to another
- Moves smoothly between sentences

Transitions:

- Uses transitional words/phrases to move clearly and smoothly between ideas
- Uses transitional words/phrases to indicate the relationship between general and specific ideas

Unity:

- Remains focused on the main idea expressed by the topic sentence

Grammar/Correctness:

- Follows the standard rules of grammar, syntax, and mechanics
- Demonstrates knowledge of MLA format

Grammatical Errors (Grouped by Level of Severity)

Category 1—Compromises both the writer's credibility and the reader's comprehension:

____ Mixed Construction   ____ Capitalization Error (severe)

____ Subject/Verb Agreement Error   ____ Article Missing / Misused

____ Comma Splice   ____ Word Omission

____ Fused Sentence   ____ Wrong Word (severe)

____ Fragment   ____ Apostrophe Missing / Misused

____ Comma Omission (compound sentence)   ____ Double Negative

___ Missing End Sentence Punctuation	___ Verb Error (wrong form)
___ Failure to Form a Plural	___ Pronoun Case Error
___ Failure to Form the Past Tense	___ Misspelled Word (severe)

Category 2—Creates ambiguity or confusion but does not indicate an ignorance of standard usage:

___ Pronoun/Antecedent Agreement Error	___ Shift in Person or Number
___ Pronoun Reference Error	___ Shift in Tense or Mood
___ Misused Semicolon	___ Shift in Subject or Voice
___ Comma Omission (words in a series)	___ Shift in Direct / Indirect Quotations
___ Comma Omission (non-essential elements)	___ Misplaced / Dangling Modifier

Category 3—Registers as incorrect but does not seriously distract or confuse the reader:

___ Lack of Parallelism	___ Awkward Phrasing / Idiom
___ Lack of Exactness / Concision	___ Failure to Spell out Numbers
___ Lack of Variety	___ Lack of Possessive before a Gerund
___ Comma Omission (introductory phrase/clause)	

Additional Comments:

MSU Honor Code:

On my honor, as a Mississippi State University student, I have neither given nor received unauthorized assistance on this academic work.

_____   _____

Signature   Date

Essay Grading Form

EN 0103/ _____   Assignment: _____

Name: _____   Date: _____

Draft 1 Grading Criteria: Score: _____ out of 20
- Identifiable introduction, body, and conclusion
- Thesis sentence (in the introduction)
- Topic sentences (in each body paragraph) and supporting details
- Correct rhetorical strategy

Peer Response Grading Criteria: Score: _____ out of 10
- Appropriate written comments on your classmate's essay
- Fully developed responses on the Peer Response Sheet
- Adequate verbal communication during the peer response session

Draft 2 Grading Criteria: Score: _____ out of 20
- Evidence of significant revision/correction of Draft 1
- Title
- Full development of introduction, body, and conclusion
- Transitional words and phrases
- Submission of Draft 1, Draft 2, and Peer Response

Final Draft Grading Criteria: Score: _____ out of 100
- Evidence of significant revision/correction of Draft 2
- MLA format
- Submission to turnitin.com
- Submission of all assignment materials in an envelope or folder

Instructors will award points on the final draft based on these evaluation standards:

Introduction: 15 points
- **Effective Hook:** The introduction begins with a surprising statistic, a provocative quotation, a vivid description, a brief passage of dialogue, or some other device to grab the reader's attention and point toward the thesis.
- **Clear Purpose:** The introduction includes one or two sentences that present appropriate information about the topic to reveal why the writer cares about the subject, answering the question, "So what?"
- **Clear Plan:** The introduction ends with a clear and defined thesis that makes a claim about the topic and a promise to the reader to support the claim.

Body: 30 points
- **Topic Sentences:** Each paragraph includes a sentence (often at the beginning) that connects with the thesis and makes a comment on one of the points set up in the plan.
- **Transitions:** Each topic sentence is preceded by a statement that links the current paragraph with the previous one, stressing the relationship between the two; also, ideas are connected within paragraphs.
- **Coherence/Organization:** Body paragraphs follow the plan set up in the introduction, emphasizing the spatial, chronological, or logical relationships between and among key points.
- **Development:** Each topic sentence receives support from relevant facts, examples, and testimony in sentences that explain the logical relationship between claims and evidence.
- **Unity:** The details presented throughout the body support the thesis and do not stray from the main idea.

Conclusion: 15 points

- **Perspective:** The writer summarizes the key points that support the thesis and stress its significance.
- **Conviction:** The writer restates why the reader should be interested in the topic and ends the essay appropriately.

Correctness: 40 points

- The writer employs correct Standard American English and avoids errors in grammar, syntax, and mechanics.
- The writer follows MLA format.

Grammatical Errors (Grouped by Level of Severity)

Category 1—Compromises both the writer's credibility and the reader's comprehension:

____ Mixed Construction	____ Capitalization Error (severe)
____ Subject/Verb Agreement Error	____ Article Missing / Misused
____ Comma Splice	____ Word Omission
____ Fused Sentence	____ Wrong Word (severe)
____ Fragment	____ Apostrophe Missing / Misused
____ Comma Omission (compound sentence)	____ Double Negative
____ Missing End Sentence Punctuation	____ Verb Error (wrong form)
____ Failure to Form a Plural	____ Pronoun Case Error
____ Failure to Form the Past Tense	____ Misspelled Word (severe)

Category 2—Creates ambiguity or confusion but does not indicate an ignorance of standard usage:

____ Pronoun/Antecedent Agreement Error	____ Shift in Person or Number
____ Pronoun Reference Error	____ Shift in Tense or Mood
____ Misused Semicolon	____ Shift in Subject or Voice
____ Comma Omission (words in a series)	____ Shift in Direct / Indirect Quotations
____ Comma Omission (non-essential elements)	____ Misplaced / Dangling ModifierCategory

Category 3—Registers on the reader's consciousness as incorrect, but does not seriously distract or confuse the reader:

____ Lack of Parallelism	____ Awkward Phrasing / Idiom
____ Lack of Exactness / Concision	____ Failure to Spell out Numbers
____ Lack of Variety	____ Lack of Possessive before a Gerund
____ Comma Omission (introductory phrase/clause)	

MSU Honor Code:

On my honor, as a Mississippi State University student, I have neither given nor received unauthorized assistance on this academic work.

_____   _____

Signature   Date

Essay Grading Form

EN 0103/ _____   Assignment: _____

Name: _____   Date: _____

Draft 1 Grading Criteria: Score: _____ out of 20
- Identifiable introduction, body, and conclusion
- Thesis sentence (in the introduction)
- Topic sentences (in each body paragraph) and supporting details
- Correct rhetorical strategy

Peer Response Grading Criteria: Score: _____ out of 10
- Appropriate written comments on your classmate's essay
- Fully developed responses on the Peer Response Sheet
- Adequate verbal communication during the peer response session

Draft 2 Grading Criteria: Score: _____ out of 20
- Evidence of significant revision/correction of Draft 1
- Title
- Full development of introduction, body, and conclusion
- Transitional words and phrases
- Submission of Draft 1, Draft 2, and Peer Response

Final Draft Grading Criteria: Score: _____ out of 100
- Evidence of significant revision/correction of Draft 2
- MLA format
- Submission to turnitin.com
- Submission of all assignment materials in an envelope or folder

Instructors will award points on the final draft based on these evaluation standards:

Introduction: 15 points
- **Effective Hook:** The introduction begins with a surprising statistic, a provocative quotation, a vivid description, a brief passage of dialogue, or some other device to grab the reader's attention and point toward the thesis.
- **Clear Purpose:** The introduction includes one or two sentences that present appropriate information about the topic to reveal why the writer cares about the subject, answering the question, "So what?"
- **Clear Plan:** The introduction ends with a clear and defined thesis that makes a claim about the topic and a promise to the reader to support the claim.

Body: 30 points
- **Topic Sentences:** Each paragraph includes a sentence (often at the beginning) that connects with the thesis and makes a comment on one of the points set up in the plan.
- **Transitions:** Each topic sentence is preceded by a statement that links the current paragraph with the previous one, stressing the relationship between the two; also, ideas are connected within paragraphs.
- **Coherence/Organization:** Body paragraphs follow the plan set up in the introduction, emphasizing the spatial, chronological, or logical relationships between and among key points.
- **Development:** Each topic sentence receives support from relevant facts, examples, and testimony in sentences that explain the logical relationship between claims and evidence.
- **Unity:** The details presented throughout the body support the thesis and do not stray from the main idea.

Conclusion: 15 points

- **Perspective:** The writer summarizes the key points that support the thesis and stress its significance.
- **Conviction:** The writer restates why the reader should be interested in the topic and ends the essay appropriately.

Correctness: 40 points

- The writer employs correct Standard American English and avoids errors in grammar, syntax, and mechanics.
- The writer follows MLA format.

Grammatical Errors (Grouped by Level of Severity)

Category 1—Compromises both the writer's credibility and the reader's comprehension:

____ Mixed Construction	____ Capitalization Error (severe)
____ Subject/Verb Agreement Error	____ Article Missing / Misused
____ Comma Splice	____ Word Omission
____ Fused Sentence	____ Wrong Word (severe)
____ Fragment	____ Apostrophe Missing / Misused
____ Comma Omission (compound sentence)	____ Double Negative
____ Missing End Sentence Punctuation	____ Verb Error (wrong form)
____ Failure to Form a Plural	____ Pronoun Case Error
____ Failure to Form the Past Tense	____ Misspelled Word (severe)

Category 2—Creates ambiguity or confusion but does not indicate an ignorance of standard usage:

____ Pronoun/Antecedent Agreement Error	____ Shift in Person or Number
____ Pronoun Reference Error	____ Shift in Tense or Mood
____ Misused Semicolon	____ Shift in Subject or Voice
____ Comma Omission (words in a series)	____ Shift in Direct / Indirect Quotations
____ Comma Omission (non-essential elements)	____ Misplaced / Dangling ModifierCategory

Category 3—Registers on the reader's consciousness as incorrect, but does not seriously distract or confuse the reader:

____ Lack of Parallelism	____ Awkward Phrasing / Idiom
____ Lack of Exactness / Concision	____ Failure to Spell out Numbers
____ Lack of Variety	____ Lack of Possessive before a Gerund
____ Comma Omission (introductory phrase/clause)	

MSU Honor Code:

On my honor, as a Mississippi State University student, I have neither given nor received unauthorized assistance on this academic work.

_____   _____
Signature   Date

Essay Grading Form

EN 0103/ _____   Assignment: _____

Name: _____   Date: _____

Draft 1 Grading Criteria: Score: _____ out of 20
- Identifiable introduction, body, and conclusion
- Thesis sentence (in the introduction)
- Topic sentences (in each body paragraph) and supporting details
- Correct rhetorical strategy

Peer Response Grading Criteria: Score: _____ out of 10
- Appropriate written comments on your classmate's essay
- Fully developed responses on the Peer Response Sheet
- Adequate verbal communication during the peer response session

Draft 2 Grading Criteria: Score: _____ out of 20
- Evidence of significant revision/correction of Draft 1
- Title
- Full development of introduction, body, and conclusion
- Transitional words and phrases
- Submission of Draft 1, Draft 2, and Peer Response

Final Draft Grading Criteria: Score: _____ out of 100
- Evidence of significant revision/correction of Draft 2
- MLA format
- Submission to turnitin.com
- Submission of all assignment materials in an envelope or folder

Instructors will award points on the final draft based on these evaluation standards:

Introduction: 15 points
- **Effective Hook:** The introduction begins with a surprising statistic, a provocative quotation, a vivid description, a brief passage of dialogue, or some other device to grab the reader's attention and point toward the thesis.
- **Clear Purpose:** The introduction includes one or two sentences that present appropriate information about the topic to reveal why the writer cares about the subject, answering the question, "So what?"
- **Clear Plan:** The introduction ends with a clear and defined thesis that makes a claim about the topic and a promise to the reader to support the claim.

Body: 30 points
- **Topic Sentences:** Each paragraph includes a sentence (often at the beginning) that connects with the thesis and makes a comment on one of the points set up in the plan.
- **Transitions:** Each topic sentence is preceded by a statement that links the current paragraph with the previous one, stressing the relationship between the two; also, ideas are connected within paragraphs.
- **Coherence/Organization:** Body paragraphs follow the plan set up in the introduction, emphasizing the spatial, chronological, or logical relationships between and among key points.
- **Development:** Each topic sentence receives support from relevant facts, examples, and testimony in sentences that explain the logical relationship between claims and evidence.
- **Unity:** The details presented throughout the body support the thesis and do not stray from the main idea.

Conclusion: 15 points
- **Perspective:** The writer summarizes the key points that support the thesis and stress its significance.
- **Conviction:** The writer restates why the reader should be interested in the topic and ends the essay appropriately.

Correctness: 40 points
- The writer employs correct Standard American English and avoids errors in grammar, syntax, and mechanics.
- The writer follows MLA format.

Grammatical Errors (Grouped by Level of Severity)

Category 1—Compromises both the writer's credibility and the reader's comprehension:

____ Mixed Construction	____ Capitalization Error (severe)
____ Subject/Verb Agreement Error	____ Article Missing / Misused
____ Comma Splice	____ Word Omission
____ Fused Sentence	____ Wrong Word (severe)
____ Fragment	____ Apostrophe Missing / Misused
____ Comma Omission (compound sentence)	____ Double Negative
____ Missing End Sentence Punctuation	____ Verb Error (wrong form)
____ Failure to Form a Plural	____ Pronoun Case Error
____ Failure to Form the Past Tense	____ Misspelled Word (severe)

Category 2—Creates ambiguity or confusion but does not indicate an ignorance of standard usage:

____ Pronoun/Antecedent Agreement Error	____ Shift in Person or Number
____ Pronoun Reference Error	____ Shift in Tense or Mood
____ Misused Semicolon	____ Shift in Subject or Voice
____ Comma Omission (words in a series)	____ Shift in Direct / Indirect Quotations
____ Comma Omission (non-essential elements)	____ Misplaced / Dangling ModifierCategory

Category 3—Registers on the reader's consciousness as incorrect, but does not seriously distract or confuse the reader:

____ Lack of Parallelism	____ Awkward Phrasing / Idiom
____ Lack of Exactness / Concision	____ Failure to Spell out Numbers
____ Lack of Variety	____ Lack of Possessive before a Gerund
____ Comma Omission (introductory phrase/clause)	

MSU Honor Code:

On my honor, as a Mississippi State University student, I have neither given nor received unauthorized assistance on this academic work.

_____   _____
Signature   Date

Statement of Composition Policies

Plagiarism

Plagiarism is a serious academic offense. Any of the following constitutes plagiarism:

- Quoting/paraphrasing/summarizing another's work without citing, or citing it incorrectly; in addition to publications, this includes ideas, data, arguments, and spoken words.
- Submitting a work or any portion of a work written by another person.
- Submitting your own writing that you submitted for a previous assignment or course (including a high school course), without the knowledge and permission of your instructor.

For a more detailed explanation of plagiarism, consult *The Little, Brown Handbook,* 4th Custom Edition. Penalties for plagiarism include a zero on the assignment, failure in the course, or dismissal from Mississippi State University.

MSU Honor Code

As a Mississippi State University Student, I will conduct myself with honor and integrity at all times. I will not lie, cheat, or steal, nor will I accept the actions of those who do.

    You are required to include the following statement, with accompanying signature, on any major assignment when you submit it for grading:

    On my honor, as a Mississippi State University student, I have neither given nor received unauthorized assistance on this academic work.

Late Submission of Work

You are expected to meet all deadlines for submission of assignments. You may not make up any daily grades (brief homework assignments, reading quizzes, in class activities, peer reviews, group work, etc.). For major graded work, you will receive a 10 percent reduction in grade for each day the assignment is late. If you have a valid university excuse, you may submit a major assignment without penalty under the following conditions.

- You must present a legitimate written excuse in accordance with MSU policy.
- You must make up the assignment within the time specified by your instructor.
- You may not make up more than two major assignments during the semester.
- You must contact your instructor to make arrangements for late submission of assignments.

_____

My instructor has reviewed the above policies, and I understand them.

_____   _____

Name (please print legibly)   Date reviewed in class

_____

Signature

Mississippi State University Standard Release Form

When you submit paragraphs and essays for grading, they become property of the English Department. Students' writing samples are often used in universities for faculty development sessions and other purposes. This form requests your permission to use copies of the paragraphs and essays you will write throughout this semester. Your decision on whether to allow the use of written work will not affect your grade in any way.

The following list describes a variety of situations for which your papers may be used:

- Your instructor maintains a teaching portfolio that may be used in hiring decisions (internally and with other universities), in promotion decisions, and in professional development situations. This portfolio usually includes sample student papers.

- The English Department conducts sessions to discuss grading and assignment criteria; student essays and paragraphs are used in these situations.

- Instructors sometimes use former students' essays and paragraphs in current classes to illustrate skills or problems. The department also compiles former students' papers to be used in supplemental texts (such as this book) for writing classes.

- For accreditation purposes, the university must periodically submit samples of student work to be reviewed by committees not affiliated with the university.

Place your initials beside the appropriate response for the use of your papers:

_____ I give permission for the use of my paragraphs and essays for teaching   portfolios, faculty development sessions, and future classes and publications.

_____ I give permission for the use of my paragraphs and essays **anonymously** for teaching portfolios, faculty development sessions, and future classes and publications.

_____ I prefer that none of my paragraphs and essays be used for teaching portfolios, faculty development sessions, and future classes and publications.

First Name: _____ Last Name: _____

Net ID: _____ _____

EN 0103 / _____ Semester: _____ Year: _____

Signature: _____ Date: _____